Forging in the Smithy

COSTERUS NEW SERIES 98

Series Editors:
C.C. Barfoot, Hans Bertens, Theo D'haen
and Erik Kooper

Forging in the Smithy

National Identity and Representation in Anglo-Irish Literary History

**Edited by Joep Leerssen,
A.H. van der Weel
and Bart Westerweel**

The Literature of Politics, The Politics of Literature

Proceedings of the Leiden
IASAIL Conference: Volume 1

*General editors: C.C. Barfoot,
Theo D'haen and Tjebbe A. Westendorp*

Rodopi   Amsterdam-Atlanta, GA 1995

CIP-gegevens Koninklijke Bibliotheek, Den Haag

Forging

Forging in the Smithy : national identity and
representation in Anglo-Irish literary history / eds.
Joep Leerssen, A.H. van der Weel, and Bart Westerweel. -
Amsterdam - Atlanta, GA 1995 : Rodopi. - (The literature
of politics,the politics of literature ; 1)
(Costerus, ISSN 0165-9618 ; 98)
ISBN 90-5183-759-3 geb.
Trefw.: nationale identiteit in de Anglo-Ierse letterkunde.

Cover design: Hendrik van Delft

© Editions Rodopi B.V.
  Amsterdam - Atlanta, GA 1995

Printed in The Netherlands

CONTENTS

INTRODUCTION: FORGING IN THE SMITHY

The interest of Anglo-Irish literature is not only that its canon includes a high proportion of literary giants — Yeats, Joyce, Beckett — but also that, as a tradition, it exemplifies the problematics of literature in a context of social and cultural tension. Irish literary history has often been studied under precisely that aspect: as the literature of a country in a marginal, in some respect almost colonial yet intra-European position; a country where a variety of cultural traditions (Gaelic, Anglo-Irish, Ulster Presbyterian) coexisted in a highly uneasy relationship; a country with intense social and economic divisions. What is more, those infrastructural tensions are by no means mere "background" or part of the "context": they have been explicitly thematized in a substantial part of Ireland's literary output, so much so that the Irish author who does not in some way address the "matter of Ireland" stands out as an anomaly, an exception to the general pattern. If Irish authors are almost invariably read under the aspect of their "Irishness", this is partly the result of their own preoccupations.

The fact that Anglo-Irish literature, more perhaps than any other literary corpus in the European canon, has generally been explicitly read in a historical context, is therefore neither surprising nor unjustified; and Jane Stevenson in her article on Maria Edgeworth and Sydney Owenson (Lady Morgan) demonstrates how the footnotes one finds in their fiction indicate the extent to which they thought of their novels as works of historiography. Stevenson argues that the function of such footnotes is "explanatory rather than entertaining", and that the different use to which the footnote is put by the two novelists stems from their common desire to genuinely enhance English understanding of Ireland.

However, the explicit reading of literature in a historical context does present us with a danger. If literary scholars call on historical information in order to cast more or fresh light on the texts they study, then it is obviously important that such historical information is not tendentious or distorting. This caveat has not always been heeded. In the recent cross-border exchanges between the departments of history and of literature, historians have often been beguiled by all too specious notions of a literary provenance — "narrativity", for instance — while literary

scholars have been heedless of recent developments and insights in the
historical disciplines, and all too often adopt a naive and simplistic notion
of what is "history" or "historical knowledge".

In the case of Irish literary history, to be specific, the crux is often
that literary scholars still tend to adopt a historical frame of reference
which is outdated and misleading. A crude manichean, national-
istically-inspired teleology is often applied, which has long fallen out of
practice in historical scholarship, but which still dominates the
perspective of literary scholars. It involves vibrant, innocent, heroic but
oppressed native Gaels, cynically exploited by English-derived colonials
with their anaemic tastes and values, and wholly ousted in the north-east
by dour Scots calvinists; it involves a grail-like quest for the recapture
of national identity, a quest which is both politically and aesthetically
justified in that it brings Ireland, after a re-Gaelicization of her
imagination, back to artistic greatness and political independence. That
usually is the implicit entelechy which is projected into Irish literary
activities; at best, one is willing to allow a bittersweet postscript to this
scenario, in which Ireland again stands in danger of losing her cultural
integrity,.this time as a result of middle-class conventionalism and Roman
Catholic backwardness — a process resisted by the literati and obviated
by the vital resources of a waning but still vibrant native culture.

Such a frame of reference, usually implicit and rarely as crudely
stated as represented here for clarity's sake, has long been abandoned by
Irish historians. Some literary scholars have also challenged the implied
Gaelocentric, nationalist and romantic slant in much of Irish literary
history; especially protestant or Ulster authors and critics who feel that
Ireland's protestant tradition deserves better than to be glossed over as
an irksome dog in the manger. Historians are now studying national
conflict as a predicament or a challenge facing people at a given point in
time, not as a moral imperative or a trajectory towards the golden aim
of regaining Ireland's authenticity and independence; and in the process,
historians have turned, with interesting results, to literary source
material.

For their part, scholars in Anglo-Irish literary history can gain much
from a refresher course in Irish history, not Irish history as taught by
outdated reference works or guidebooks, not the all too comfortable
master grid of nationalist or (what amounts to much the same) "post-
colonial" binaries, but history as currently practised by historians.

The present collection brings together some essays which illustrate the
possibilities open to a proper historical understanding of Anglo-Irish
literature. What is more, these essays appear to illustrate, between them,
two interesting trends. One is that attention is increasingly being paid to

the period before 1800 — a period which (with the exception of Swift) was frequently underrepresented in traditional Anglo-Irish literary historiography. The other is that the corpus which is being studied by literary historians is widening far beyond the traditional, narrowly aesthetical, canon of "literature". Thus, Wim Tigges in his article on Wolfe Tone argues that Tone was a man of letters as much as a man of action, and that his autobiographical writings are legitimate objects of literary analysis. Indeed, the history of ideas and attitudes in and about Ireland can be studied through the evidence not only of literary forms, styles and statements, but also of arts such as garden architecture and music. Ciaran Murray's analysis of the influence of Japanese concepts of artlessness in garden architecture makes a powerful case for the Irish-Dutch intermediacy in the spread of this early straw in the wind of pre-romantic aesthetics; and Peter Davidson's contribution on a music manuscript of a member of an Italian family of professional musicians is an illustration of what Davidson calls "the colonization of music" that was taking place in Ireland and Scotland in the late eighteenth and early nineteenth centuries. The manuscript, copied for Anna Corri around 1805, demonstrates the ways in which indigenous music is adapted to suit the tastes of those who follow the trends of "the style of the European mainstream".

The essays gathered here address three interrelated areas of interest in particular: language, territory and politics; the role of historical consciousness in Irish authors and in their dissemination; and the representation of Irish affairs as it gives rise to specific literary strategies.

The political burden on Ireland's linguistic and territorial situation is charted by Wall, Leerssen, Green and Westerweel. Richard Wall, in his article on "Politics and Language in Anglo-Irish Literature", focuses on the vocabulary connected with English attempts to subdue and assimilate Ireland, and distinguishes between words (frequently taking the form of code words) praising the Irish, and words criticizing or satirizing Ireland and its customs, behaviour or religious convictions; this distinction reflects the outlook of the suppressed and the suppressor, respectively. As the title of Joep Leerssen's article, "Language Revivalism before the Twilight", indicates, his contribution traces the social and political implications of the revival of interest in the Gaelic language in the course of the nineteenth century. Leerssen shows how the interest in the Celtic heritage moved from a conservative, antiquarian stage in the first Celtic revival of the late eighteenth century towards the much more revolutionary oriented second revival taking place a century later. Arthur Green's homage to Arthur Heslinga, author of *The Irish Border as a Cultural Divide*, is a highly polemical plea for a reappraisal of the relationship between Ireland and Great Britain on the grounds of geographical realities which the Irish nationalist temper has too often refused to recognize. Bart Westerweel discusses Spenser's use, especially in Book V of *The Faerie Queene*, of "imagotypes" of Irishness, stereotypes based on the ideology of conquest and colonization that Spenser subscribed to in his own dealings in Ireland.

Irish texts are doubly implicated in history: they are often produced by writers for whom authorship is in itself a form of historical consciousness; and they are read by readers and critics who likewise impose an often urgent and explicit set of historical demands. The historical awareness of Irish men of letters as diverse as the antiquarian Charles Vallancey and the nationalist John Mitchel is discussed by Clare O'Halloran and Christopher Morash, respectively; Vallancey imposing a mythical, orientalist complexion on the obscure origins of Gaelic Ireland, Mitchel caught up, ironically, in the British imperialist thinking of Thomas Carlyle, especially in his notion that human rights and freedom are earned through force: "right equals might". An intermediary position between Vallancey and Mitchel is taken up by the United Irishman and book publisher Mathew Carey, whose seminal nationalist history *Vindiciae Hibernicae* is discussed by Martin J. Burke. Robert Mahony analyses the reputation of Swift among later readers, as gauged against his own political concerns, and demonstrates the resulting tensions and complexities. James M. Murphy challenges the generally accepted view that the literary revival of the late nineteenth and early twentieth centuries, led by Anglo-Irish Protestants, forms the canon of literature of the period. Irish Roman Catholic fiction is rarely discussed and even Joyce is placed in a category of his own. Murphy focuses on fiction by Rosa Mulholland (1886) and W.P. Ryan (1910) as representatives of two sides of the watershed of the 1890s, thus dividing the outlook of the Catholic upper class from the concerns of an emerging Catholic intelligentsia. The interaction between historical context and self-image, both in the actions and aspirations of historical persons and in their later reputation, is analysed by Barbara Freitag, who addresses the case of the lives and myths of James Connolly and James Larkin. The matter of historical consciousness is addressed in a thematical rather than an author-oriented sense by Norman Vance, who, using New Grange as an example of a *lieu de mémoire*, illustrates the tenacious hold of colonial and nationalist ideologies on Irish archaeology over the centuries.

Finally, many contributions in this volume relate historical predicaments to textual strategies. A number of contributors (some of them already mentioned) offer analyses of "literary" ways of addressing historical predicaments or conflicts. In her analysis of an undergraduate poem by Swift, Susan Fisher Miller shows how its rollicking humour reflects some of the conditions of Trinity student life and exhibits characteristics that were later to become more pronounced in Swift's writing. C.C. Barfoot provides an account of the intricate ways in which Jacobin and anti-Jacobin feelings emerge in the various press accounts of the trial and execution of the Irishman James Coigly in 1798. Basing himself on the newspaper coverage of the events, in the "Jacobin" papers *The Morning Post* and *The Morning Chronicle* on the one hand, and *The Times* on the other, Barfoot brings out the whole repertoire of rhetorical ploys used by editors to match fact and political alliance.

From Spenser, by way of Swift and Wolfe Tone, to Connolly, the topics addressed in this volume span a large period in Irish history and Anglo-Irish literature. In all their diversity, the contributions between them testify to the continuing preoccupation with history on the part of Irish authors, and to the challenges and opportunities that this preoccupation offers to present-day critics.

Joep Leerssen, A.H. van der Weel
and Bart Westerweel

SPENSER'S IRELAND

BART WESTERWEEL

Their native barbarism and idle desert life ... impose upon their minds every form of vicious pleasure. In faithlessness, inconstancy, lying, cheating, treachery, and infamous concern with every kind of lust they exercise their villainy .... Those Africans who gave you your triumphal name, O Scipio Africanus, lofty exemplar of culture and sainthood, must have been more humane, more chaste, than these.[1]

It is admitted by all that the Hottentots hold no obligation more sacred than that of comforting a distressed soul by hospitality .... I only wish that our citizens would rival them in their respect for strangers, and learn from the natives never to break the laws of hospitality and to rid themselves of their inhuman and savage temper.[2]

Notwithstanding the obvious differences between these accounts they share the notions of cultural classification and of predetermined attitudes towards the Other. The former description of an African people seen through the eyes of white man is by Willem ten Rhyne, whose *An Account of the Cape of Good Hope* dates from 1686; the latter is taken from J.G. de Grevenbrock's *An Account of the Hottentots*, written in 1695.[3]

Roughly a century after these two distinguished Dutch travellers expressed their widely divergent opinions about their African experience we read in the Diary of John Scott, Earl of Clonmell,[4] under the

---

1. I. Schapera, *The Early Cape Hottentots*, Cape Town, 1933, 125.

2. *Ibid.*, 239.

3. I owe these quotations to Richard M. Santalla's unpublished MA thesis (University of Leiden, 1991).

4. Clonmel in modern spelling.

heading, "The Irish Oppressed like Hottentot Slaves — their Weakness
for Liquor makes them an easy prey for the Designing Stranger":

> English governors, and, in generall, Englishmen, treat the Irish,
> great and small, like slaves, and nearly as the Dutch do the
> Hottentot; and the Irish submit to almost the same indignities as
> the Hottentots do. Irish stuffing and guzzling lower and injure the
> Irish exceedingly. Drunkenness gives such advantages to sober
> observers and watchful English and Scotch swindlers and
> adventurers that the Irish are actually imposed upon and duped,
> and the poor are undone by a constant excess in drinking spirits,
> as bad as the Hottentots. A man in station, in Ireland, is really like
> a traveller in Africa, in a forest among Hottentots and wild beasts
> .... Irish government resembles extremely the state of the
> Hottentots in Africa. The common Irish, divided, oppressed,
> pillaged, and abused as they are, are the Hottentots; the English
> Administration are the Dutch planters; the followers of Lord
> Lieutenants are the bushmen or spies, and swindlers; and their
> wild beasts — viz., lions, tigers, &c. — are the Irish satraps. The
> man who would live in this country, especially in public station,
> should, like Mons. Vaillant, the traveller, guard himself hourly
> against serpents, tigers, hyenas, elephants, jackals, monkeys in
> human form, and against the planters and bushmen besides.[5]

As we know, Edmund Spenser once lived in the country that John
Scott writes about and, like the ambitious Earl of Clonmell, who became
Chief Justice of the king's bench in 1784, in public station at that. From
1580 to 1582 Spenser was secretary to Arthur Grey of Wilton, Lord
Deputy of Ireland, and subsequently occupied the modest estate of
Kilcolman castle where he spent most of his time between 1589 and
1599. Kilcolman is only a small number of miles removed from
Clonmell, whose earl John Scott became towards the end of the
eighteenth century and the name Clonmell appears in the topographical
list of rivers attending the poetic marriage between the Thames and the
Medway in Book IV, xi of *The Faerie Queene*. Arlo Hill, mentioned
several times in Spenser's poetry, is situated in between Kilcolman and
Clonmell. In 1599 Tyrone besieged Kilcolman on his march through
Munster.

-----

5. Dr P.J.C.M. Franssen (University of Utrecht) first drew my attention to John
Scott's diary. Extracts from it were edited in *Ireland before the Union: With Extracts
from the Unpublished Diary of John Scott, LL.D., Earl of Clonmell, ...* , ed.
William J. Fitzpatrick, Dublin, 1867. The quotation in the text is at 32-33.

Widely divergent in time and place as the previous quotations may be, it is all the more remarkable that they exhibit structural elements that are quite similar, even if they serve a different purpose. Cultural and national classification and its corollary, the view of the Other, apparently avail themselves of imagotypes, i.e. stereotypes turned into a literary topos.[6] Nicholas Canny has argued in several publications that the view of Ireland as a plantation is more often accompanied by equations with the Amerindians of the New World than with the native tribes of Africa, but when cultural classification is in operation geographical distances matter preciously little and Hottentots, Indians, Irish, Tartars and Goths are all regarded as members of the same ubiquitous, barbarous, savage, wild and pagan family.[7] Spenser, in his prose treatise *A View of the Present State of Ireland* (1596), frequently invokes the help of imagotypes based on cultural classification to prove a point. This is the case, for instance, in the following passage in which Irenius, one of the two participants in the dialogue and representative of Spenser's point of view, objects to the efficacy of "heavy laws and penalties" in taming the wild Irish:

> I think sure that will do small good; for when a people are inclined to any vice or have no touch of conscience, nor sense of their evil doing, it is bootless to think to restrain them by any penalties or fear of punishment; but either the occasion is to be taken away, or a more understanding of the right and shame of the fault is to be imprinted. For if Lycurgus should have made it death for the Lacedemonians to steal, they being a people which naturally delighted in stealth, or if it should be made a capital crime for the Flemings to be taken in drunkenness, there should have been few Lacedemonians soon left, and fewer Flemings. So impossible is it to remove any fault so general in a people with terror of laws, or most sharp restraints.[8]

---

6. For a related use of the imagotype, see my article "Astrophel and Ulster: Sidney's Ireland", *Dutch Quarterly Review*, XVIII (1988), 169–85 (later reprinted in *The Clash of Ireland: Literary Contrasts and Connections*, eds C.C. Barfoot and Theo D'haen, Amsterdam and Atlanta: GA, 1989, 5-22). Cf. J.Th.Leerssen, *Mere Irish & Fíór-Ghael*, Amsterdam and Philadelphia, 1986, esp. 3f. and *passim*.

7. See, for instance, Nicholas Canny, *Kingdom and Colony: Ireland in the Atlantic World 1560–1800*, Baltimore & London, 1988, esp. ch.1. Cf. also D.B. Quinn, *The Elizabethans and the Irish*, Ithaca: NY, 1966, 22–23: "Of course it was easy for Englishmen to lump all non-Englishmen together, or at least to throw together those who were distinctively different from the English" (23).

8. Edmund Spenser, *A View of the Present State of Ireland*, ed. W.L. Renwick, Oxford, 1970, 24–25. All subsequent references to *A View* will be to this edition.

What Spenser's images have in common is not just the language of cultural classification but the ideology of conquest and colonization. In order to understand and interpret the former, one should be well acquainted with the historical dimensions of the latter. The situation in Ireland had always been in need of image systems of this kind and Spenser could have found models for them in Gerald of Wales (thirteenth century) or in contemporary historians such as Edmund Campion and Richard Stanihurst.[9] Towards the end of the sixteenth century the debate about the relationship between England and Ireland was particularly fierce, concerning the legal system to be adopted and the sometimes conflicting policies of conquest and colonization. Since the English Act of Succession of 1544 made Henry VIII king and head of the Church in both England and Ireland the implications of that Act had caused more turmoil and cost more human lives than at any other period.[10] As J.D. Mackie points out, it is significant that the first Jesuit mission appeared in Ireland the July following the adoption of the Act of Succession. "Henry had 'scotch'd the snake', not killed it." "His monarchy, like other attempts to coerce Ireland, rested in the end on no surer foundations than the rewarding of the king's enemies and the mutual animosities of the Irish leaders. They were enriched with the lands of the abbeys, but the 'island of the saints' still turned her eyes towards Rome."[11]

Sir Henry Sidney, the poet's father, served three terms as Lord Deputy of Ireland between 1565 and 1578, preceding Lord Grey in that capacity. He recommended a number of regulatory measures for Munster and Connaught. Among the measures suggested by Henry Sidney, wisely from the perspective of the English government, were the establishment of presidencies, the introduction of land tenure by royal patent, which would give the Crown a direct means of control over the chiefs, and the plantation of English colonists. Several of Sidney's ideas were put into practice and Spenser became involved with all of these in one way or another. After his employment as secretary of the Lord Deputy between 1580 and 1582 he served as Clerk of the Council of Munster and as such

---

9. For a more elaborate account of Anglo-Irish historiography and Spenser's place in it, see Jane Stephenson's article "The Politics of Historiography: Or, Novels with Footnotes", in this volume (195-206 below).

10. Cf. Canny: "... the Act of Kingship ... made it incumbent upon all English monarchs to win the loyalty of their subjects in Ireland rather than to attempt their extirpation" (3).

11. J.D. Mackie, *The Earlier Tudors, 1485–1558*, Oxford, 1952, 366.

he was secretary to the Presidents of the Council, Sir John and Sir Thomas Norris. In 1588/89 Spenser became an undertaker for the settlement of Munster and occupied Kilcolman Castle, dispossessing Lord Roche, its Anglo-Irish claimant. After a brief visit to England with Sir Walter Raleigh to present the first three books of *The Faerie Queene* to Elizabeth he returned to be a planter himself at Kilcolman in 1591. *A View of the Present State of Ireland* was written in 1595/96 during another visit to London.[12] In 1598 he became sheriff of Cork, a position he was to hold but briefly, since in 1599 the O'Neills swept across Munster, the numbers of the English planters being far too few to put up any sort of serious resistance, and sacked Kilcolman in the process. Spenser had to flee, reported the fate of Munster duly to the Queen and died three weeks later in rather miserable circumstances.

A few points should be made at this stage before these bare facts of Spenser's life can be fruitfully connected with his work. One of these is the simple but important fact that the greater part of *The Faerie Queene*, in which the Irish matter is presented under the cloak of allegory, was written in Ireland, whereas *A View*, although it obviously had its roots in Ireland, was actually written in England. The other poem in which Ireland figures prominently, "Colin Clouts Come Home Againe", although published in 1595, was written in 1591, after Spenser's return from his visit to England. Spenser's point of view, then, is essentially English and Ireland is regarded as a colony. The point Renwick, the modern editor of *A View*, makes about the prose treatise is valid for the other works mentioned as well: "England is referred to as *here*, Ireland as *there*, with a consistency difficult to preserve if the placing were imaginary."[13] In Bakhtinian terms, the chronotope of Ireland in Spenser's work is invariably a chronotope of the threshold, a crossing from one world to another.[14] As I will argue later in this paper, this crossing is shaped in a particular way that demonstrates both Spenser's qualities as a poet and his inability to come to terms with the problem of finding an adequate way of talking politics in allegory about issues whose impact on the senses was perhaps too direct to allow for the abstract sensuousness that characterizes most scenes of *The Faerie Queene*.

---

12. *A View* was published much later than it was written, in 1633 by James Ware.

13. Renwick, 171.

14. The idea or theory of the chronotope is described in M.M. Bakhtin, *The Dialogic Imagination: Four Essays by M.M. Bakhtin*, tr. Caryl Emerson and Michael Holquist, Austin, 1981, 84–258.

Part of that uncertainty of expression was no doubt caused by
Spenser's station in life, an ambivalence that frequently characterizes the
attitude of a colonizer who sympathizes to a certain extent with the
colonized. It is likely that Spenser, as secretary of Lord Grey, witnessed
the Smerwick massacre of 1580, where Lord Grey and the Earl of
Ormonde, with the support of the English fleet, made the fort surrender
and had its defenders, more than six hundred papal soldiers, executed as
pirates.[15] The early period of Spenser's Irish experience is inextricably
interwoven with the systematic devastation of Munster by the English
following the Smerwick incident in an attempt to eradicate the last traces
of the revolt of Fitzgerald and his supporters. More than 30,000 native
Irish perished in the brief space of six months.[16] This is what Spenser
writes about the episode in a famous passage of *A View*:

> ... ere one year and a half they were brought to such
> wretchedness, as that any stony heart would have rued the same.
> Out of every corner of the woods and glens they came creeping
> forth upon their hands, for their legs could not bear them. They
> looked anatomies of death, they spake like ghosts crying out of
> their graves, they did eat of the dead carrions, happy were they
> could find them, yea and one another soon after in so much as the
> very carcasses they spared not to scrape out of their graves, and
> if they found a plot of water cress or shamrocks, there they
> flocked as to a feast for the time, yet not able long to continue
> there withal, that in short space there were none almost left and a
> most populous and plentiful country suddenly left void of man and
> beast (104).

The final blow to the revolt was dealt when the Earl of Desmond was
captured and beheaded in 1583 and all his estates fell to the Crown. In
the wake of that process Spenser acquired Kilcolman.

The years 1595/96, when *A View* was written, were yet again full of
tensions and turmoil: these were the days of the famous, notorious,

---

15. See J.B. Black, *The Reign of Elizabeth 1558-1603*, 2nd edn, Oxford, 1959,
476-79. Spenser describes the execution of the Spaniards at Smerwick in *A View*,
107-108, in a passage devoted to a spirited defence of Lord Grey against the
accusation that the latter had broken a promise to the Spaniards to spare their lives:
"... most untruly and maliciously do these evil tongues backbite and slander the
sacred ashes of that most just and honourable personage, whose least virtue of many
most excellent which abounded in his heroic spirit, they were never able to aspire
unto" (108).

16. See Black, 478-79.

brilliant, shrewd Hugh O'Neill, Earl of Tyrone, called by one English historian "an accomplished disciple of Machiavelli — flexible, suave, incalculable" (Black, 481). Tyrone alternately played the cards of Elizabeth and Philip in the hope of playing his own trump card at either Carlingford or Galway, where the Spaniards were supposed to land.[17] A planter's scheme hesitantly and incompletely executed, which made the new arrivals from England feel insecure and insufficiently protected and the growing threat of "The O'Neill" whose popular appeal made many forces rally to his side were some of the shaping forces behind the writing of *A View*. Many of Spenser's statements about the Irish problem seem exceedingly harsh and cruel, even to near contemporaries. James Ware, the editor of the first edition of 1633, felt it necessary to apologize for this aspect of the work in the Preface:

> As for his worke now published, although it sufficiently testifieth his learning and deepe judgement, yet we may wish that in some passages it had bin tempered with more moderation. The troubles and miseries of the time when he wrote it, doe partly excuse him (3v).

Spenser was, it should be remembered, an Englishman with a subservient official position and in view of the meagre rewards reaped by such loyal followers of Queen, Church and Country as Sir Henry Sidney and Lord Arthur Grey for voicing an opinion of their own or acting at their own initiative, it is small wonder that by and large Spenser toed the official line.

Spenser's outspoken support of the ideology of conquest in *A View* appears in many areas, a few of which will be briefly discussed. One is the system of transhumance. This is classified by Spenser as one of the "Scythian, or Scottish manners" and consists in the "pasturing upon the mountain and waste wild places, and removing still to fresh land as they have depastured the former days" (49). This custom of "Bollyng" as it is called in the sparsely populated Bollies seems innocent enough to Eudoxus:

---

17. Philip was prepared to send the fleet notwithstanding the losses suffered at the hands of Essex and Howard in their attack on Cadiz where many ships intended for the Irish enterprise were either burnt or sunk. The Armada finally left for Ireland in October 1595, but a heavy storm prevented the flotilla from ever reaching its destination.

> What fault can ye find with this custom, for though it be an old
> Scythian use, yet it is very behoveful in this country of Ireland
> where there are great mountains and waste deserts full of grass,
> that the same should be eaten down and nourish many thousand of
> cattle, for the good of the whole realm ...? (49)

Irenius responds by indicating the threat of disruption caused by the
practice of Bollyng since it provides "outlaws or loose people" with a
place of relief and shelter "where else they should be driven shortly to
starve, or to come down to the towns ... where by one means or another
they would soon be caught" (49-50). Bollyng also facilitates the hiding
of stolen cattle and, finally "the people that live thus in these Bollies
grow thereby the more barbarous and live more licentiously than they
could in towns ..." (50).[18] Elsewhere in *A View* Spenser advocates:

> that whatsoever keepeth 20 kine should keep a plough going, for
> otherwise all men would fall to pasturage and none to husbandry,
> which is a great cause of this dearth now in England, and a cause
> of the usual stealths now in Ireland ....

And the argument is buttressed up with yet another piece of national
classification:

> ... for look into all countries that live in such sort by keeping of
> cattle, and you shall find that they are both very barbarous and
> uncivil and also greatly given to war, The Tartarians, the
> Muscovites, the Norways, the Goths, the Armenians and many
> other do witness the same (158).

Another custom said by Spenser to derive from the Scythians is "the
wearing of mantles and long glibs, which is a thick curled bush of hair
hanging down over their eyes, and monstrously disguising them, which

---

18. The strong resentment of the English against transhumance should be seen
against the background of the pride of the English in their own orderly rural
communities, which were thought to contribute substantially to England's peaceful
prosperity. This stability was continually threatened by the ever-increasing number
of inclosures for pasture. As J.B. Black explains, "the blessed state of England" was
thought to be dependent on the abundance of arable land. He quotes a poem by
Thomas Churchyard eulogizing the rural riches of England in 1579 (*op. cit.*,
253-54). The same Thomas Churchyard had, ten years before, accompanied Sir
Humphrey Gilbert on his march through Munster in 1569 to break down the
resistance of the Irish against the attempts at colonization of the province. See my
article "Astrophel and Ulster: Sidney's Ireland", 173-74.

are both very bad and hurtful" (50). The main reason for mantle and glib being obnoxious to a planter is that they prevent easy recognition. The mantle being worn night and day by both men and women, "it is a fit house for an outlaw, a meet bed for a rebel, and an apt cloak for a thief" (51). It is easy to hide stolen goods or weapons under the mantle and, for "a bad housewife" it is "a coverlet for her lewd exercise, and when she hath filled her vessel, under it she can hide both her burden and her blame; yea, and when her bastard is born it serves instead of all her swaddling clothes, her mantles, her cradles with which others are vainly cumbered" (53). The glib, too, is objectionable, because a thief to prevent recognition "either cutteth off his glib quite, by which he becometh nothing like himself, or pulleth it so low down over his eyes that it is very hard to discern his thievish countenance" (53).

Besides customs that were felt to be a threat to the colonizing English another area of dispute was in the field of the law. Irenius is particularly vehement about the Brehon laws which allow for a financial settlement between, say, a murderer and the family or friends of the victim. The judge of these cases, the so-called Lord's Brehon, takes care that to both his Lord and himself is given "for his judgement a greater portion than unto the plaintiffs or parties grieved" (5). Eudoxus, ever the voice of reason and common sense, wonders how it can be that the Irish still maintain their own laws notwithstanding their acknowledgement of the sovereignty of the English monarch. Irenius responds:

> True it is that thereby they bound themselves to his law and obedience, and in case it had been followed upon them as it should have been, and a government thereupon presently settled amongst them agreeable thereunto, they should have been reduced to perpetual civility and contained in continual duty: but what boots it to break a colt and to let him straight run loose at random? (6)

As I have argued elsewhere, the metaphor of breaking a colt belongs to a familiar colonial imagotype in which the subjection of one nation to the domination of another is expressed in images of the control of a human over an animal, especially a horse, although, as one of the first quotations of this paper made clear, other, more exotic animals may well belong to the same metaphoric field.[19] The imagotype of the unruly

---

19. "Astrophel and Ulster: Sidney's Ireland", 181–84; on the iconography of bit and bridle and the cardinal Virtue of Temperantia, see also Bart Westerweel, "The Well-Tempered Lady and the Unruly Horse: Convention and Submerged Metaphor in Renaissance Literature and Art", in *Convention and Innovation in Literature*, eds

horse as an expression of disobedience to the law is introduced in the
first pages of the book:

> ... yet with the state of Ireland peradventure it doth not so well
> agree, being a people altogether stubborn and untamed, and if it
> were once tamed, yet now lately having quite shaken off their
> yoke and broken the bands of their obedience (4).

The Irish, unfortunately, are not so readily bridled and tamed as the
prescriptions of the English example would have them be. They will feed
their cattle in the Bollies, wear their mantles and glibs and exercise the
Brehon laws. In addition and worst of all in the eyes of a loyal servant
of the Tudor monarchy there is the Irish right of succession, called the
Tanist or Tanistry, which refers to the way of appointing the Lord or
Captain of a tribe, who is not the eldest son or any of the other children
of the deceased Lord, but "the next to him of blood, that is the eldest and
worthiest" (7). Eudoxus asks, with his customary bluntness:

> Do they use any ceremony in this election? For all barbarous
> nations are commonly great observers of ceremonies and
> superstitious rites (7).

Irenius duly explains the rites observed during the election ceremony.
The tanistry has obvious advantages for the Irish, since it guarantees that
the leadership is in the hands of "a man of stronger years and better
experience to maintain the inheritance and to defend the country" (8). To
defend it, to be sure, not only against rivalling tribes but "against the
English which they think lie still in wait to wipe them out of their lands
and territories" (8). Needless to say the English were a little less than
enthusiastic about the custom of Tanistry.

Notwithstanding the imagotypes of colonial domination and cultural
and national classification Spenser demonstrates an interest in Irish
culture that may best be termed antiquarian.[20] He was interested in Irish
literature, even got some of it translated for his benefit and tried to find
out about its techniques.[21] He granted that "Ireland hath had the use of

---

Theo D'haen *et al.*, Amsterdam and Philadelphia, 1989, 105–22.

20. Spenser uses the term himself in *A View* (for instance in the final sentence
of the work, 170).

21. *A View*, 75. See D.B. Quinn, *The Elizabethans and the Irish*, Ithaca: NY,
1966, 30. Quinn adds: "Yet he set his description of Irish life in the context of a
program for complete Anglicization and he therefore inevitably adopted an

letters very anciently, and long before England" (40). On the other hand he objects to the Old English speaking Irish "for it hath been ever the use of the conquerer to despise the language of the conquered, and to force him by all means to learn his" (67). He also resented the habit of the Irish bards to spend their creative energy in glorifying those leaders that are the most rebellious, licentious and lawless (73).

In assessing Spenser's attitude towards the Irish in the dialogue between Eudoxus and Irenius in *A View* by means of the imagotypes of domination and classification employed in it we have tended so far to emphasize its contemporary context. However, since imagotypes are conventional ways of expressing attitudes towards the Other, pressures of a historical–linguistic kind should not be disregarded either. As Nicholas Canny put it, "the vocabulary of abuse that was used by English authors to castigate the Gaelic Irish was largely derived from earlier writings by Old English spokesmen, and no sixteenth-century Englishman surpassed the twelfth-century Anglo-Norman Giraldus Cambrensis (Gerald of Wales) in his vituperative dismissal of Gaelic culture".[22] What Spenser added to the conventional discourse of conquest in *A View*, besides a marked interest in the origins and development of Irish culture, is the rhetorical form of the dialogue, which he adopted as naturally as he did the pastoral or epic form elsewhere. The Ciceronian form of the dialogue enabled Spenser at least to suggest that Irish problems could be looked at in more ways than one and Eudoxus occasionally has this role in the debate with Irenius, although usually his speeches are no more than just a foil to the words of Irenius.

In *The Faerie Queene* the Irish matter is, of course, presented differently. One critic claims that *A View* returns in poetic shape in *The Faerie Queene*.[23] Be that as it may, it goes without saying that Spenser's experiences in Ireland exercised a profound influence upon the form and substance of *The Faerie Queene*.[24] On the whole I tend to agree with the point made by Gray that the misery, starvation and atrocities that Spenser witnessed or experienced in Ireland must have had an impact on the writing of *The Faerie Queene*. One should, however, be careful not to connect life experience and artistic expression in ways

---

overriding attitude of hostility to the Irish polity, even where parts of his description are objective and some of his comments both friendly and perspicacious."

22. Canny, 3.

23. M.M. Gray, "The Influence of Spenser's Irish Experiences on *The Faerie Queene*", *RES*, VI (1930), 413–28.

24. See Raymond Jenkins, "Spenser and Ireland", *ELH*, XIX (1952), 131–42.

that are too narrowly literal. Besides being an English planter in Ireland Spenser was also *poetus doctus* and his wide reading had at least as much sway over his writing as his immediate experience. If this is true of many of the colonial images in *A View* it is even more important to recognize it with respect to *The Faerie Queene*. The point is nicely illustrated by a brief response of C.S. Lewis to the article by Gray about the influence of Spenser's Irish experience on his epic poem. Gray had suggested that *The Faerie Queene*, unlike the models of Malory and earlier romance writers, frequently describes encounters between the errant knights and the "rascal many", which he attributes to Spenser's experience as a government official with the Irish rebels. Lewis quarrels with Gray's method by pointing out that, in so far as *The Faerie Queene* is a romantic epic, Spenser followed Italian models rather than English ones, where he "[f]ound precedent for the type of episode in which knights are attacked by a rabble of robbers or cannibals". "Is it not rather a canon of Spenserian *Quellenforschung*: 'Never look further for the source of a passage until you have satisfied yourself that it does not come out of the Italian epics'?", Lewis concludes drily.[25]

I would like to devote the final part of this article to an aspect of Spenser's view of Ireland in *The Faerie Queene* that has not been studied in the context of his colonial experience as far as I know. The text of Spenser's poem "Colin Clouts Come Home Againe" is preceded by a short dedicatory epistle to Sir Walter Raleigh. The final sentence of the letter reads: "From my house of Kilcolman the 27. of December. 1591", followed by Spenser's name.[26] There is something special about the use of the possessive pronoun here, particularly when one connects its use here with other, similar occurrences in contexts where one would least expect it. The first is part of the topographical enumeration of Irish rivers in Book IV, xi, 41, who join the pageant of rivers and sea-gods — even old Ocean is present — to celebrate the marriage of the Thames and the Medway:

> There was the Liffy rolling downe the lea,
> The sandy Slane, the stony Aubrian,
> The spacious Shenan spreading like a sea,
> The pleasant Boyne, the fishy fruitfull Ban,
> Swift Awniduff, which of the English man

---

25. C.S. Lewis, "Spenser's Irish Experiences and *The Faerie Queene*", *RES*, VII (1931), 83–85.

26. *Spenser's Minor Poems*, ed. E. de Sélincourt, Oxford, 1910, 308. All subsequent references will be to this edition.

Is cal'de Blacke water, and the Liffar deep,
Sad Trowis, that once his people ouerran,
Strong Allo, tombling from Slewlogher steep,
And Mulla mine, whose waues I whilom aught to weep.[27]

The veil of allegory is suddenly lifted to reveal a different viewpoint, that of the poet himself celebrating the beauty of the Irish rivers, with special emphasis on those surrounding "my house of Kilcolman". In "Colin Clouts Come Home Againe" Colin, Spenser's spokesman, sings "of my riuer *Bregogs* loue" (l. 92), the love of the river Bregog for the "shiny Mulla". The river Mulla has been identified as the Awbeg which runs just south of Kilcolman. And in the "Mutabilitie Cantos" "my old father Mole" (Book VII, vi, 36) appears, whom we also know from Colin's story. Mole refers to the Ballyhoura and Galtee Mountains, whose highest peak is Galtymore or Dawson's Table, "Arlo-hill" in Spenser.[28] "Who knowes not *Arlo-hill*?" the poet asks between brackets. As Jack B. Oruch answered that question: "Nobody except Mrs. Spenser, Lodowick Bryskett, and Sir Walter Ralegh."[29]

Why did Spenser appropriate the rivers and mountains surrounding his Irish home in this way, breaking the rules of decorum by inserting himself as speaker in an allegorical context? Oruch suggests that the myths of which the quoted passages are part were "private poetry written to please the author's own fancy and to be fully understood by a small group of friends and patrons" (622). I believe that there is a more fundamental reason for the intrusion of the possessive pronoun in these texts. In order to make the point let us return for a moment to *A View*. One of the rare passages in which Irenius expresses himself with real enthusiasm about Ireland is when he describes a part of Northern Ireland, now desolate and waste:

And sure it is yet a most beautiful and sweet country as any is under heaven, seamed throughout with many goodly rivers replenished with all sorts of fish most abundantly, sprinkled with

---

27. *Spenser's Faerie Queene*, ed. J.C. Smith, 2 vols, Oxford, 1909, II, 146. All subsequent references to the poem are to this edition.

28. See Patrick W. Joyce, "Spenser's Irish Rivers", in *The Wonders of Ireland*, London, 1911, 72–114; also Roland M. Smith, "Spenser's Irish River Stories", *PMLA*, L (1935), 1047–56; *idem*, "Spenser's 'Stony Aubrian'", *MLN*, LIX (1944), 1–5; *idem*, "Irish Names in the *Faerie Queene*", *MLN*, LXI (1946), 27–38.

29. Jack B. Oruch, "Spenser, Camden, and the Poetic Marriages of Rivers", *SP*, LXIV (1967), 622.

> very many sweet islands and goodly lakes like little inland seas,
> that will carry even ships upon their waters, adorned with goodly
> woods fit for the building of houses and ships so commodiously,
> as that if some princes in the world had them, they would soon
> hope to be lords of all the seas and ere long of all the world ...
> (18–19).

The passage smacks of the Golden Age. The rivers leading out to sea are
here described as the life-source of the country. They provide food,
transport, plenty of building material both for "my house of Kilcolman"
and for ships sailing the seas, that allow England to conquer the world.

My point is that the images of the river stream and, by extension, the
seas that it leads out into, constitute a medium between two aspects of
Spenser's world that represent mutually exclusive chronotopes: the world
of the planter's home, epitomized in the possessive pronoun "my",
representing ideally a chronotope of stability and natural growth on the
one hand, and the world of expansion, of ships sailing the seas,
representative of a chronotope of travel and conquest on the other.[30]

There is dramatic irony in the fact that Spenser's idealization of the
water is the corollary of the miserable state of the land. Owning property
in Ireland did not correlate with the ideal chronotope. Instead of stability
and growth it meant being hemmed in and arrested in one's movements,
because of the threat of unexpected inroads of rebels and it meant land
laid waste and famine instead of plenty.

The rivers and the sea indicate chronotopes of the threshold, both in
A View and in the poetry. The chaos and lawlessness that permeate the
pages of *A View* are set off against the Golden Age vision of the Irish
rivers. As William Nelson has pointed out, the myth of the poetic
marriage of rivers in Book IV is symbolic not only of nationalism and
patriotism but also "of cosmic harmony and plenitude".[31]

A similar function is allotted to images of water in that part of *The
Faerie Queene* that is generally seen as a thinly disguised commentary on
Lord Grey's Irish policy and the lack of understanding and mistrust with
which he was regarded at home. Book V is the Legend of Justice and

---

30. W.W. Gray suggested that it is a "curious characteristic of Spenser as a poet
— his seeming capacity for holding two beliefs, or experiencing two emotions which
are incompatible with one another" (22).

31. Quoted in Oruch, 618n.

Artegall (read: Lord Grey) is its hero. He represents that aspect of Justice which is called equity.[32] Pauline Parker says of equity:

> The principle of equity enables even law to be set aside when, by some circumstance, it becomes clear that slavish insistence on the literal legal position would defeat the ends of real justice (216).

Artegall's quest is to help the Lady Irena (read: Ireland) against the tyrant Grantorto who keeps her in thraldom and usurps her heritage. We hear of his quest in Canto i after which a number of adventures follow, with Sir Sanglier, Pollente the Sarazin, the Giant, Radigund, Mercilla, and so forth, in each of which, according to W. Nicholas Knight, the principle of equity plays a part. Were it not for the assistance of Talus, the iron arm of the law and his loyal servant who conveniently does most of the dirty work for him, and for Britomart who comes to the rescue when Artegall has been unarmed by Radigund and made to wear women's clothes and do women's chores, Artegall would not have survived to uphold the high principles of equity. Artegall only returns to his original quest in the penultimate Canto of the Book. He duly performs his deed, fights and kills Grantorto, without assistance this time, and, like Lord Grey, has to return to "Faerie Court" prematurely, before he had the chance to "reform the country thoroughly" (xii, 27).

Although most of Artegall's adventures take place on land, Book V is curiously embedded in two images of the sea. The end of Book IV tells the myth of Neptune, one of the guests at the wedding of rivers, who frees Florimell by using the principles of equity in response to the plea of Marinell's mother: "For death t'adward I ween'd did appertaine/To none, but to the seas sole Soueraine" (xii, 30). That extra-remedial justice is not to be found on land is also exemplified in the story of the two brothers Amidas and Bracidas (iv, 4-20). Artegall settles the dispute between them by invoking the principle of equity:

> For equall right in equall things doth stand,
> For what the mighty Sea hath once possest,
> And plucked quite from all possessors hand,
> Whether by rage of waues, that neuer rest,
> Or else by wracke, that wretches hath distrest,

---

32. See W. Nicholas Knight, "The Narrative Unity of Book V of *The Faerie Queene*: 'That Part of Justice which is Equity'", *RES*, XXI (1970), 267-94. On equity, see M. Pauline Parker, *The Allegory of The Faerie Queene*, Oxford, 1960, 202-27.

> He may dispose by that imperiall might,
> As thing at randon left, to whom he list.
> So *Amidas*, the land was yours first hight,
> And so the threasure yours is *Bracidas* by right. (19)

By sweeping land away from the island of Bracidas and depositing it on
the island of his brother and by removing a chest filled with treasure
from Amidas' island and carrying it across to the island of Bracidas, the
sea establishes an equitable rule that human justice could not have
provided.

   At the end of Book V Artegall is recalled from Ireland, which forces
him to interrupt the "course of Iustice" (xii, 27). On his way back:

> He had not passed farre vpon the strand,
> When as two old ill fauour'd Hags he met. (28)

They turn out to be Envy and Detraction. Artegall meets them on the
"strand", the border line between two worlds, a threshold. In the sombre
perspective of Book V neither England nor Ireland live up to the high
ideals of harmony and equity. Spenser throws the anchor of his hope into
the element that surrounds both islands and keeps them divided.

ANGLO-DUTCH AND ANGLO-IRISH:
THE POLITICS OF ROMANTICISM

CIARAN MURRAY

Sir William Temple is best known to us as the mentor of Swift; I have previously set forth what I believe that troubled relationship to have been.[1] He was, indeed, an Anglo-Irishman in his own right, a landlord in Co. Carlow and Member of Parliament; but his most obvious claim to fame arises from his dealings with another country. It was as British ambassador to the United Provinces that he forged the first of the series of alliances that were to limit the power of Louis XIV, and negotiated the marriage between the Prince of Orange and the Princess Mary which gave William his claim on the throne of England and so brought about the revolution which made government a mandate extended by the governed. It was a principle that Temple passionately believed in. "The safety and firmness of any frame of government", he wrote, "may be best judged by the rules of Architecture, which teach us that the Pyramid is of all figures the firmest". "The ground", he went on, "upon which all government stands, is the consent of the people".[2]

It is, of course, one of the great ironies of history that that revolution was carried out through the medium of a man who resented bitterly the restrictions that it placed upon him. William was King in Holland, it was observed, and Stadtholder in England;[3] and you have only to think of his great garden over at Het Loo, with its obvious echoes of Versailles, to recall that he had something in him of the arbitrary temper of his enemy Louis. Temple detected this at an early stage, recommending as a motto for him *potius inservire patriae liberae quam dominari servienti*.[4] What

---

1. "The Japanese Garden and the Mystery of Swift": paper delivered to the IASAIL conference, Kyoto, 1990.

2. William Temple, *Works*, London, 1757, I, 50–51.

3. J.P. Kenyon, *The Stuarts*, Glasgow, 1981, 178.

4. H.E. Woodbridge, *Sir William Temple*, New York, 1940, 95.

Temple valued, then, beyond William, was the ethos of his country. One of his first impressions here was of the "strange freedom" — to an Englishman of that day — "that all men took ... of talking openly whatever they thought upon all the public affairs"; and, in his *Observations upon the United Provinces*, while he affected some of the fashionable disdain of an aristocratic for a merchant society, he was generous in his praise of its virtues: "the beauty and strength of their towns, the commodiousness of travelling in their country by their canals, bridges, and cawseys, the pleasantness of their walks ... and, in short, the beauty, convenience, and sometimes magnificence, of all public works."

He saw these as the the result of natural advantages improved upon by character: making, I am afraid, a rather painful contrast with Ireland in this regard. After pointing out that there were so many Irish harbours superior to those of Holland, he observed: "it is not a haven that draws trade, but trade that fills a haven." "The time of labouring or industrious men", he remarked, "is the greatest native commodity of any country". The concentration on, and pride in, public works he considered superior to what he described as "the constant excesses and luxury" of an aristocratic lifestyle: so that under cover of sharing his countrymen's prejudices he appears to be quietly criticizing them: as the book as a whole was intended to bring England back to what he considered its natural alliance with the Netherlands.

This alliance he did not think of merely as one of temporary advantage, or the accident of proximity, but of deep-seated affinity. He traces the parallels in language and institutions between the two countries to a common origin: making the Anglo-Saxons, in effect, transplanted Frieslanders. The ancient Batavians, he points out, were regarded by the Roman writers as "the most obstinate lovers and defenders of their liberties". This quality, he goes on, "seems to have continued constant and national among them, ever since that time, and never to have more appeared, than in the rise and constitutions of their present State".

Of all the liberties asserted in the Netherlands, Temple was most visibly impressed by that of religion. "No man can here complain", he writes, "of pressure in his conscience: of being forced to any public profession of his private faith: of being restrained from his own manner of worship in his house, or obliged to any other abroad". "They argue", he observes, "without interest or anger; they differ without enmity or scorn; and they agree without confederacy. Men live together, like citizens of the world, associated by the common ties of humanity, and by the bonds of peace .... The power of religion among them, where it is, lies in every man's heart."[5]

This eloquent account of the openness and generosity of spirit that Temple had found in the Dutch commonwealth brought him, in his own country, the kind of response that might have been expected. When he stood for parliament in the University of Cambridge, he was opposed, on the basis of this passage, by the Bishop of Ely: unsuccessfully, I am happy to relate.[6]

Temple had equally little influence on his royal master Charles, or his brother James: the result of whose experiments in despotism was the revolution which brought the Dutch king to England and vindicated Temple.

The second of his notable achievements was less deliberate, but it has been no less fundamental. And this, too, was rooted in his experience of this country. I have argued elsewhere that the first manifestation of romanticism in the arts is the English landscape garden; and that this is to be traced to an account by Temple of the naturalistic gardens created by the people he describes as "Chineses". Since, however, contemporary references to China, Japan, and what were still known as "the Indies" in general were extremely fluid, since no Chinese equivalent has been found for the word that Temple cites describing the irregular principle of these gardens, and since this word — *sharawadgi* — corresponds closely to the Japanese word *sorowaji*, meaning that a pattern is asymmetrical, it seems clear that Temple's source was Japanese. What is of particular interest, in this context, is that this form had become obsolete in the standard language by the time that Temple wrote, but that it survived in the south, where the Dutch settlement lay. And in the south of Japan you can still hear the trick of speech by which a word such as *sorowaji* would have turned into *shorowaji*. The final transition, from *shorowaji* to *sharawaji*, would have taken place, I am assured, as a result of its having been filtered through the Dutch language. Since this was then the only country in Europe permitted to carry on trade with Japan, and since Temple, in the summer of 1669, visited the directors of the East India Company, which managed that trade, in Haarlem, Amsterdam and Leiden, I think we may say, with a fair degree of certainty, that he might have met men who had stood in Japanese gardens, and that these in fact — since he speaks of having had his information at first hand — were the source of

---

5. Woodbridge, 81, 128–31. Temple, I, 154, 158, 182–83, 149, 159, 141–45, 164, 180–81.

6. Woodbridge, 197.

his description. What is extraordinary about Temple, however, is not that he picked up this piece of information, or even that he propagated it, but that he gave its principle such very high prestige, placing it above the formality in gardens which was the norm for Europe in his time.[7]

Each of this unusual Anglo-Irishman's significant achievements, then, was made possible by his sojourn in the Netherlands, and the influences he received there. And each of them is the prefiguring of a specifically modern idea: the decentralization of society bodied forth in the English revolution, and the decentralization of landscape, and ultimately of consciousness, which we describe as romanticism. For us, with the benefit of hindsight, the principle in common between the two — the principle of liberation — may seem perfectly obvious; and it may seem obvious, too, that one should be linked with the other, and that the landscape garden should become the specific attribute of a land with a then-revolutionary constitution, and should express a flight from centrality, in a kind of anti-Versailles. But as Arthur Koestler has pointed out, such retrospective obviousness requires, at the time, enormous reserves of imagination and persistence, in order to sift through countless irrelevancies and detect the essential analogy where no-one had observed it before.[8]

The person responsible for the achievement in this case — who spent, indeed, the greater part of a lifetime in working it through — was the unlikely figure (unlikely, that is to say, given current assumptions) of Joseph Addison. And Addison first appears upon the stage, both of history and of literature, as the author of a panegyric on the enthronement of the Anglo-Dutch king and his queen. The poem is modelled on the eclogues of Vergil, and when, in the first line, we find his shepherds meeting *inter corylos densas*, we are prepared for the theme of restoration. The song of the shepherds in fact is an encomium on those who have saved the kingdom from ruin — *qui dignabantur Regni fulcire ruinas* — and, after some little preamble, we are given their names: *Ipse Tuas, Gulielme, canam laudesque Mariae.*

As Vergil, in the beautiful language of the ninth eclogue, had placed Caesar's star above the older constellations — *Ecce Dionaei processit Caesaris astrum* — so Addison performs a similar service for William and Mary: he is the sun, she the moon:

7. "Swift's Mentor, Japan and the Origins of Romanticism", *The Harp*, V (1990), 1–21.

8. *The Act of Creation*, London, 1970, 103–105.

Primus hic Imperio, nulli est Virtute secundus,
Sic Sol, quam stellae, majori luce refulget.
Sed qualis stellas micat inter luna minores,
Talis, cum cincta est Sociis, Regina videtur.[9]

Exaggerated as all this may seem to us, who are so far removed from the conventions of baroque apotheosis, I believe every syllable of it to be sincere. I have not space here to go into the details of why I consider the whole current conception of Addison radically false: I hope to do so elsewhere. Let me simply say that the documentary evidence, when read without any tinge of subsequent mythologizing, indicates that, far from being the "First Victorian", or standard-bearer of conformity, he was a born, or at least a bred, rebel: that he was the subject of severe repression at the hands of his family; that he ran away from them; that he headed a revolt at school; and that his break with his own people culminated when, in defiance of their principles, he identified himself with the national revolution. This poem, and its reception, marked the turning-point of his life. His talent as a propagandist was immediately recognized. He was given a scholarship at Oxford, which was followed by a fellowship; he received the patronage of the Whig architects of the revolution settlement, Somers and Montagu; and through their influence he was awarded a Treasury grant to travel in Europe and prepare himself for public office.

This journey was to have momentous results. Everywhere that Addison travelled, his biographer Smithers remarks, he observed the revolution through its opposites;[10] and also through its parallels. In the lush plain of the Papal States, he noted decadence as the result of despotism; on the barren mountain of San Marino, he found prosperity as the consequence of freedom; and this reinforced certain thoughts he had earlier had about the analogy between liberty and landscape. Even before he had travelled abroad, he had considered the simple garden described by Vergil in the Georgics as superior to all the artificial elaborations of the gardens of France;[11] and, when he actually encountered the French gardens, he used this principle to differentiate them. "For my part", he writes, "I ... woud as soon see a River winding through Woods & Meadows as it dos near Fontaine-bleau than as when

---

9. Addison, *Miscellaneous Works*, ed. A.C. Guthkelch, London, 1914, I, 237–38.

10. P. Smithers, *The Life of Joseph Addison*, London, 1954, 63.

11. *Misc. Works*, II, 71, 76, 11.

it is toss'd up in such a Variety of figures at Versailles".[12] By the time
he reached Italy, and stood before the great waterfall at Terni, he was
ready to discard the French garden completely. "I think", he observed,
"there is something more astonishing in this *Cascade*, than in all the
water-works of *Versailles*".[13]

Gradually, in the course of Addison's travels, a formula had been
gathering force: as artifice is to tyranny, so is nature to liberty. As he
wrote in a poem to his Whig patron Montagu on crossing the Alps: "'Tis
Liberty that crowns Britannia's Isle,/And makes her barren Rocks, and
her bleak mountains smile."[14]

One does not think of Britain as predominantly a land of bleak
mountains or barren rocks: what has happened here, quite obviously, is
that the sight of the Alps has reawakened in Addison the memory of San
Marino, and transposed it over his thoughts of returning home. England,
as a result, is seen in its aspect of a land of liberty, and accordingly as
a landscape of wild nature.

It is tantalizing to see how close Addison has come to the principles
of the future English garden; but it was to be many more years before
that was to be realized. At this point the Dutch king died, Addison's
patrons fell from power, and Addison himself wandered, somewhat
aimlessly, in the general direction of home. He spent some time in
Holland and visited the university of Leiden. A rather lugubrious letter
of his has survived, in which he makes a contrast between his own
meditations amongst the anatomical exhibits and a more ebullient friend's
encounters with the fine women of The Hague.[15] It was a time of great
depression for him: he was impoverished and without prospects; but he
was observant enough to notice the good taste shown in the public
buildings and monuments, which he regarded as an index of a people's
culture.[16]

Queen Anne had had no great love for her Dutch predecessor: the
story goes that she even had the box hedges at Hampton Court rooted up
because they reminded her of him.[17] But she had wisdom enough to
follow his grand strategy for Europe and contain the ambitions of Louis

---

12. Addison, *Letters*, ed. W. Graham, Oxford, 1941, 10–11.

13. *Misc. Works*, II, 83.

14. *Ibid.*, I, 58.

15. *Letters*, 40–41.

16. *Spectator*, ed. D.F. Bond, Oxford, 1965, I, 111.

17. D. Clifford, *A History of Garden Design*, London, 1962, 98.

XIV. It was something the more insular Tories, then as now, found it impossible to comprehend: so that she was obliged to find support among the Whigs. As a result of this, Addison arrived in Dublin as secretary to the Lord Lieutenant. "I ... do not at all", he wrote, "regrette the leaving of England whilst I am going to a place where I shall have the satisfaction and Honour of Dr. Swift's conversation".[18] It would be pleasing to be able to assume that it was in the course of conversation with Temple's former secretary that Addison hit upon the idea of making the Japanese garden, as communicated to Temple in the Netherlands, the prototype of the English one. Intellectual history in that case would have taken on a peculiarly satisfying personal symmetry. I do not think, however, that we can do so. "Where he touched", observed a Whig historian of Swift, "he scorched";[19] and few passages are more blistering than that in which Swift attacks Holland precisely on the point of its communications with Japan. You will remember that the most improbable of all students of Leiden university was one Lemuel Gulliver; that he was fluent in Dutch; and that he was therefore able to pass himself off as a native of this country in Japan. There, he appealed to the shogun not to have to trample on the crucifix; whereupon that dignitary "began to doubt whether I were a real *Hollander* or no; but rather suspected I must be a CHRISTIAN".[20]

Here is the Swiftian irony at its most virulent; and it has been suggested that what has been termed his "vindictiveness against the Dutch" first surfaced when he was engaged by the Tory ministers to help dissolve the alliance which had so successfully thwarted the King of France.[21] But Swift's animosity had far deeper roots. Republicanism, Calvinism, religious toleration: any one of these was a threat to the establishment that he upheld. And in the country that embodied all of them he saw, says Ehrenpreis, "moral and social chaos ... brazenly exalted".[22] By the time he conversed in Dublin with Addison, he had already written that the Dutch "have no Religion, and are the worst constituted Government in the world".[23]

---

18. *Letters*, 210.

19. G.M. Trevelyan, *England under Queen Anne*, London, 1930-34, III, 99.

20. Swift, *Prose Works*, ed. H. Davis, Oxford, 1939–74, XI, 216–17.

21. E.D. Leyburn, "Swift's View of the Dutch", *PMLA*, LXVI (1951), 734–45.

22. I. Ehrenpreis, *Swift*, London, 1962–83, II, 542.

23. Swift, *Prose Works*, II, 100.

No, what happened to Addison in Dublin, the impetus that he encountered there and that changed his life and our history, came to him from his other close Irish friend, Richard Steele. It was in Dublin that Addison came upon that strange new publication, the *Tatler*, recognized Steele's hand in it from an observation that he himself had once made to him, submitted contributions, was taken into partnership, and, while Swift and his party drove Steele and himself out of office, found in journalism an alternative career and his true vocation.[24] Queen Anne, recognizing that the time had come to offer peace to the French, allowed a Tory government to return to office. But for Addison there was far more involved here than the loss of place or the temporary overshadowing of a friendship. Addison, like so many of the Whigs, saw in the devious figures who manipulated Swift the possibility that an understanding by them with France would lead to intrigues to bring back the Stuart pretender, and ultimately to the negating of the gains of the Williamite revolution. Subsequent research in the archives of the French Foreign Office has proved him right;[25] and though, through a combination of circumstances, this did not come to pass, it seemed at the time a very tangible threat. It was this moment of apprehension which led to Addison's next advance in the development of the landscape garden. In an essay of the *Tatler*, he sketched his vision of an England under siege: beleaguered by the French and the pretender in a fertile valley among the Alps. "I was wonderfully astonished", he relates,

> at the Discovery of such a Paradise amidst the Wildness of those cold, hoary Landskips which lay about it; but found at length, that this happy Region was inhabited by the Goddess of *Liberty*; whose Presence softened the Rigours of the Climate, enriched the Barrenness of the Soil, and more than supplied the Absence of the Sun.

Here Addison has taken up the theme where he had left it off in the poem he had written on his own crossing of the Alps, of English liberty and natural landscape; but where he carries it further is that this landscape of liberty is disposed internally according to the principles of an irregular garden. "The Place", he says,

---

24. Smithers, 160–64. *Tatler*, ed. D.F. Bond, Oxford, 1987, I, 56. A. Beljame, *Men of Letters and the English Public in the Eighteenth Century*, London, 1948, 261.

25. Trevelyan, III, 89–94, 248–49.

was covered with a wonderful Profusion of Flowers, that without being disposed into regular Borders and Parterres, grew promiscuously, and had a greater Beauty in their natural Luxuriancy and Disorder, than they could have received from the Checks and Restraints of Art.[26]

This is one of the great turning-points in intellectual history. Addison, through the inexorable intertwining of aesthetic and political thought, has made the natural garden the inevitable symbol of the England of the Williamite revolution: so reversing millenia of development in the attitude to nature in the west. But this reversal has occurred, as yet, on the emblematic level alone. It was only when Addison, deepening his virtuosity in the medium given him by Steele, replaced the *Tatler* with the *Spectator* — a journal in which he became the dominant power and the dominant personality — that the expression of his thought became complete. It was here, in his great series of essays on the "Pleasures of the Imagination" that Addison, in the year that Rousseau was born, "laid the foundation of the whole romantic aesthetics in England".[27] And at the core of this was the paper in which he suggested that the English garden return to nature. As a prototype he puts forward the usage of the people he knew as Chinese; and his account is a paraphrase of Temple. At the end he remarks: "They have a Word, it seems, in their Language, by which they express the particular Beauty" of the irregular garden.[28] That word, unspoken, is *sharawadgi*; and Temple's quest is complete. The two parts of his vision, government and the garden, have been brought together: they have fused in the crucible of another psyche. So the world we know begins, in the consciousness of two inhabitants of Anglo-Ireland, and through their encounter with an Anglo-Dutch king. The fruit of that encounter was romanticism, which we are now in a position to define: aesthetic manifestation of the English revolution.

---

26. *Tatler*, II, 397–401.

27. J.G. Roberston, *Studies in the Genesis of Romantic Theory in the Eighteenth Century*, Cambridge, 1923, 241.

28. *Spectator*, III, 548–63.

"THE GENTLEMEN AT LARGE": DUBLIN CASTLE, TRINITY COLLEGE, AND JONATHAN SWIFT

SUSAN FISHER MILLER

In an appendix to his landmark edition of Swift's poems, Sir Harold Williams devoted considerable attention to an early eighteenth-century Dublin commonplace book that includes satiric poems once attributed to Swift.[1] Though Williams found few grounds in the verses for claiming Swift's authorship, he did acknowledge that the "distinct Dublin interest" and "relative and intrinsic" merit of one ten-stanza poem, "The Gentlemen at Larges Litany", invites speculation about its provenance (pp. 1062–63). Closer examination now reveals a hand that may well be that of the author of *A Tale of a Tub*.[2]

Williams's transcription of "The Gentlemen at Larges Litany" follows here:

> 1   From leaving fair England y^t goodly old seat
>   And comeing to Ireland to serve for our meat
>   In hopes of being made all verry great
>   Libera nos Domine

---

1. *The Poems of Jonathan Swift*, ed. Harold Williams, 3 vols, Oxford, 1958, III, 1058–68. The owner (or owners) of the commonplace book transcribed poems into an interleaved copy of Harwards's Almanack for 1666. Sir William R. Wilde first drew critical attention to the Harward manuscript. F. Elrington Ball, *Swift's Verse*, London, 1929, 11–13, also treats the manuscript, correcting Wilde's mistaken ordering of the poems, as well as Wilde's mistaken assumption that all the poems were compositions by Swift. I am indebted to Professor John J. Fisher of Goshen College, Goshen, Indiana, who first brought "The Gentlemen at Larges Litany" to my attention, and gave valuable critical suggestions regarding this article. I also wish to thank professors Donald T. Torchiana and Christopher Herbert, Northwestern University, for their critique of an earlier form of the manuscript.

2. Jonathan Swift, *A Tale of a Tub with Other Early Works*, ed. Herbert Davis, Oxford, 1939.

2   From staying at Dublin till we have spent
     Our ready Coine all in following ye sent
     Of what we could never catch; Preferment
                              Libera nos &c

3   From liveing upon one short meale a day
     Without bit of breakfast our stomach to stay
     Or supper to drive ye long night away
                              Libera nos &c

4   From dwelling where folks to prayers doe fall
     Thrice for each meal, and where they doe call
     To ye Chappell oftner than to ye Hall
                              Libera nos &c

5   From drinking and whoreing and staying [out late]
     And being locked out of ye Castle gate
     And returning again to ye bonny Kate
                              Libera nos &c

6   From lying all night with a Lowsie whore
     And bringing away from her ye Glandore
     And running with Monsr Roboe on ye score
                              Libera nos &c

7   From quarrelling amongst our selves; without
     Some body to hold us from goeing out
     From handling cold iron being stout
                              Libera nos &c

8   From playing Cards in ye room above stairs
     And loosing our mony with a bon air
     To gratifie ye Lady thats not verry fair
                              Libera nos &c

9   From ye Stewards rebuke and Controllers smile
     Bestow'd with a grace enough to beguile
     One out of his way a Yorkshire mile
                              Libera nos &c

10   From turning Tory or Highwaymen
     And leaveing our bones near Stephens green
     Now let us all say I pray God Amen
                              Libera nos Domine

This Litany would have been Longer but that the Author knew those Gentlemens Constitutions, can as ill endure long as frequent Prayers.

(1063–64, stanza numbers added).

The poem is a parodic litany, a form frequently employed by political versifiers of the age.[3] Its pattern is typical: a series of three-line stanzas cataloguing, with sham piety, an assortment of calamities, each followed by the petitionary refrain "Libera nos Domine".

Williams assigned "The Gentlemen at Larges Litany" to 1690–91 (1063). In fact, this poem's allusions to particular circumstances at Trinity College point to a somewhat earlier composition — before, rather than after, the Battle of the Boyne. The "Litany" involves, then, a crucial period in Irish history: the panic from 1687 to 1689, when James II, having produced a Catholic heir to the English throne, was supplanted by William of Orange but then mounted with Tyrconnel a brief but potent threat to Ireland until his defeat in 1690. The poem's uneasy tone properly reflects the anxieties of Irish Protestants before the Boyne.

The poem's title phrase, "gentlemen at large", in its colloquial sense refers to young gentlemen from respectable families, "attached to the court but having no specific duties assigned to them" (*OED*). Such gentlemen, attached to viceregal Dublin Castle but caught in the confusion before William's military victory, would indeed be "at large".

Against this backdrop rises the plaint of the gentlemen. The litany's petitions mark a progressive decline which begins with "leaving fair England"; moves on to "staying", "living", and "dwelling" at Dublin; points to various modes of dissipation offered in that city; and ends with a prospect of these gentlemen "turning Tory" and "leaveing their bones near Stephens green" — the latter an allusion to the gallows at Baggot Street where executions were performed.[4]

---

3. *Poems on Affairs of State: Augustan Satirical Verse, 1660–1714*, gen. ed. G. de F. Lord, 7 vols, Yale University Press, 1963–1971, V, 218.

4. William R. Wilde, *The Closing Years of Dean Swift's Life*, Dublin, 1849, 140n.; George Mayhew, "Swift and the Tripos Tradition", *PQ*, VL (1966), 85–101, at 100. For definitions of "turning tory", see J.G. Simms, "The Restoration and the Jacobite War", in *The Course of Irish History*, eds T.W. Moody and F.X. Martin, Cork, 1978, 204–16: "Many Catholics failing to recover [lands] following the Act of Settlement (and second Act) turned 'tory', took to the hills and woods, and raided the new settlers" (205); and Máire O'Brien and Conor Cruise O'Brien, *A Concise History of Ireland*, 3rd edn, London, 1985, 70: "The 'tories' — outlaws drawn from the ranks of the dispossessed — threatened the new rulers and owners throughout

Besides the Castle and the town, and still considered to be outside Dublin proper,[5] Trinity College felt the force of the same political storms. Indeed, Jacobite agitation for Catholic appointments to the faculty and increasingly restricted college incomes forced the college's temporary closure early in 1689. At the Commencement of July 1688, the annual free-for-all of students known as the Tripos featured, along with the usual outrageous in-house humour and jibes at the town residents assembled for the occasion, satiric treatments of the college's political foes.[6] This strong Tripos tradition suggests a Trinity College source for "The Gentlemen at Larges Litany". These verses could have been material assembled for the July 1688 Tripos but withheld from performance, or omitted from the record.[7] One can imagine the effect of such a mock prayer voiced by Trinity students, whose own required daily devotions were numerous,[8] in which city swells beg release from those misdemeanours sternly prohibited to the scholars. The "Litany's" antiphonal form would have made it a perfect burlesque performance

---

much of the country" in the period of Protestant settlement from 1650 onwards.

5. Edward MacLysaght, *Irish Life in the Seventeenth Century*, Cork, 1950, 185; Irvin Ehrenpreis, *Swift: The Man, His Works, and the Age*, 3 vols, London, 1962–1967, I, 44.

6. *The Whimsical Medley*, TCD ms I.5.1, Trinity College Library, Dublin, 142–77; Mayhew, 90–95. I have relied on George Mayhew's article "Swift and the Tripos Tradition" for its thorough history of the Tripos at Oxford, Cambridge and Dublin. Ehrenpreis, *Swift: The Man, His Works and the Age*, also treats the Tripos tradition at Trinity College (67). While John Barrett (*An Essay on the Earlier Part of the Life of Swift*, London, 1808) had argued over-confidently that the entire Tripos of 1688 was the secret work of the student Swift (it is known to have been delivered by Swift's classmate, John Jones), Mayhew holds out the possibility that Swift may have collaborated in producing this Tripos.

7. While the Trinity College Tripos of 1688, as preserved in *The Whimsical Medley*, does not include "The Gentlemen at Larges Litany", it is worth remembering that this version may not be complete. As Mayhew points out, the Tripos speeches by this late period in the tradition consisted of "parts" composed by a number of student contributors. In an effort to avoid college authorities requisitioning his script following a libelous performance, the deliverer of the speech likely "attempted to keep his script down to the minimum in a single, easily disposed of copy" and "was expected to do a certain amount of witty and offensive improvising" (96–97). Mayhew also establishes that the *Whimsical Medley* version could not have been transcribed until some time following 1700 (91n.).

8. Constantia Maxwell, *A History of Trinity College Dublin*, Dublin, 1946, 49.

piece: the leader solemnly intoning each set of petitions, and his audience roaring back "Libera nos Domine!".

A closer look at the poem strengthens the case for its Trinity origins. Half of the Litany's stanzas allude to recorded historical circumstances of the period before the college's 1689 closure. These allusions suggest that in "The Gentlemen at Larges Litany" a student author facetiously equates two types of Dublin gentlemen — the "boys" at Trinity College preparing to enter the world, and the "men" from the Castle already out there. For example, Maxwell reports in *A History of Trinity College* that college officials of the late seventeenth century found it necessary to decree that, on pain of punishment, "gowns had to be worn both in the College and in the city of Dublin, and no one was to wear boots with his gown or 'affect the pomp of a Court in his dress, hair, or gait, but everyone shall observe that modesty and gravity that befits an academical state'" (47). If we remember that "at large" can also refer to a group of people taken "as a whole, as a body, in general; taken together" (*OED*), then the title can also imply town and gown gentlemen satirically united.

The "Litany" sends up both courtiers and scholars. The poem's first direct reference to Dublin student life occurs in stanza three. "By the beginning of 1689", Irvin Ehrenpreis writes, "none of the tenants of the college properties was paying rent, and supplies fell so low that 'but one meal a-day' was ordered to be provided in hall, 'and that a dinner, because supper is the more expensive meal'" (88).

Ehrenpreis also confirms the poem's claim in stanza four of a prayer "thrice for each meal": "Undergraduates and bachelors of arts had the exercise of giving the blessing before meals, the thanks afterward, and the Bible-reading at dinner", hence the call to chapel more often than to hall. At least three daily visits to chapel for devotions were required as well (60).

As for "quarrelling" and "handling of cold iron" (stanza seven) Maxwell cites, among other student vagrancies, "rioting in the streets ... wearing swords, daggers or poniards ... wounding fellow-students, or Dublin citizens" (46).

Stanza eight alludes to another documented college vice, playing cards. Surreptitious card-playing took place in the seclusion of the Porter's Lodge or of the Steeple, a tower remaining on campus from the days of an early Augustinian monastery (Maxwell, 46–47) — thus the Litany's "room above stairs". As for stanzas nine and ten, the "Steward" and "Controller" mentioned are standard staff members in the English-model university.

We now return to stanzas five and six and the question of Castle or College gentlemen. The "Castle gate" (stanza 5) clearly alludes to the home base of wastrel Dublin gentlemen attached to the viceregal court. Edward MacLysaght quoted the journal of one John Steven, who observed in 1698 that Dublin "seemed to be a seminary of vice, and an academy of luxury, or rather a sink of corruption and living emplem [*sic*] of Sodom". Prostitution was a common feature of city taverns (58–59).

Yet "drinking and whoreing and staying out late" were known to Trinity students as well. To refer once more to Maxwell's account, college records list "lodging in the town, resorting to the ale houses, climbing the college walls and insulting women" among examples of student disobedience (46). Jonathan Swift himself was on several occasions punished for staying in town, as well as for inciting riot within college and failure to attend prayers (Ehrenpreis, 68–70). Certainly, the Litany's author in stanza five affects censure of the tardy society gents, "locked out of ye Castle gate" and stranded on Dame Street. But he hints as well that we need only read "College" for "Castle" to envision marauding Trinity lads, barred late at night from entry at College Green. Of after-hours misbehaviour in Trinity Irvin Ehrenpreis comments, "A desperate comment may be heard in an order of the house, July 1688, that the walls of the College should be built three feet higher" (66).

If the Litany was meant to figure in a public Tripos oration, the defiant disrespect of "The Gentlemen at Large" is especially daring. As a student piece it sends barbs in at least four directions: toward the Castle (its gentlemen and ladies present in Trinity Commencement Tripos audiences) (*Whimsical Medley*, 142–77, Mayhew, 88–89), toward the town, toward College disciplinarians, and, in an engaging self-skewering, back toward its feckless student petitioners and their leader.

The Litany poet's nonchalantly tossing our way more gentlemen and points of view than we can comfortably juggle and his merging of their Dublin settings suggest a distinctive talent, one intent not simply on totting up clever contemporary allusions, but on stretching the limits of his satiric form. William J. Cameron remarks that in the conventional parodic litany, the stanzas' complaints are frequently too wide-ranging to make effective satire (Lord v, 218). In "The Gentlemen at Large", on the other hand, expatriation in Dublin does provide a unifying focus. In contrast to other mock litanies of the period that single out various people for ridicule, this litany's gentlemen pray to be quit of Dublin itself. An entire place — like the London of Swift's "A Description of a Shower" — rather than persons, becomes the ostensible target of the satirist.

Even more impressive than his use of place as unifying conceit is the author's control of his *dramatis personae*, the gentlemen. Parody of the litany genre typically presents two choices: either the poet may employ the litany's spokesmen as his mouthpieces in a direct attack on his enemies, or he may create ironic petitioners whose prayers expose them as fools. In this case, the author behind "The Gentlemen" manages to do both.

If mouthpieces, a mock litany's speakers may simply voice their author's grievances; an example is the "Litany in the Year 1684",[9] sensitive to the conventional French and Dutch religious polarities:

> From the Partial Preaching that is now in Fashion
> From divinity to undo a Nation
> From Wooden shoes and Transubstantiation
>   Libera nos, &c.

"The Gentlemen at Large", too, employs straightforward spokesmen, the expatriate Englishmen associated with Dublin Castle, who expose Dublin's hard-luck conditions, moral pitfalls, and threat of Catholic coercion. "The Gentlemen at Large" manuscript takes its place among a collection of Protestant, Williamite verses, and its author presumably shared these sympathies.

But a litany author can also choose self-ironic spokesmen. One example from the 1680s, "A Loyal Litany", dramatizes supporters of James II who face the impending threat of William's invasion: "We humbly do beseech Thee, Lord/That we may govern by the sword" (*Third Collection*, 30). The outrageous temptations that these Catholic loyalists show themselves prey to, and the alarming boons they request, work against the pious tone of their appeal.

This convention of creating a spokesman whose own words condemn him is not limited to mock litanies, of course; putting words into enemy mouths was one standard way to frame adversaries in print. The classic example is "Lillibullero", the mock-Gaelic doggerel originally written to poke fun at native Irish hopes when, in January 1687, the Catholic Earl of Tyrconnel was appointed by James as lord deputy in Ireland. "The Gentlemen at Larges Litany" does not employ native Irish speakers in its exposure of Irish manners; it maintains the vantage point of condescending English observers who must endure an assignment in Ireland. Yet the Litany nonetheless partakes of the "Lillibullero" satiric strategy.

And, if we return for a moment to the anti-Catholic "Loyal Litany" (*Third Collection*, 30), we see that its opening lines, created to self-destruct in the mouths of the Catholic spokesmen, also call to mind

---

9. *A Third Collection of the Newest ... Poems ... Relating to the Times*, London, 1689, 30.

the arrogant accusations of our litanists, accusations which in fact metamorphose into confessions:

> From all the women we have whored.
> From being bound to keep our word
> From Civil Broiles and Foreign Sword.
>   Libera nos domine.

Much of the special effect, then, in "The Gentlemen at Large" comes from the reader's recognition that these penitents should plead, "From *ourselves*/Libera nos Domine".

Yet the poem outdistances contemporary litanies even beyond the comic effect achieved when the prayers turn back on their speakers. Bewildered in this litany by the mutually subversive vindication and satirization of the gentlemen, in its confusion the audience itself is made to feel "at large" and somehow ridiculed. In short, the poet is capable of composing reflexive satire of the kind we have come to know as "Swiftian".[10]

In light of the preceding perceptions of the Litany, we must once more consider the possibility that "The Gentlemen at Large" could in fact be a juvenile effort by Swift. Other Swiftian aspects present themselves. By mentioning "yᵉ Glandore", for instance, as a threat to gentlemen consorting with Dublin ladies, the author refers to no human malady, but to a livestock disease (*OED*). We note also the equivocal nature of the "Litany's" political stance; while he ostensibly defends the position of Ireland's Anglo-Irish residents, in a back-handed way the author hints at some degree of sympathy with the dispossessed Catholic landowners, the "tories" or outlaws — they, too, are alienated "gentlemen at large", perhaps analogous to the politically alienated Sir William Temple or the non-juring Archbishop Sancroft, heroes of Swift's youthful idealism.[11] Finally, readers of Swift cannot help noticing the parallel between the Litany author-speaker's abrupt sign-off, after ten rambling stanzas ("This Litany would have been Longer ..."), and the closing lines from the crazed narrator of *A Tale of a Tub*, another scribbler "at large": "I already discover, that the Issues of my Observanda begin to grow too large for the Receipts. Therefore, I shall here pause ..." (*Tale*, 135).

---

    10. David M. Veith, "Toward an Anti-Aristotelian Poetic: Rochester's *Satyr against Mankind* and *Artemisia to Chloe*, with Notes on Swift's *Tale of a Tub* and *Gulliver's Travels*", *Language and Style*, V (1972), 123–45.

    11. A.C. Elias, *Swift at Moor Park*, Philadelphia: Pa, 1982, 78n.

Even if the possibility of Swift's hand in "The Gentlemen at Larges Litany" should remain in the realm of speculation, we can recognize the poem's precocious Swiftian signs: sophistication, Irish "double vision",[12] and "anti-Aristotelian poetic" (Veith, 123–45). In any case, "The Gentlemen at Larges Litany" offers some hitherto neglected insight into the troubled political milieu and witty academic atmosphere from which Jonathan Swift emerged in 1689 — a gentleman at large himself — to enter Sir William Temple's service at Moor Park and to generate *A Tale of a Tub*.

---

12. Andrew Carpenter, "Double Vision in Anglo-Irish Literature", in *Place, Personality, and the Irish Writer*, ed. Andrew Carpenter, Gerrards Cross, 1977, 173–89.

"PRINCE POSTERITY" AS AN IRISH NATIONALIST: THE POSTHUMOUS COURSE OF SWIFT'S PATRIOTIC REPUTATION

ROBERT MAHONY

Jonathan Swift may have been no more concerned than many other writers with the reception later generations would accord him, but in his case that concern is definitely and repeatedly evident. Early in his writing career he taunted those later generations by dedicating *A Tale of a Tub* to "Prince Posterity"; close to its end, he made his posthumous reputation the subject of his most famous poem, "Verses on the Death of Dr. Swift", which he concluded with an extended eulogy on himself. Finally, he composed the Latin epitaph, inscribed on a marble tablet that adorns his grave in St. Patrick's Cathedral, Dublin. Here, as in "Verses on the Death of Dr. Swift", he tried to shape his reputation in terms of his defence of human freedom: "Fair *Liberty* was all his cry", the poem has it; the epitaph enjoins the onlooker to imitate his vindication of liberty, "if you can". At least ostensibly, it was as a lover of liberty that he wished to be remembered. And in Ireland, this has long had a distinct local significance, stemming from his support for domestic manufactures, from his sympathy for the oppressed, and especially from his articulating the Irish popular resistance to the London government's award of a patent for Irish coinage to the Englishman, William Wood. From the very appearance of *The Drapier's Letters* opposing Wood's patent in 1724, Swift was hailed as a great Irish patriot, and oftentimes since he has been regarded as an ancestor of Irish nationalism. His patriotic reputation has hardly had a steady course over the two and a half centuries since his death, however, and among Irish Catholics he has only in this century been accepted as a patriot without equivocation.

As recently as 1934, indeed, Daniel Corkery, reviewing a few biographies of Swift for the journal *Studies*, doubted the validity of Swift's patriotism on the ground that he was not really Irish at all. Rather, Swift's identity was English, which Corkery determined more surely than he felt that he, or any living Anglophone Irishman, could his own. "For there is no living Irishman who is Irish through and through as the first Englishman we may light upon is English. The best of us, even the people of the Gaeltacht, practically all of them educated in English, are little more than piebald nationalists". But Swift was none such: "the dominant factor in his mind was English",[1] and further, the Irish patriotism often attributed to him was actual only if he had sympathized with Gaelic Ireland, which manifestly he did not. Corkery was particularly addressing notions such as W.D. Taylor's comment on the fourth *Drapier's Letter*, which Swift addressed "To the Whole People of Ireland": "with his mind full of the ignorance, servility and destitution of the 'native Irish' he insensibly begins to speak for them".[2] Corkery knew, as we know, that the "whole people" Swift really had in mind in this letter comprised Protestant Ireland, and that he laments here the helotized state this people had been reduced to by their dependence upon England. The actual degradation of the native Irish, Swift implies again and again, is a metaphor for the less obvious political and psychological degradation of Protestant Ireland. But Corkery hardly stops there, for he would not have accepted the term "Protestant Ireland", which suggests the existence of two nations in Ireland. When Aodh De Blácam pressed the idea of a Protestant Ireland in another *Studies* article in 1934, "The Other Hidden Ireland", Corkery rejected it in yet another piece in that journal, "The Nation that was not a Nation". The Protestant settlement was thoroughly imbued with "the spirit of English imperialism, to which spirit Bedell the Gaeliciser, as well as Ussher the Angliciser, had both surrendered themselves".[3] There might be two religions, two cultures even, but only one national identity; the effect of this, of course, is to exclude the non-Gaelic in culture and the non-Catholic in religion — even if contemporary Gaels are but piebald nationalists!

In our time, most Irish people, however nationalist, can accept more easily than Corkery could the significance to national history and culture of both Protestant Ireland and an Anglo-Irish literature, in both of which Swift is a leading figure. Seamus Deane, for instance, has recently maintained that "Anglo-Irish writing does not begin with Swift, but Anglo-Irish literature does". To Deane the political Swift, like his older contemporary William Molyneux, is beginning "to identify what was

1. Daniel Corkery, "Ourselves and Dean Swift", *Studies*, XXIII (1934), 210–11.

2. W.D. Taylor, *Jonathan Swift: A Critical Essay*, London, 1933, 167.

3. Daniel Corkery, "The Nation that was not a Nation", *Studies*, XXIII (1934), 615.

later to be understood as colonialism".[4] Where Corkery identified Protestant Ireland with English interests, Deane sees it as an early version of modern Anglophone Ireland. Corkery could not have accepted this; opposed to the very notion of an Anglo-Irish literature as central to modern Irish culture, he could hardly have taken its inauguration as analogous to the colonial beginnings of a modern emergent nation. To him, Ireland was no emergent nation, but then he did not have other post-colonial cultures to compare it with. Underscoring the implications of such tentative, retroactive assimilation, Deane notes further that in defending Protestant Ireland, taking the part of a country he despised, Swift became "a man and mind subverted rather than subversive. Ireland enriched his rhetoric and undermined his beliefs. In the end he appeared to himself to have become one of his own foolish projectors, a man preaching improvement to a doomed people ... beginning to see his own reflection in his reformist writings. The Irish world would not be mended, but the Irish writer would be transmogrified in his attempt to improve it."[5] In concert with the dominant tendency of Anglo-Irish literary historiography since Yeats, Swift is thus absorbed into the mainstream of Irish literature. Rather as he seemed to Yeats, he becomes a generic prototype of the modern, discontented Irish writer, recognizable as a cultural ancestor.

This is a long way from being Corkery's outsider, yet Corkery was probably more accurate about what we can discover of Swift's own perspective. Certainly his references to the religion and the language of most Irish people in his time, the two elements of culture that determine for Corkery their national identity, indicate that they are tangential to his patriotic concerns. Their plight may, as I have said, work as a metaphor for that of Irish Protestants, but since Swift's patriotism was defensive, Irish Catholics hardly figured because they posed no threat to the Protestant nation or its interests. To accept that they did, in religious terms, would be to play into the hands of the English latitudinarians, and those of the dissenters, especially Presbyterians, whose cause the latitudinarians promoted. Swift was always a strong Churchman, who generally identified Ireland's best interest as that of the Anglican establishment. The great strength of Presbyterianism in Ireland was, moreover, not merely a real problem for that establishment but offered the English an important means of controlling the fortunes of Anglicans in Ireland, often adversely to their interests and thus the good of the

---

4. Seamus Deane, *A Short History of Irish Literature*, London, 1986, 37, 47-48.

5. *Ibid.*, 48-49.

country as a whole. Hence it is from Presbyterianism that Swift saw the real threat to the religious establishment and social harmony. By contrast, Catholics were checked by the penal laws, and the language of most of them mattered very little to Swift. It is true that in his "Answer to Several Letters sent me from Unknown Hands" of 1729 he comments that "It would be a noble achievement to abolish the Irish language in this Kingdom".[6] This is a very brief reference to the subject, actually concerned with the benefits of an exclusive use of English for commerce; while it probably reflects his sentiments accurately, there is little else in his works to suggest that he cared about the language.

The Ireland whose cause Swift advocated, then, was not the Gaelic, Catholic country Corkery championed. And the reactions of ordinary Catholic people to him in the eighteenth and early nineteenth centuries, as measured by the anecdotes collected by the Irish Folklore Commission and preserved at University College, Dublin, render a picture not so much of a patriot as of a wit, a "character".[7] Of course, during the Wood's halfpence controversy, according to Lord Orrery, Swift's friend late in life, he had the allegiance of Catholics along with that of others: "The Papist, the Fanatic, the Tory, the Whig, all listed themselves under the banner of M.B. Drapier, and were all equally zealous to serve the common cause."[8] But after his death Swift was not a figure much invoked by the leaders of the respectable classes of Catholics in their campaigns for the relaxation of the Penal Laws in the latter part of the century. Both Dr John Curry and Charles O'Conor of Belanagar, who were prominent in these campaigns, praised Swift as a great patriot,[9] but they were brief references, and very unusual. A major reason that such references are so sparse is of course their implausibility, as Swift himself had never advocated a specifically Catholic cause or taken issue with the Penal Laws. A second, less obvious reason is that Swift's patriotic efforts

---

6. *The Prose Works of Jonathan Swift*, ed. Herbert Davis, Oxford, 1955, XII, 89.

7. See Mackie L. Jarrell, "'Jack and the Dane': Swift Traditions in Ireland", in *Fair Liberty was all his Cry: A Tercentenary Tribute to Jonathan Swift*, ed. A.N. Jeffares, London, 1967, 311–41.

8. John Boyle, Earl of Orrery, *Remarks on the Life and Writings of Dr. Jonathan Swift*, London, 1752, 73.

9. John Curry, *Observations on the Popery Laws*, Dublin, 1771, 50; Charles O'Conor, introducing Curry, *The State of the Catholics of Ireland*, appended to *An Historical and Critical Review of the Civil Wars in Ireland*, Dublin, 1786, II, iii–iv (second pagination).

were frequently regarded in England as spurious, motivated by disappointment at the thwarting of his ambitions for preferment or influence there rather than by a real love of his own country. Since it was to the British establishment, more than to the Irish Parliament, that Catholics looked for relief, Swift was hardly a political writer that they could serviceably invoke to advance their case among that establishment. He had, moreover, a popular reputation in England as an eccentric, ribald parson, unduly given to scatology; Irish Catholic leaders, anxious to demonstrate their respectability, had all the greater reason therefore to make little mention of him.

Irish Protestants generally had a better opinion of the Dean who had showed himself outspoken for their economic well-being. But the praise they showered upon him was often shallow, a form of words like "that great patriot Dr Swift", and the ever-present fear of Popery could uncover ambiguities about the defensive patriotism he represented. Following a proposition that a statue be erected to celebrate the Drapier, an anonymous writer in 1732 suggested that it was more necessary for Ireland to recall her deliverance by King William III not only from the "Popery and Slavery" of Jacobitism, but also from "King *James's* Brass money, ... an Evil of a hundred Times greater Consequence than that which provoked the *Splendida bilis* of the honest *Drapier*".[10] And after Swift's death, the popular memory of him as a patriot did not necessarily include remembering the substance of his patriotism, so that he could be made to seem an opponent of what, if living, he might well have supported. When in 1748–49 the Dublin apothecary Charles Lucas stood for Parliament as an advocate of municipal and parliamentary reform, his establishment adversaries felt free to raise Swift's ghost in their own favour. A pamphlet addressed especially to the city's weavers cautions them against Lucas, since "it is *your Interest, more particularly than any other Set of People,* to be well with those in *Power,* who can *serve* or *disserve* you! You may have Favours to ask of them! then be *wise* — be *prudent* — do not *offend* them — do not kick against the Pricks!"[11] Lucas himself, on the other hand, hardly mentioned Swift at all, since he was a wholehearted Whig and Swift was remembered as a Tory.

Swift's reputation as a patriot was actually pressed during the eighteenth century less in discussions of Ireland's national rights or the

---

10. "Philostelus", *A Letter to the Right Honourable Sir Ralph Gore ...*, Dublin, 1732, 12.

11. Anon., *Dean Swift's Ghost: To the Citizens of Dublin: Concluding with a Word Particularly to the Weavers*, Dublin, 1749, 7.

need for reform, than in discussions of the Dean himself, raised by the
frequent republication of his collected *Works* in the eighteenth century
and the attendant host of literary and biographical treatments. George
Faulkner, Swift's publisher, who was responsible for most Irish
eighteenth-century editions of the *Works*, noted him as "that great and
eminent Patriot" in recording his death in the *Dublin Journal* of 19–22
October 1745. After Faulkner published the Irish edition of Orrery's
largely pejorative *Remarks* in 1752, however, the Dean's ghost was
resurrected to protest against Faulkner's disloyalty to his memory in so
joining "Issue with the Enemies of Ireland", whom Orrery's attacks on
Swift had encouraged.[12] For, as another anonymous pamphleteer put it,
"what Friend of Ireland ... would not be grieved at seeing the Infirmities
of such a Man ever become the subject of malevolent Criticism?"[13] But
it was not only Orrery's seeming character assassination that his own
detractors rebuked. He had remarked of Swift's *Short View of the State
of Ireland* (1727) that "Of this I need take little notice, since the present
state of Ireland is, in general, as flourishing as possible ... in the space
of eighteen years, which is almost the full time that I have known it, no
Kingdom can be more improved".[14] Swift's cousin Deane Swift
responded in 1755 that Orrery was clearly "a Stranger to the Groans and
Miseries of that unfortunate kingdom", and wondered that he could
"possibly reside for the greater part of eighteen years in Ireland, without
remarking ... that no People in the Christian World are so destitute".[15]
Deane Swift's *Essay*, like Orrery's *Remarks*, was first published in
London, and both spoke therefore to more than an Irish audience; hence,
perhaps, Samuel Johnson a quarter century later could at once accept
Orrery's view of Irish prosperity and count Swift a great patriot: "It was
from the time when he first began to patronize the Irish that they may
date their riches and prosperity. He taught them first to know their own
interest ... and gave them spirit to assert that equality with their fellow

---

12. Anon., "A Letter from Dean Swift to G---E F----R", in *A Letter from a
Primate to a Pretender Found by a Patriot Stander-by: To Which Is Added* [etc.],
Isle of Man, n.d., 15.

13. Anon., *A Letter from a Gentleman in the Country to his Son in the College
of Dublin*, Dublin, 1752, 9.

14. *Remarks*, 199–200.

15. Deane Swift, *An Essay upon the Life, Writings and Character of Dr.
Jonathan Swift*, London, 1755, 199–200.

subjects to which they have ever since been making vigorous advances".[16]

Swift's continuing eminence as a literary figure, indeed, and the pride his fellow Irish Protestants took in him as such, were more the factors that kept his patriotic reputation fresh than were any admiring references by Irish reformers in the latter part of the eighteenth century. The most famous such reference, Henry Grattan's invocation in his 1782 speech on the achievement of Irish legislative independence — "Spirit of Swift! spirit of Molyneux! your genius has prevailed! Ireland is now a Nation!" — has been shown actually to have been inserted in editions of Grattan's speeches in 1821 and 1822, rather than delivered forty years earlier.[17] But Thomas Sheridan did dedicate his 1784 edition of Swift's *Works* to Grattan as "Founder of the Liberties of Ireland" and disciple of Swift, "his great Precursor, the immortal Drapier, in whose footsteps he has trodden, and whose ideas realized".[18]

Outside such a literary context, however, this was hardly a notion universally accepted. Grattan's fierce adversary in the Irish Parliament, Patrick Duigenan, was himself likened to Swift in 1798 by the poet T.J. Mathias, and Grattan compared to William Wood.[19] The recognition of Swift as an Irish patriot, then, remained sufficiently casual to be turned, as it was earlier in the century, to surprising purposes.

Nonetheless the verdict of commentators like Johnson gained ground, and the Drapier was hailed in early nineteenth-century accounts of Irish history as an instructive champion against English oppression. The Rev. James Gordon noted in 1805, for instance, that Swift was "deeply affected by the wretched poverty of his countrymen, occasioned by an absurdly cruel system of government",[20] while J.W. Croker regarded him as a "distinguished and magnanimous patriot" whose example, if emulated, might redeem his country.[21] Even Catholic writers like

---

16. Samuel Johnson, *Lives of the English Poets*, ed. G.B. Hill, Oxford, 1905, III, 50.

17. See Gerard O'Brien, "The Grattan Mystique", *Eighteenth-Century Ireland*, I (1986), 190–94.

18. *The Works of the Rev. Dr. Jonathan Swift*, London, 1784, II [sig A2].

19. [Thomas James Mathias], *The Shade of Alexander Pope on the Banks of the Thames*, London, 1799, 5.

20. James Gordon, *A History of Ireland*, Dublin, 1805, II, 212.

21. J.W. Croker, *A Sketch of the State of Ireland Past and Present*, Dublin, 1808, 10–11.

Francis Plowden and Denis Taafe joined in the chorus of approbation.[22] All of these maintained a view of Swift's patriotism that lacked significant reference to his attitude towards Catholics, and it was asserted again at greatest length in Sir Walter Scott's biographical and critical introduction to his edition of the *Works* in 1814. This remained the standard edition of Swift throughout the nineteenth century, and the major impetus for dismissive or negative criticism of Swift was Francis Jeffrey's harsh treatment of the Dean in his review of Scott's edition for the *Edinburgh Review* in 1816. Jeffrey concentrated upon Swift's character defects, especially his unrelenting malevolence towards the English Whig ministry which had spelled the end of his hopes for political power and advancement; this, rather than disinterested patriotism, lay behind the *Drapier's Letters*. Though such a view had often been pressed in England during the eighteenth century, it had never been so thoroughly articulated. Where Jeffrey advanced most notably upon his predecessors in this vein, however, was in stressing that Swift's regard for Ireland ignored "its radical grievance, the oppression of its Catholic population", who "are not so much as named above two or three times in his writings, and then only with scorn and reprobation".[23] His not attending to the Catholic cause, Jeffrey holds, betrays the selfishness behind Swift's supposed patriotism; by the same token, few Catholic commentators after Plowden and Taafe were moved to hail Swift as a patriot. Although Jeffrey did not go unchallenged, it remained difficult for later defenders of Swift to counter this feature of his criticism effectively. The continuing authority of Scott's edition, on the one hand, and the comprehensiveness of Jeffrey's attack, on the other, mark the polarities of British considerations of Swift in the nineteenth century.

And in Ireland, Jeffrey's attacking Swift's patriotism by all but identifying the national cause with that of the Catholics was tacitly endorsed by most Catholic leaders and writers in the decades between the Union and Emancipation, who ignored Swift because his kind of patriotism seemed irrelevant. Daniel O'Connell, to cite the most obvious instance, hardly ever mentioned him. Thomas Moore was a rare exception to the general Catholic silence on Swift, noting in 1824 that though the Dean had been influential, his "patriotism was little more than a graft of English faction upon an Irish stock" and that he had cared

22. Francis Plowden, *An Historical Review of the State of Ireland*, London, 1803, 389–91; Taafe, *An Impartial History of Ireland*, Dublin, 1809–11, IV, 20–30.

23. *Edinburgh Review*, XXVII (September 1816), 22.

nothing "for the misery and degradation of his Roman Catholic countrymen".[24] Irish Protestants continued, in the main, to cherish Swift's memory as a literary classic who fought for their interests, and among the foremost of those who favoured the Catholic claims, Grattan advanced a new dimension in the treatment of Swift as patriot. For in adding the "Spirit of Swift! spirit of Molyneux!" passage to his address of 1782 for an edition of his speeches forty years later, he built upon the suggestion inherent in Thomas Sheridan's dedication of the 1784 *Works* to him, establishing a line, or implicit genealogy, of Protestant Irish patriots. Thus Grattan takes his place in an eighteenth-century patriot tradition, the successive generations of which are represented by Molyneux, Swift and himself. By so fixing his own eminence genealogically, Grattan composed a neat synthesis. This is not a notion that O'Connell adopted, as his movement for Catholic Emancipation developed into that for repeal of the Union, perhaps in part because of Swift's lingering reputation as a disrespectable and malevolent Tory among the English Whigs — the party that O'Connell was attempting to cultivate in the 1830s; perhaps simply because the patriot genealogy smacked of Ascendancy apologetics. Indeed, Francis Mahony used one of his early "Father Prout" essays in *Fraser's Magazine* in 1834 to contrast O'Connell's party-political nationalism to Swift's noble and disinterested patriotism, sharpening the contrast and avoiding any hint of such apologetics by ignoring Grattan's patriotic genealogy.[25] With the emergence of *The Nation* newspaper and the Young Ireland movement in the 1840s, however, the idea of a patriot tradition began to exert a strong appeal.

Thomas Davis and *The Nation* are perhaps best remembered today for promoting a more strident nationalism than O'Connell's and attempting to arouse in the paper's readers a sense of Anglo-Irish literary culture. In the latter respect, of course, *The Nation* was heralded by George Petrie's *Irish Penny Journal* in the 1830s, as well as the forthrightly Unionist *Dublin University Magazine*; and indeed the *D.U.M.* in 1840 devoted a long article to Swift, running over four issues, and treating him as the ancestor of Irish political agitation, implicitly including that of

---

24. Thomas Moore, *Memoirs of Captain Rock*, London, 1824, 123.

25. Francis Mahony, "Dean Swift's Madness: The Tale of a Churn", *Fraser's Magazine*, X (July 1834), 20. Though a Catholic priest, Mahony had a deep-seated antipathy to O'Connell; see Ethel Mannin, *Two Studies in Integrity: Gerald Griffin and the Rev. Francis Mahony (Father Prout)*, New York, 1954, 140–41, 165.

O'Connell himself.[26] The article makes no specific mention of the patriot tradition, but, as though drawing out its implications, Thomas Davis does so repeatedly in *The Nation*. The concept fitted very neatly his plan of appealing to his fellow Protestants' Irishness, not merely because the patriot line (often at his hands including Molyneux, Swift, Lucas, Grattan and Tone) was Protestant, but also because it dated to the 1690s, when Molyneux' *Case of Ireland ... Stated* appeared. By coincidence, the 1690s also saw the Treaty of Limerick and the abrogation of its guarantees of Catholic religious rights. It was from this decade, thus, that the modern legitimacy of Catholic grievances could be dated. Molyneux had argued for the independence of the Irish Parliament, which was in fact the progenitor of the penal legislation against Catholics. But he voiced this essentially Protestant grievance in terms of the English government's oppressiveness as ultimate arbiter of Irish affairs, a perception shared by nationalists of the 1840s; hence he, and those like Swift who took a similar viewpoint, could indeed be hailed as nationalist ancestors. It is of signal importance to the development of Swift's patriotic reputation that he was conspicuous in this nationalist line, for it diminishes the significance of anti-Catholicism among Protestant patriots. However differently motivated Protestant and Catholic complaints about the condition of Ireland may have been, what counted most was that both could be said to have begun at about the same time, and both were directed against English domination. Thus they could be composed into a tradition, a nationalist synthesis. The Protestant element in this, the patriot line or genealogy, was particularly felicitous, for it provided a propagandistic means of reminding contemporary Protestants both of their Irishness and of their advanced place in the emergence of nationalism. Protestant attachment to the Union in the mid-nineteenth century could be characterized, then, as a concession to expediency on their part which flew in the face of both principle and tradition.

Hence *The Nation*, in a leader early in 1845, addressed them as "Poor, deluded Irish Protestants ... you have denied the country for which a race of Protestant patriots ... Molyneux, Swift, Lucas, Flood, Grattan, Tone ... fought and spoke".[27] And, reviewing a volume on Irish ballad poetry, Davis noted of Anglo-Irish ballads that "before the time of Swift, they were chiefly written by followers of the court .... Swift snatched these weapons out of the hands of the English faction, and

---

26. Anon., "Gallery of Illustrious Irishmen, No. XI: Swift", *D.U.M.* XV (February–May, 1840), 131–44; 333–44; 538–56; 634–61.

27. "The Betrayed Protestants", *The Nation*, 25 January 1845, 248.

turned them against their own breasts. He rescued our popular poetry ...
and gave it a vigour and concentration which it has never wholly lost ...
it became a power in the country, the obscure predecessor of a free
press".[28] As such, of course, Swift becomes a predecessor of Davis
himself, for within the nationalist synthesis the concept of a patriotic
genealogy, whatever its objective accuracy, is certainly a means of self-
validation for the modern patriot. It is not Swift's morally-determined
economic nationalism or literary eminence, on the one hand, or the self-
interested motives of his antipathy to English control, on the other, which
are probed — the two viewpoints between which many nineteenth-century
opinions of the Dean are polarized. Instead, it is simply the fact of his
being a forceful and effective propagandist that is emphasized, within a
line of patriots. This approach is infectious: one of Davis's Catholic
colleagues, the poet Denis Florence MacCarthy, could regard Swift in
1846, after Davis's death, as "unquestionably the greatest [name] in our
literature ... the first Anglo-Irish writer who felt that he was an Irishman
... if on the roll of our patriots the names of Lucas, of Flood, and of
Grattan ... of Tone and Fitzgerald, of Drennan and Davis, and the great
living embodiment of the principles of Swift — O'Connell — stand
emblazoned, we may thank for all these the illustrious ... Dean of St.
Patrick's".[29] Thus at Catholic hands the patriot line itself becomes
ecumenical.

Self-validation through invoking it, moreover, continued as the
informal Young Ireland movement seceded from the O'Connellite Repeal
Association and became the Irish Confederation. At its inaugural meeting
in 1847, T.F. Meagher identified its spirit as that which "made the walls
of Limerick impregnable ... that dictated the letters of Swift" and also
inspired Grattan, Thomas Moore, Thomas Davis, and even O'Connell in
his more vigorous days.[30] One of the Confederate Clubs in Dublin was
named for Swift, with John Mitchel as its vice-president, and Mitchel
also wrote an introduction to a reprint of Swift's *Short View of the State
of Ireland* for the first "Irish Confederation" pamphlet. Here he noted
that the rural degradation the Dean had described in 1727, and his
"warnings, advice and remonstrances ... suit our condition exactly to this

---

28. "Ballad Poetry of Ireland", *The Nation*, 2 August 1845, 698.

29. Denis Florence MacCarthy, *The Poets and Dramatists of Ireland*, Dublin,
1846, 1, 130.

30. T.F. Meagher [speech of 13 January 1847], *The Nation*, 16 January 1847,
229.

day".[31] In all likelihood, the condition of Ireland in 1847, at the height of the Famine, was considerably worse than the picture Swift had given in 1727, which suggests that defining a heritage is more important than describing reality.

Buttressing the effect of the nationalist synthesis among Catholics was the fact that, while O'Connell as "The Liberator" was the most successful political nationalist from their standpoint, Protestants like Davis, at first, and then Mitchel and William Smith O'Brien, were among the leading spirits in the journalistic and political agitation culminating in the abortive Rising of 1848. And for the next forty years the major parliamentary leadership of the nationalist movement was Protestant as well. Protestants were thus perceived as fostering the Irish spirit through maintaining the tradition of a patriot genealogy. But this feature of the nationalist synthesis did not persuade the majority of Irish Protestants to embrace the nationalist cause. There had arisen, however, even before Davis's time, and would continue long afterward, an apparently more prudent combination of political Unionism with varying degrees of pride in Gaelic and Anglo-Irish literary culture and in the Protestant aspects of Irish nationalist history. These tendencies never coalesced so surely as those which make up the nationalist synthesis: such figures as Ferguson, Lecky and Standish O'Grady are hardly a "school". Of major significance to each of them, however, as also to Davis, is the Protestant contribution to Irish culture and history. That contribution is not synthesized with the contemporary claims of nationalism; rather, it is perceived as intermediary, as a buffer between England and Catholic Ireland. Of course, like the nationalist synthesis of the 1840s onward, this perception is predicated upon the circumstances of the present, rendering a re-reading of the past necessary. Thus Lecky in *The Leaders of Public Opinion in Ireland* (1861) emphasized the tradition of Protestant patriotism through such figures as Swift, Flood and Grattan, because by this time public opinion was increasingly nationalist in politics and Catholic in ethos. Swift, for example, "was admirably calculated to be the leader of public opinion in Ireland, from his complete freedom from the characteristic defects of the Irish temperament. His writings exhibit no tendency to exaggeration or bombast; no fallacious images or farfetched analogies; no tumid phrases in which the expression hangs loosely and inaccurately around the meaning."[32] We may wonder

31. John Mitchel, *Irish Political Economy*, Dublin, 1847, iii.

32. William Lecky, *The Leaders of Public Opinion in Ireland*, London, 1861, 48–49.

how a reading of "A Modest Proposal", just to take one obvious instance, would support such a conclusion; but it is actually O'Connell, the final figure examined in his book, characterized by an extravagant personality and florid oratory, that Lecky is criticizing in this description of Swift. Latent in Lecky's analysis is the contrast between his Protestant heroes, who formed public opinion and were thereby able to mediate it to the English establishment, and O'Connell, who expressed it with all "characteristic defects of the Irish temperament" that necessarily confused the English view of Irish conditions.

The mediating role of Irish Protestants that Lecky implies was for many years as important to his community's sense of Irish identity as had been the idea of a patriot genealogy out of which the mediatory notion grew. Lecky himself, with the passage of time, increasingly reflected and expressed his community's Unionism; but — though this is difficult to measure — such a role for Irish Protestants lent itself also to Catholic perceptions of the nationalist synthesis, at least in reinforcing some Catholic nationalists' sense of the validity of their cause when Protestants became associated with it. In cultural respects, moreover, that role is analogous to the efforts of Unionists like Ferguson and O'Grady in representing Irish poetry and history for Anglophone readers. Their mediating function appeared enhanced by the success of the Literary Renaissance about the turn of the century, when Irish Protestant writers could be seen as having brought about the modernization of Anglo-Irish literature through their openness to international trends. It was a role, finally, which encouraged Yeats to see Swift, and ultimately Goldsmith and Burke, as precursors. But nationalists were not altogether pleased by the assertion of such a role for Protestants. One of the first to criticize it was John Mitchel, himself a Protestant and formerly a champion of Swift's patriotic reputation, who a few years after Lecky's *Leaders* appeared raised, in modified form, the objections to Swift that Francis Jeffrey had outlined in the *Edinburgh Review* in 1816. Mitchel's polemical emphasis in his highly-coloured *History of Ireland*, published in 1869, was the oppression of the Catholic nation by an anti-national Protestantism. Swift's indignation, however, Mitchel noted, "was inflamed to the highest pitch — not by the ferocity of the legislature against Catholics, but by Wood's copper halfpence. The country, he thought, was on the verge of ruin, not by reason of the tempest of intolerance, rapcity, fraud and cruelty, which raged over it on every side, but by reason of a certain copper coinage …. Here was the crying grievance of Ireland." For his part, Swift was "the most offensive and disdainful enemy" Irish Catholics ever had, and even his would-be patriotism is compromised by "senseless ribaldry". Admittedly, Swift "opposed English domination over Ireland, yet equally opposed the union of Irishmen to resist it ... the verdict of history must for ever be, that he was neither an English patriot nor an Irish one".[33]

Mitchel had a larger object than Swift in view, of course. In adopting an uncompromising majoritarianism that pits the real historical grievances of Catholics against the comparatively trivial concerns of Protestants, he attacked the credentials of constituents of the patriot genealogy to undermine the nationalist synthesis itself. Thus he anticipates Corkery's dismissal of Swift in 1934, but just as Mitchel's treatment looks back to Jeffrey's, Corkery's derives directly from the Irish Ireland movement and its most energetically articulate proponent, D.P. Moran. For to Moran, as to Corkery, the decline of Ireland could be laid not so much to the domination of England or the Protestants, as to the Catholic absorbtion of their values, a process Moran traced to Grattan's legislative victory in 1782. Writing in 1899, Moran maintained that "the spirit of Molyneux and Swift — that same spirit Grattan apostrophized, the spirit which 99 out of every 100 of us still look up to as our polar star — was the death of those elements of the Irish race that could have defied the attacks that were to come". More trenchantly, he describes Swift as "that great Irishman, as we love to call him, who had not a drop of Irish blood in his veins, no Irish characteristics, and an utter contempt for the entire pack of us ... This Englishman, whom, with characteristic latter-day Irish cringe we claim for ourselves." With the gathering wind of the language revival movement in his sails, Moran counterposes the assimilative philosophy of Irish Ireland to what he regards as the spirit of the Pale, the ethos to which Swift, and later O'Connell, gave credibility. For if Ireland is to be rescued from a provincial English mentality it is necessary to recognize that "The Foundation of Ireland is the Gael, and the Gael must be the element that absorbs. On no other basis can an Irish nation be reared that would not topple over by force of the very ridicule it would beget".[34]

Whatever the enduring effects of the Irish Ireland movement, Moran's view of Swift and of the patriot tradition never gained dominance. Not only did most Irish treatments of the Dean from a literary perspective, from the last quarter of the nineteenth century onwards, recite his patriotic purpose and his achievement in establishing a spirit of self-reliance in Ireland, but he kept his honoured place in the patriotic roster

---

33. John Mitchel, *History of Ireland*, Dublin, 1869, II, 79, 92, 81, 94.

34. D.P. Moran, "The Pale and the Gael", *New Ireland Review*, XI/4 (June 1899), 230, 232, 233.

that was as insistently recited by Home Rulers and advanced nationalists alike, and by their successors. The nationalist synthesis was simply too valuable to be dispensed with. Thus D.J. O'Donoghue in 1912, tacitly responding to Moran's dismissal of Swift as patriot on more or less racial grounds, could assert that standing "by Ireland whenever the question is one between this country and England is not a bad definition of an Irishman", a test from which Swift emerges triumphant. He was, further, "with the people and against their oppressors all the time",[35] which convinced O'Donoghue that Swift's "suggested identification of himself with the [Protestant] settlers was an unmistakable pose, and that he spoke for the whole of the Irish people".[36] Indeed, O'Donoghue admits that he is tempted to title his article, in the context of 1912, "Jonathan Swift, Sinn Feiner and Cattle Driver".[37]

If this seems utterly fanciful to us, knowing what we do of Swift, it is as well to bear in mind that the Irish popular view of the Dean retains much of O'Donoghue's characterization. It is also true, however, that in each generation Irish treatments of Swift have reflected contemporary currents of thought about Ireland's relationship with Britain, and about relationships within Ireland between the Protestant and Catholic communities. Swift's own concerns, especially with the former, have appeared to justify integrating him in some way with successive modern analyses. Hence Lecky, for instance, advances a picture of Swift almost as an early type of a Victorian gentleman, urbane and balanced, in implicit contrast to O'Connell's impropriety as an intermediary for Ireland's claims with the British establishment. Moran in turn accepts Lecky's characterization but rejects the whole notion of a mediatory role, either for Protestants or anglicized Catholic nationalists, as undermining Gaelic or truly Irish values. O'Donoghue by contrast sees Swift as truly Irish himself, in terms of Sinn Féin *circa* 1912. Corkery and De Blácam, a quarter-century later, go over much the the same ground as Moran and O'Donoghue, with De Blácam reintroducing the Protestant nation as an implicit analogue of the patriot tradition. And J.J. Hogan in 1945 finds in Swift's lack of pronounced concern for the Catholics a freedom to "attack the complex Irish problem with a fierce simplicity",[38] so that the

---

35. D.J. O'Donoghue, "Swift as an Irishman" (Part 1), *The Irish Review*, II/4 (June 1912), 210.

36. "Swift as an Irishman" (Part 3), *The Irish Review*, II/6 (August 1912), 311.

37. "Swift as an Irishman" (Part 1), 209.

38. J.J. Hogan, "Bicentenary of Jonathan Swift (1667–1745)", *Studies*, XXXIV (1945), 504.

Dean favours at once political independence from England and a comprehensive anglicization of Ireland in language and culture, a vision that fits the facts as they actually developed.

The process is remarkably Hegelian, and seems propelled by the enduring difficulty in Ireland of determining somehow the radical ambiguity posed by Swift's evident patriotism, on the one hand, and his espoused Protestantism, on the other. Outside of Ireland Swift is regarded all but exclusively as a literary figure, whose ambiguities can be analysed in rhetorical, moral and psychological terms. His ribaldry, therefore, becomes more important than his national identity. But in Ireland Swift's ambiguities have a local value that broadens beyond literature, though raising paradoxes analogous to his own literary practice. If, to take one instance, the Dean as patriot is an ancestor for Irish nationalism, is he not equally one for Ulster loyalism, given his own Protestantism and the fact that Northern Ireland is governed even more like a colony than even eighteenth-century Ireland as a whole, engendering at least as much resentment among its Protestant political leaders? Or, in a cultural context, his personal and political ambiguities might be seen as prefiguring in some ways the current doubts about identity in Anglophone but sociologically Catholic Ireland. In Ireland, indeed, the peculiarities that make Swift difficult to fix in place allow him a currency denied to most other long dead writers. Prince Posterity still finds him useful, whether as a guide or a goad.

PUBLIC, PRIVATE AND POETIC:
WOLFE TONE'S AUTOBIOGRAPHICAL WRITINGS

WIM TIGGES

In this essay I intend to demonstrate that the autobiographical documents written by the Irish revolutionary Theobald Wolfe Tone (1763-98), edited by his son William in 1826, and given a more final form by R. Barry O'Brien in 1893, can be legitimately read as a literary artefact. Although never intended to be more than an account of Tone's day-to-day experiences, recorded for the sake of his wife and children, from whom he was frequently separated for long stretches of time due to his legal and political activities, the text that has come down to us strikes a remarkably sophisticated literary tone, both in structure, style and subject matter. My thesis is that the *Autobiography* can be read as a "political" novel, in a mixed mode of reminiscence, essay and journal, containing many elements that are characteristic of the *Bildungsroman*. This latter genre is generally said to originate with Goethe's famous *Wilhelm Meister's Lehrjahre*, first published in 1795-96, almost simultaneously with the moment Tone started to write an account of his "Birth, Family, and Early Life", on 7 August 1796, when he was about to participate in the risky French expedition to Bantry Bay under General Hoche.

> As I shall embark in a business, within a few days, the event of which is uncertain, I take the opportunity of a vacant hour to throw on paper a few memorandums relative to myself and my family, which may amuse my boys, for whom I write them, in case they should here-after fall into their hands (I, 1).[1]

William Wolfe Tone's composition of the *Life* is closely followed by O'Brien in the *Autobiography*, which, however, omits "the letters, the

---

1. Unless otherwise indicated, all references following quotations from Tone's Autobiography will be to *The Autobiography of Theobald Wolfe Tone, 1763-98*, ed. R. Barry O'Brien, 2 vols, London, 1893, henceforth to be referred to as *Autobiography*.

political essays (as being 'of little interest or importance now'), the
account of Tone's family after his death, and some minor material";[2]
from the *Life* we get a more or less chronological account of the political
and private development of a late-eighteenth-century character at least as
fascinating as Godwin's Caleb Williams or Bage's Hermsprong, whose
fictional "lives" were first published in 1794 and 1796 respectively.

In terms of Anglo-Irish literary history, it is interesting to note that,
as has been stated by James M. Cahalan in *The Irish Novel*, the earliest
Anglo-Irish novel (William Chaigneau's *The History of Jack Connor*,
1752), "like many an Irish novel that came after it"[3] was a
Bildungsroman. As prominent characteristics of many Anglo-Irish novels
Cahalan mentions formlessness or loose, plotless and episodic structure,
a colloquial narrative voice (14), a Dublin student as the protagonist (32),
and the theme of exile (33). Cahalan also speaks of "the seeming
predisposition of Irish novelists to use the bildungsroman form and focus
on the transformations of youth" (137). May we regard Theobald Wolfe
Tone, whose stylistic qualities are in my opinion not surpassed by those
of Maria Edgeworth or Lady Morgan, as not only the first Anglo-Irish
(political) novelist but also as the "wandering hero" of his own
Bildungsroman? I would tend to answer this question in the affirmative.

Picturing himself somewhat paradoxically as "a sanguine young man"
with "a rooted habit of idleness" (I, 25; 10), Wolfe Tone develops from
a "mild conspirator" (the term is O'Faolain's) to a committed republican;
his heroic reputation is strictly posthumous. Tone never postures as an
ambitious author, nor does he present himself as a "literary" character,
although, as will be seen, he was not averse to a certain amount of self-
dramatization. "As to literary fame", he writes with regard to the review
articles he composed for the *European Magazine* in 1787, during his
student days at the Middle Temple, "I had then no great ambition to
attain it" (I, 16). And as to his "memorandums", he later on states with
characteristic modesty: "There are about six persons in the world who
will read these detached memorandums with pleasure; to every one else
they would appear sad stuff" (I, 239). "What makes these notes valuable
(that is to say, to myself and to my dearest life and love) is, that they are
a faithful transcript of all that passes in my mind, of my hopes and fears,
my doubts and expectations, in this important business" (II, 18). "To
divert the spleen which is devouring me, I have been, for some days

---

2. *The Autobiography of Theobald Wolfe Tone*, abr. and ed. Sean O'Faolain,
London etc., 1937, xxvii.

3. James M. Cahalan, *The Irish Novel: A Critical History*, Dublin, 1988, 11.

past, throwing memorandums of my life and opinions on paper, from recollection. They are very ill done" (II, 104).

Tone was not merely the well-educated and well-read man that transpires from the frequent use of literary quotations in his journals[4] and from his respectably-sized library of some six hundred volumes, all of which he went to the trouble of packing up for his American exile in 1795 (see I, 212, 214). In 1788 he had collaborated with two fellow students, Richard Jebb and Thomas Radcliffe, on a *roman à clef* called *Belmont Castle*, which, according to his most recent biographer, Marianne Elliott, contains much autobiographical material as well as self-mockery (Elliott, 16). This epistolary novel, which he managed to get launched by a friendly Dublin publisher, Patrick Byrne, in 1790,[5] was "a parody of contemporary romantic fiction" (Elliott, 28). According to Elliott,

> The entire work is a kitsch pastiche of stock themes of the romantic novels and plays of the day: the glorification of true love and female virtue, denunciation of the arranged marriage and the negligent husband, the conspirational role of servants, the value of a good heart, disciplined by prudence (of which Scudamore [Tone's *persona*], and by implication Tone, is totally devoid), and the whole written in the epistolary form so popular at the time. Few of the characters are credible, and when in danger of becoming so, the authors contrive to introduce an element of the ridiculous (53).[6]

---

4. Marianne Elliott, *Wolfe Tone: Prophet of Irish Independence*, New Haven and London, 1989, 145, discusses Tone's "tendency to speak through witty and often ludicrous quotations" as "a trait common in eighteenth-century journals, though it figures to an unusual degree in Tone", and mentions some of his "favourite texts". She also states here that "the journals read like the Top Twenty of the eighteenth-century educated man's reading list, Pope, Swift, Defoe, Richardson, Goldsmith, Sterne, Smollett, Fielding and the occasional if predictable foreign work such as Voltaire or Laclos. One will search in vain for Montesquieu or Rousseau. These journals were never intended to be a political treatise."

5. Byrne also published revolutionary pamphlets by Tone and others.

6. See Elliott 52-54 for an account of *Belmont Castle*. She also mentions that a copy of the book was among Tone's rifled possessions when he was captured and sentenced by court-martial in November 1798. For a description of the book, and of other writings by Wolfe Tone, see M.J. MacManus, "Bibliography of Theobald Wolfe Tone", *Dublin Magazine*, XV (1940), 52-64.

In this light it is all the more interesting that Tone's own "amorous
adventures" in the manuscript journals were omitted by his widow and
his son in the 1826 *Life*.[7] Obviously, they, as well as the other
omissions, ought to be restored in a comprehensive definitive edition.

That Tone was well aware of the foibles of contemporary literature
is also clear from the account we get of his reviews for the London
European Magazine and later for the Dublin *Universal Magazine*. In
these, Elliott reports, Tone attacked "the many trashy romantic novels of
the day" (55). All the same, Tone was himself clearly a product of the
early Romantic period. Elliott refers to him as "a typical product of the
Enlightenment" (364, 395), but more frequently as a "romantic" (e.g.,
37, 43, 56, 104, 160, 181, 361). In his memorandums Tone himself
refers to his proposal for colonizing the Sandwich Islands as an
"adventure" which is "additional proof of the romantic spirit I have
mentioned in the beginning of my memoirs, as a trait in our family" (I,
31), and to his Paris machinations of 1796 as "absolutely like a
romance" (II, 97; cf. Elliott, 310). "Everything about his life", Elliott
concludes, " — his intense loyalty to friends, his capacity for sacrifice,
his inflated sense of honour, his rakish youth and dramatic death — is the
very stuff of romantic legend" (419), that element of his career that made
him almost at once a hero of the Young Irelanders, and made his grave
in Bodenstown churchyard into a place of pilgrimage for Irish
nationalists.[8] It is all the more remarkable that Tone, whose knowledge
of Irish history is said to have been poor (Elliott, 310), never
romanticized the Irish past or the Irish peasant (see e.g. I, 83, and cf.
Elliott, 339, 418); nor does he in fact romanticize his own life or his role
as a political activist.

If one wishes to call Tone's *Autobiography* romantic, it is so
inasmuch as it does not restrict itself to a mere description of deeds and
opinions, but also depicts his inward thoughts and emotions. A most
notable passage in this respect are the entries for 27 April and 17 May

---

7. See Elliott, 24, 51, 144. What was omitted from Tone's journals by his son
and widow in the 1826 printed version, and subsequently by O'Brien, are, besides
the references to women, the criticisms of his wife Matilda's family, of America
(where the Tones settled in 1817), and of friends still alive in 1826. Nevertheless,
Elliott remarks that on the whole "the pruning exercise was far more restrained than
it might have been" (144). Most are from the 1796 Paris journal (284). Some of
these omissions are reinserted in Sean O'Faolain's 1937 abridged edition (see also
Elliott 438, n.27).

8. Cf., for example, the famous anthology piece by Thomas Davis, "Tone's
Grave".

1798 (II, 306-12), in which he first meditates on the "present" state of Ireland and immediately afterward muses on his personal affairs and those of his nearest relatives. Some time before, after a very busy period, he had written: "The only good in my journals is, that they are written at the moment, and represent things exactly as they strike me, whereas, when I write after an interval of some time — " (II, 271-72).

It has been rightly remarked that the "rakishness" of the *Autobiography* (a rakishness which, it should be added here, is realistic rather than romantic) does not correspond with Tone's public image (Elliott, 167), so that it can be argued that, at least after the event, Tone has to some extent "fictionalized" himself. The very manuscript title of his "Memorandums, relative to my Life and Opinions", written in Paris between 7 August and 8 September 1796, seems to cock a familiar eye at the "autobiography" of that fictional Irish gentleman of literary fame, Tristram Shandy.[9] This self-dramatization is also reflected in the many "nicknames" and pseudonyms he went by. Thus, Elliott reports that he signed himself "Mirabeau" in some letters to his wife Matilda (Tone's "Dear Jenny"!); in *Belmont Castle* he is "Scudamore"; in his journals "Mr Hutton" (a nickname his friend Thomas Russell had playfully given him); his legal acquaintances had nicknamed him "Marat", and in his reopened journals, when operating as a republican agent on his mission in France in 1796, he features as "Citizen Smith", "James Smith" being the name in his passport (Elliott, 165; 53; 96; 173; 189; 278).

Elliott is certainly right in concluding that the journals are not those of "Tone creating his own myth for posterity" (309). He never glorified himself; he considered his motives legitimate, and saw his efforts to execute them as a failure. In his trial speech he is reported to have remarked that "in this world success is everything" (Elliott, 393).[10] Tone's main characteristics are dignity, integrity, and a very warm humanity, which transpires in spite of or perhaps rather because of his modesty and relativizing humour and self-mockery. But what becomes most prominently clear is that Theobald Wolfe Tone, although he presents himself in his journals first and foremost as a politician, does not become dehumanized by his political activities. It is the balanced account of Tone the man (in all senses of the word), and Tone the

---

9. See Elliott 309-12 for a brief discussion of the discrepancy between the manuscript version of Tone's journals and memorandums and the first printed version. Cf. also 193, and 171: "The journals ... are not the public Tone."

10. *Autobiography*, II, 359, has "In a cause like this, success is everything". No absolutely authentic account of the trial speech appears to have survived.

political man, that makes him so fascinating as a "character", historically but also in a very literary sense. Tone was indeed what Elliott succinctly calls him on the very first page of her biography: "a gifted writer"; his prose was not equalled by any Anglo-Irish writer until George Moore (*pace* Cahalan's brave vindications of the nineteenth-century novelists).

Before we can go a little further into the "literariness" of this political document, into its aesthetics, we must first devote a few paragraphs to the theoretical aspects of the relationship between autobiography and literature, a topic that has been much discussed in recent years.

The fictional autobiography as a genre antedates the very introduction of the word "autobiography" into the English language, which according to the *Oxford English Dictionary* was done by Robert Southey in an article dated 1809. Laurence Sterne's *Tristram Shandy* (1759-67) has already been referred to, and another work with which Tone may well have been acquainted is Daniel Defoe's *Life of Captain Singleton* (1720). Tone, of course, was not writing such a fictional life, nor was he entirely working along the lines of autobiography "proper", i.e. writing an account of his past life from a vantage point. In fact, as stated before, he only embarked upon the memorandums when a major event, perhaps *the* major event in it was to be broached, the liberation of his country from English rule. The day-to-day accounts of his life start in 1789, and most of the *Autobiography* is in this journal or diary form, which is essentially a different technique. A diary refers to the present, with outriders into the future perhaps rather than into the past, which it takes for granted in the form of the previous days' account, whereas an autobiography (or, as Tone would still call it, a "memorandum" or "memoir") recalls selected details from the past, often commenting on their coherence, lack of foresight, etc., in passing. Tone's *Autobiography*, then, edited from seventeen surviving notebooks (Elliott, 309) with other written material added in appropiate places, is a mixture of memorandum or memoirs, journals, letters, pamphlets, minutes etc., and contains items which perhaps ought to be called travelogues. Incidentally, the very point of its being edited by a survivor into whose hands these papers have come is a well-known literary technique that has been often applied in fictional autobiography, as in the Preface to Maria Edgeworth's *Castle Rackrent* (1800) and "The Editor's Narrative" prefacing James Hogg's *Private Memoirs and Confessions of a Justified Sinner* (1824), both of which present the novel they introduce as "memoirs".

In what follows, I will for convenience's and economy's sake use the term "autobiography" in a very broad sense, including "memoirs" as well as "diaries" or "journals", if only because the structurally important element of selection applies to the whole genre, albeit with a difference. I shall come back to this later on.

In recent discussions of autobiographical texts much is made of a seminal article by Paul De Man, "Autobiography as Defacement".[11] In this article De Man argues that "the distinction between fiction and autobiography ... is undecidable" (70), and he follows this up with: "The interest of autobiography ... is not that it reveals reliable self-knowledge — it does not — but that it demonstrates in a striking way the impossibility of closure and of totalization (that is the impossibility of coming into being) of all textual systems made up of tropological substitutions" (71), a fact already well understood more than two centuries earlier by Tristram Shandy and his creator. We find a similar view in a monograph by Patricia Meyer Spacks: "To read an autobiography is to encounter a self as an imaginative being";[12] she continues: "This statement describes autobiographies written in the eighteenth century, *whose authors would not have assented to its truth*, as accurately as those composed with full consciousness of the power and ambiguity of imagination" (20; italics mine). Compare to this a statement made more recently by Paul John Eakin: "the self that is the center of all autobiographical narrative is necessarily a fictive structure."[13]

Statements like these seem to justify a literary-critical approach to the autobiographical genre, especially if we take to heart a useful distinction made by Barrett J. Mandel, who questions the (by now) common thesis

---

11. In Paul De Man, *The Rhetoric of Romanticism*, New York, 1984, 67–81 (first published in *Modern Language Notes*, LXXXXIV (1979), 919–30).

12. Patricia Meyer Spacks, *Imagining a Self: Autobiography and Novel in Eighteenth-Century England*, Cambridge: Mass. and London, 1976, 19.

13. Paul John Eakin, *Fictions in Autobiography: Studies in the Art of Self-Invention*, Princeton: NJ, 1985, 3. See ch. 4 for a summary of modern and postmodern notions about autobiography, esp. the relationship between "self" and "language", which is now a much disputed topic in the wake of deconstructionist views. For a review of available scholarship on autobiography, see William C. Spengemann, *The Forms of Autobiography: Episodes in the History of a Literary Genre*, New Haven & London, 1980, 170–245 ("The Study of Autobiography: A Bibliographical Essay"). On diaries, see Felicity A. Nussbaum, "Toward Conceptualizing Diary", in *Studies in Autobiography*, ed. James Olney, Oxford, 1988, 128–40. Tone's *Autobiography* is listed in both William Matthews, *British Diaries: An Annotated Bibliography of British Diaries Written between 1442 and 1942*, Berkeley, Los Angeles, London, 1950, 132 ("an important and interesting diary") and William Matthews, *British Autobiographies: An Annotated Bibliography of British Autobiographies Published or Written Before 1951*, Berkeley and Los Angeles, 1955, 306.

that (auto)-biography is fiction,[14] but admits that it may borrow devices from fiction (53), and goes on to categorize both fiction (e.g. the novel) and non-fiction (e.g. autobiography) under the common denominator of "literature" (55), accepting autobiography as a literary genre (*ibid.*; also 62).[15] Or, as formulated even more concretely by Fowler in his authoritative monograph on literary genres: "many would now agree that Pepys' *Diary* and Boswell's *London Journal* belong to literature",[16] to which we may confidently add Tone's *Autobiography*, without having to enter into the "aporia" of the deceptive self-image of the autobiographer.

In a very illuminating article, William L. Howarth discusses three types of autobiography, the "oratorical", the "dramatic" and the "poetical", respectively presenting the protagonist in terms of what he "stands for" (his ideology or vocation), what role he plays, and who he really is; various examples of each type are adduced.[17] Tone's *Autobiography*, partly because of its combination of memoir and diary, is arguably a perfect mixture of all three. It is oratorical in that it can be read first of all as an allegory, in which the protagonist stands for the ideology he represents, in this case that of the Irish nationalist.[18] As its subsequent popularity, especially in Ireland and in contexts of Irish or Anglo-Irish Studies attests, Tone has indeed "carved a public monument out of his private life", to paraphrase one of Howarth's definitional phrases (92). The journals may never have been intended as a political treatise, as Elliott argues (145) (and, it will be recalled, William Wolfe Tone omitted the political sections as being of little topical interest), but

---

14. Barrett J. Mandel, "Full of Life Now", in *Autobiography: Essays Theoretical and Critical*, ed. James Olney, Princeton: NJ, 1980, 49–72, at 52 ff.

15. Also, cf. Georges Gusdorf, "Conditions and Limits of Autobiography", [1956], in *Autobiography: Essays Theoretical and Critical*, 28–48: "Every autobiography is a work of art" (45). See esp. 43–44 for a reasoned account of the artistic function of autobiographical writing.

16. Alistair Fowler, *Kinds of Literature: An Introduction to the Theory of Genres and Modes*, Oxford, 1982, 13.

17. William L. Howarth, "Some Principles of Autobiography", in *Autobiography: Essays Theoretical and Critical*, 84–114. First published in *New Literary History*, V (1974), 363–81.

18. Cf. Olney's introductory essay to *Autobiography: Essays Theoretical and Critical*, in which he draws the link between the personal autobiography and that of a nation, a culture, or a genre (3–27, esp. 13 ff.). Olney here lists American autobiography, Black autobiography and Women's autobiography, to which may of course be added Irish autobiography.

in their later nineteenth as well as in their twentieth-century redactions they definitely have that effect upon even the most a-political reader.[19]

This ideological aspect of Tone's *Autobiography* is reflected in the bursts of often downright hackneyed oratory, as when he speaks of "the luminary of truth and freedom in France" which "advanced rapidly to its meridian splendour" (I, 43), or in the following, oft-quoted passage:

> To subvert the tyranny of our execrable Government, to break the connection with England, the never-failing source of all our political evils, and to assert the independence of my country — these were my objects. To unite the whole people of Ireland, to abolish the memory of all past dissensions, and to substitute the common name of Irishman in place of the denominations of Protestant, Catholic and Dissenter — these were my means (I, 50–51).

As to the dramatic aspect of Tone's *Autobiography*, this appears most prominently in the journal parts. According to Howarth, the dramatic autobiographer "is unpretentious and impertinent, viewing life as a staged performance that he may attend, applaud, or attack, just as he pleases" (96–97). Plenty of examples could be adduced, such as the following brief entry for 1 September 1792:

> Dress myself in the Belfast uniform, and go to dine at Dixon's. All the soldiers salute me as I pass, and the sentries carry their arms; pleased as Punch at this, and a great fool for my pains. Suppose they take me for the Duke of Brunswick, or some foreign officer of distinction. Puppy! (I, 125);

or the ending of the entry for 5 October of the same year, on the eve of a journey by post-chaise from Dublin to Ballinasloe, during which the travellers were to be held up by a gang of robbers. "For the miraculous events in that journey", Tone writes, building up tension for what is to follow in the diary account, "see book — wherein they are fully detailed, being *'moving accidents by flood and field; how we were taken by the insolent foe, and sold to slavery, and our redemption thence'*, &c., &c." (I, 135, italics in original). Here Tone has unmistakeably put on the impersonating mask of the romantic hero.

---

19. See e.g. Elliott's Epilogue "The Cult of Tone" (411 ff.). I think it is in particular this aspect of the Life which explains the favourable reviews immediately upon its first appearance in 1826 (Elliott, 411).

Thirdly, then, we have to consider Tone as a "poetical" autobiographer, who is "given to intellectual brooding and sharp critical dissent, searching always for private discoveries, uncertain of the proper course to follow", a character charged with Keatsian "negative capability", the power to be in uncertainties (Howarth, 110). Again, examples to illustrate this point abound, and a small random selection must suffice. Already concerning his schooldays, which he writes about in retrospect, Tone says: "I was very idle, and it was only the fear of shame which could induce me to exertion" (I, 8). On 21 January 1791 he writes: "I find it very hard to keep those journals regularly ... I wish I could bring myself to set apart some certain time for journalising; but, as that would be something approaching to system, I despair of ever reaching it" (I, 176). From the start of his political career until the very end of his life, elation at the progress he thinks he is making is repeatedly alternated by expressions of doubt or resignation. In the account of his Paris sojourn in 1796 we find a characteristic passage in the entry for 4 April:

> I am heartily glad the system of *Chouannerie* is knocked in the head, and I hope it is partly owing to my representations against it. I am now absolutely idle for three or four days, and I am truly weary of this life. "*Fie upon't, I want work!*" Well, if ever I get to Ireland I shall have work enough to make me amends for this. Strolled, as usual, to the Champs Elysées, and dined alone. Delicious weather, and all the world diverting themselves except me. "*Poor moralist, and what art thou? A solitary fly.*" I declare I am as much alone here as if I were in the deserts of Arabia, and that is hard in such a city as Paris ... (I, 319; italics in original).

From the foregoing examples the complexity of Tone's *Autobiography* will already have become apparent. If the "memorandums" enable him to put his political activities into perspective, the journals make for emphasis on privacy and momentariness. In these diary parts details are selected that might have been rejected in long-term flash-backs: his dealings with nonentities, such as the foolish priest Fitzsimons who is proposed as an informant on present affairs in Ireland, but appears to think that the despatches of the Portuguese Ministry to the Governor of Rio de Janeiro are written in English, which elicits Tone's lamentation: "Oh Lord! Oh Lord! I thought I should have choked, endeavouring to smother the irresistable propensity I felt to laugh in his face. Yes, he is a pretty devil of an agent. I suppose he will talk Portuguese to the Irish, by way of keeping the secret. Damn him sempiternally!" (I, 317); the Dutch Jew, who tries to cheat him in exchanging money on the "trakschuyt, a villainous barge" (II, 207); his indulgence in wine and late hours (*passim!*); and his infatuations (cut out, but in any case rarely overstepping the bounds of propriety). It is gratifying that he generally approves of Dutch women (II, 204), although he is occasionally disappointed: "After dinner a concert, as yesterday, but the band was differently composed: '*On n'y voyait ni tetons ni beaux yeux*'" (II, 221). Tone, who came to France with hardly a word of its language, picked up the correct expressions with his natural talent for observation. He is rightly proud at being able to order a "genever" in a Dutch pub, for, as he rightly remarks: "I do not see why I should come to the Hague without tasting some Holland gin" (II, 221). And so he muses:

> I am tempted, as I walk about the Hague, to cry out: "*Thou almost persuadest me to be a Dutchman.*" Whoever may be Ambassador from the Republic of Ireland to Holland will not be the worst off of the future Corps Diplomatique. Returned to the *auberge*; demanded of the waiter "*if he could help me to a glass of genever, or so?*" (I defy man, woman, or child, to track me in that quotation.) The waiter produced the needful ... (II, 222).

Such details may be more important, more revealing, more "telling" than their author thinks either at the time or by hindsight. Tone's concentration on external action is said to be typical of eighteenth-century autobiography, but we must not lose sight of the fact that "external action ... reflects the internal" (Spacks, 23-24). The crucial question to be addressed, then, is: what did Tone select, rather than: what did Tone's widow and son select? Ultimately, the question is not: who is the "real" Theobald Wolfe Tone (an "aporia" anyhow), but: how universal is his life, how is it aesthetically pleasing? It will by now be evident that his life is "interesting" both in its individuality and in its universality.

That we call this *Autobiography* a political work is due to the emphasis that Tone places in his selection on the political schemes and movements he was involved in: the Sandwich project, the French Revolution, the Whig Club, the Volunteer movement and the tenuous alignment between Catholics and Dissenters, the Catholic Committee, the founding of the United Irishmen, the French and Dutch expeditions to invade Ireland, and the Rising of 1798. Both in their public nature and in his own life these events become bigger as the autobiography proceeds, and we closely observe how one event leads to another, not so much in an inexorably fatal chain of cause and effect, but mainly because of Tone's free decisions to strike into certain paths, although he appears to be acting intuitively rather than rationally.

His first "essay in what I may call politics" (I, 19) is a project Tone proposed to the then Prime Minister, William Pitt the Younger, "to establish a colony in one of Cook's newly-discovered islands in the South Sea on a military plan" (I, 18). This "Sandwich scheme", devised in 1788, Tone looks upon in hindsight somewhat as a boyish dream, enabling himself, his brother William and a friend, to read every book on South America they could lay hands on, and to write and talk about the project as prospective buccaneers. At the time, however, Tone was so angry with the entire lack of notice from the authorities and with his father's complaints about the "embarrassments" of his affairs, that he decided to enlist for India, an impulsive move wich came to nothing — reputedly because it was the wrong season, but really, one suspects, because it was too ridiculous for words (Tone had been willing to abandon his family!). "In my anger", Tone writes in retrospect in 1796, "I made something like a vow, that, if ever I had an opportunity, I would make Mr. Pitt sorry, and perhaps fortune may yet enable me to fulfil that resolution". As to the misfired India project, Tone continues: "Thus were we [Tone himself and his brother William] stopped, and I believe we were the single instance, since the beginning of the world, of two men, absolutely bent on ruining themselves, who could not find the means" (I, 19–20). The whole affair is recounted in a curiously polyvalent note. There is youthful ambition and a generation conflict, an almost suicidal counterreaction, self-mockery and a prevision which is in itself ambiguous.

Interestingly, the "enlistment-for-India" theme features again near the end of Tone's journals, where he declares himself willing to serve under Napoleon in India, if an expedition were to be moved there (II, 317, 327), thereby providing a kind of circularity, not only to his life, but also to the unity of the *Autobiography* as a composition.

The Sandwich scheme was not to be Tone's only mishap which turned out to be a blessing in disguise, and Tone frequently puts on this mask of resignation and long-suffering, which reveals impatience and impulsiveness under the surface. A favourite quotation, repeated literally dozens of times in the journal, occasionally twice within a single entry, is the phrase: "*'tis but in vain, for soldiers to complain*" (see e.g. I, 103, 124, 126, 137, 138, 140, 145, 155, 178, 243, 247 (twice, once with comment), etc.). On one occasion later on in the journals, having found himself "moralising like an ass", he says, "Well, *'Tis but in vain for soldiers to complain*' (for the 595th time)" (II, 246).

Tone always looked upon himself as a soldier (he was a Volunteer, a United Irishman, and ended up as Chef de Brigade and ultimately an Adjutant-General in the French army), and so we need not be surprised to find that his comparisons (which he used sparingly) are often military, as in the following account of a session of the Irish House of Commons in 1792:

> All parties were now fully employed preparing for the ensuing session of Parliament. The Government, through the organ of the corporations and grand juries, opened a heavy fire upon us [the Catholic Committee, of which Tone was secretary] of manifestoes and resolutions. At first we were like young soldiers, a little stunned with the noise, but after a few rounds we began to look about us, and seeing nobody drop with all this furious cannonade, we took courage and determined to return the fire. In consequence, whenever there was a meeting of the Protestant ascendancy, which was the title assumed by that party (and a very impudent one it was), we took care it should be followed by a meeting of the Catholics, who spoke as loud, and louder than their adversaries, and, as we had the right clearly on our side, we found no great difficulty in silencing the enemy on this quarter (I, 69).

Other key concepts that pervade the *Autobiography* are the notions of friendship and justice. Tone, who did not, as we have seen, suffer fools gladly, repeatedly expresses the intention to "do justice" to others, his father, his schoolfellows, his friends, even his adversaries. Incidentally, the topic of the inept but loving father, which appears in Anglo-Irish characters from Sterne's Walter Shandy to John McGahern's old Moran in *Amongst Women* (1990), occurs early in the *Autobiography* and in a sense reflects on Tone's own position, not only as a son, but as a father who scarcely saw his own children because of his frequent absence from wherever "home" happened to be. As to Tone's father, a charming paragraph concludes the psychologically very revealing description of the family Tone grew up in. On pages 2–4 of the first volume, Tone provides an extensive account of his younger brother William in India, whom he lost sight of — this opening passage reflects the idea of preserving the reputation not only of himself, but of relatives and friends as well. His brothers, though different from him in some respects, are also very much like him: cultivated, like William (I, 2), or with a "rambling, enthusiastic spirit" and with "a dash of coxcombry", like Matthew (I, 5–6), and "something of a poet" like both of them (I, 5). Even of his sister Mary he writes: "If she were a man, she would be exactly like one of us" (I, 7). Then he starts off the concluding paragraph of this family portrait as follows:

> My father and mother were pretty much like other people; but, from this short sketch, with what I have to add concerning myself, I think it will appear that their children were not at all like other people, but have had, every one of them, a wild spirit of adventure, which, though sometimes found in an individual, rarely pervades a whole family, including even the females (I, 7).

It is as if Tone on the one hand wishes to avoid any suspicion of blame on the parents of this remarkable family, while on the other presenting himself as just one member of an extraordinary breed rather than as the odd one out.

There is one other early passage I wish to say a few words about, before concluding on a more general note. This is the account of the housebreaking described on pages 14–15. After his precipitate marriage, the young Tones (Matilda was only sixteen) moved in with Tone's father, who was then living at Bodenstown. On 16 October 1786 six armed robbers broke into the house and started to demolish the furniture after tying up its inmates, causing no small alarm, although in the event the Tones remained unharmed. This "most terrible event" left a great impression on Tone's mind, and although he never explicitly draws a link between it and his later career, I think the event is both traumatic and symbolic. It is, indeed, arguable to see the pointless, destructive and psychologically damaging burglary as a symbol of the "rape" of Ireland by the English, and as the ultimate cause for Tone's political activities, which carry a strong element of personal retribution. In any case, it caused Tone to be from then onwards undauntedly prepared for any attack upon his person, as appears from various later accounts, such as that of the aforementioned hold-up on the way to Ballinasloe. The episode, like that of the Sandwich scheme, fits extremely well into a "fictional" account explaining the development of its protagonist's character and career. Obviously, Tone "selected" it from his memories because of its psychological impact, but the "literary" effect it attains is that of a *mise-en-abyme*. Both his grandfather and his father incapacitated themselves by a fall — his grandfather was killed by falling off a stack of corn; his father was lamed by falling down a flight of stairs (I, 9), and had to retire from business as a consequence. Tone himself at least would be careful where he put his feet.

The quotations presented thus far to illustrate various points will have demonstrated the variety of subject and style of these delightful documents. The style of the memorandums is elegant and highly periodic, without, however, ever becoming pedantic or abstruse.[20] In the original version they are occasionally so frank about personal affairs that they make O'Faolain wonder if Tone "wrote these autobiographical notes, as he wrote his diary, for other eyes" (21n.). The journals are written in a brisk, telegraphic style, in places slangy. Here is an account of 13 July 1792, in Belfast:

> 13th. Rise again with a headache. Go to the Donegal Arms. No Catholics by the mail; very odd. Saw them take places for last night. Will they come or not? No letters. The Jacobin party up here; Lafayette down; think they are all wrong. Belfast not half so pleasant this time as the last. Politics just as good or better; everything else worse. Grievous want of P.P. [Russell]; the Keeper [Whitley Stokes] not equal to him. By-the-bye, the Hypocrite [Dr McDonnell] made the Keeper drunk last night. Fine doings. Miss that unfortunate Digges. Weather bad. Afraid for to-morrow every way; generally in low spirits. Hear that the Tribune [J. Napper Tandy], with his suite, is arrived; go to the Donegal Arms and say *O* to him (*vide* "Robinson Crusoe"). The Harpers again. *Strum strum* and be hanged ... (I, 97).

The reference to Defoe attests Tone's un-pedantic use of literary quotations, and once he finds a quotation "wears well" it is repeated several times (see e.g. I, 107, 143). Commenting on the failed French naval expedition against Britain to capture the "Isles Marcou", Tone paraphrases Sterne by exclaiming: *"They do not order this thing better in France"* (II, 314). When he becomes humorous, the joke is as often as not directed at least partly against himself, as when he writes: "Breakfast, more beefsteak and onions. *Go gentle gales.* Fragrant and pretty" (I, 137).

It is impossible not to be charmed and intrigued by the life history of this fascinating and humane man, and one wonders how interesting his life would have been if he had not been a political activist, but, let us say, an amateur musician and composer. Successfully pacifying his unpleasant but violin-playing future brother-in-law by forming a duet with him (I, 12), we later find Tone playing duets on the flute with the Dutch Admiral De Winter (II, 243), and while waiting for the French fleet to set sail for Bantry Bay, Tone reports himself as having written

---

20. After 30 June 1798 the account of Tone's life was completed by William Wolfe Tone in a businesslike and movingly dignified manner, albeit not without some rhetorical flourishes (II, ch. 14).

"about thirty Irish airs for the band of my regiment", ominously adding: "if I am to have one" (II, 116).

Wolfe Tone's *Autobiography* is indeed a political document. The life of Theobald Wolfe Tone is also the life of Ireland in the 1780s and '90s. In it, we see the country shifting its mood as if it were that of the protagonist himself: now ready for a rising, then lukewarm; now in peaceful harmony with itself, then at internal strife; now enjoying itself with a drink, then execrating the English oppressors. In the end Tone misjudged the political consciousness of his countrymen, and the rising of 1798 turned out to be wrongly timed. It meant the end of Ireland's relative political freedom, and the end of Tone's life.

"WHY HANG O'QUIGLEY?":
TREASON AND THE PRESS IN 1798

C.C. BARFOOT

"Why hang O'QUIGLEY? — he, misguided man,
"In sober thought his Country's weal *might* plan.
"And, though his deep laid Treason sapp'd the Throne,
"*Might* act from *taste in morals*, all his own."[1]

When George Canning, Under-Secretary of State in the Foreign Office, asked the question, not, it need hardly be said, *in propria persona*, there was no doubt that personally he considered "O'Quigley" fittingly hanged. He probably thought too that at least one of the other defendants at the Maidstone Treason Trials on 21 and 22 May 1798, and some not even on trial, should have been hanged with him. The question put in the poem, later to be entitled *New Morality*,[2] and the other sentiments expressed there, amounting to an argument of a familiar liberal kind, are put into the mouths of those Canning wants to condemn. Speaking for himself Canning is:

Content for good men's guidance, bad men's awe,
On moral truth to rest, and gospel law;
Who owns, when Traitors feel th'avenging rod,
Just retribution, and the hand of God —[3]

---

1. *The Anti-Jacobin*, 36, Monday, 9 July 1798, 284, ll. 215–18. For a general account of *The Anti-Jacobin* (which published its first issue on 21 November 1797 and its last on 9 July 1798), see my "Parody and the Classic Art of Political Partisanship in *The Anti-Jacobin*", in *Tropes of Revolution: Writers' Reactions to Real and Imagined Revolutions 1789–1989*, eds C.C. Barfoot and Theo D'haen, Amsterdam and Atlanta, 1991, 127–93.

2. In the *Poetry of the Anti-Jacobin*, London, 1799; and the two volume reprint of *The Anti-Jacobin* (a revised and corrected fourth edition) in the same year.

3. *The Anti-Jacobin*, 285, ll. 229–32.

From the Ministerial point-of-view, at least some partial "just retribution" had been felt the previous month. On 8 June 1798 *The Times* announced:

> His Majesty has been pleased to remit part of the sentence of Mr. O'COIGLEY, which still stands in the judgment for High Treason. The sentence to be executed is, that he shall be hanged until he is dead, and his head be severed from his body.[4]

And the next day, Saturday (a day later than might have been expected), the following report, with an unexpected misprint, appeared in the same newspaper: "*O'Coigley* was executed on Monday [*sic*]; and his execution has been detailed in the Opposition Papers with as much form and precision as if they were announcing the most interesting information." *The Times* continued:

> The reason for their doing so is obvious, and intended to draw forth the compassion of the public for the fate of as great a traitor as ever was sent to the gallows. It is really disgusting to read the affected manner in which one of the Jacobin Papers records the dying moments of this villain.
>
> So many reports have been circulated respecting the precise time when he was to be executed, that few people were informed of the fact, and his journey to the gallows was not even attended by the ordinary concourse of persons who usually attend executions. At eleven o'clock, on Thursday [7 June], he was carried on a hurdle from Maidstone to Pennenden Heath. On the gallows, he said — that he could not deprive himself of the *glory* of dying in that manner. He persisted to the last in his innocence of ever having carried on an improper correspondence with the French. Those who are acquainted with the history of the last six years of *O'Coigley*'s life, will know what degree of credit to give to this assertion.

---

4. Apart from the various aliases that he adopted, the name of the executed man took various forms in the writings of friends and foes alike — Coigly, Coigley, O'Coigley, Quigley — and one suspects that *The Anti-Jacobin* picked on "O'Quigley" as the most demeaning version (cf. Gurney's treatment of his name on the title page of his report of the Trials, n.12 below). Throughout this article, except in quotations, I use the form of the name as it appears on the title page and under various documents in *The Life of the Rev. James Coigly: Observations upon His Trial, an Address to the People of Ireland, and Several Interesting Letters, All Written by Himself during His Confinement in Maidstone Gaol*, ed. Valentine Derry, London, 1798.

Mr. O'Coigley came on the ground about a quarter past twelve; and was turned off about a quarter before one.

After hanging near a quarter of an hour, *O'Coigley* was taken down, the head taken off by a Surgeon, and the Executioner held up the head to the populace, saying, "This is a head of a traitor!" Both the head and the body were then put into a shell, and buried at the foot of the gallows.

What this account indicates both in its sentiment and in its tone, as well as in the self-righteous brevity with which it dismisses the treatment of the story in other newspapers, are divisions in political opinion and in the style and rhetoric of newspapers on either side of the divide. My reason for writing this article in the first place is a concern with the story of what one might call, in order to reflect a tradition of British injustice to Irish people that continues to this day, the Margate Five. But of almost equal interest is the way that the story from the time of the arrest to the execution of Coigly was presented to the public.

The arrests — how the story broke: Friday 2 March 1798

On the day the story of the arrest of the Margate Five broke *The Times* offered its readers the following account:

Last Friday, in consequence of private information being received at the Duke of PORTLAND'S Office, that a person had left London on board a hoy on Thursday, and was to be joined by several others, who were in treasonable correspondence with the FRENCH DIRECTORY, two Officers belonging to Bow-street left London on Saturday in pursuit of him, but could hear no tidings of him till on Tuesday morning about one o'clock an express came to them at Gravesend, from the Secretary of State's Office, informing them that information had been received that five suspicious persons were at *Whitstable*, in Kent; upon which the Officers set off for that place, where they arrived in the afternoon. On enquiry, they learnt that five persons had left that town in disguise, after having offered 130 guineas for a passage to France, besides making a deposit of 300 guineas as a security for the vessel. These offers led them to be suspected, on which they decamped. They had besides with them very heavy luggage; and the officers having traced out by what means the luggage was taken away, which was in a small cart, and having found the owner of it, he informed them that he had driven the property to Margate, and that the five persons who belonged to it walked by the side of the cart. Upon this the officers set off for Margate, and meeting with a party of light horse, took them with them.

On their arrival at Margate early on Wednesday morning, they traced them to the King's Head Inn, where two of them were found in the parlour, going to breakfast. Upon one of them there was discovered a dagger; the other three were up stairs, upon one of whom they found a brace of pistols. In one of their great coats was found a most seditious paper, purporting to be an address from a secret Committee of United Irishmen to the Executive Directory of France. Drawings and bearings of the English coast were also found on them; with a list of the houses where the Meetings of the Corresponding and other Democratic Societies are held in this country. On searching their luggage, the trunks were discovered to be made of such materials as to sink when put into the water. The Officers learnt, before they left the town, that the Prisoners had been offering considerable sums of money to fishermen to carry them to France; but not being able to succeed, were about to leave that place for Deal.

The Officers arrived with them at Bow-street yesterday afternoon, attended by a party of Light Horse, in three post chaises, and a post-coach and four, conveying also several witnesses, when they underwent a private examination before Sir WM. ADDINGTON, Mr. KING, under Secretary of State, and Mr. Justice FORD. Their names are *O'Connor, Binns, Fevey*, who assumed the name of Col. Morris, *Leary*, and *Alley*. They were committed to different prisons, and their luggage was not opened, nor will it be till this day, when it is expected they will be examined before the Privy Council.

The Magistrates ordered them to be kept separate.

Lord ROMNEY and Mr. FLOOD were present at the examination, which lasted near an hour.

As a newspaper favourable to the Government, and receiving favours in return from the Treasury,[5] *The Times* presents this story in a circumstantial but circumspect manner. One would not expect modern headlines of the "Five Traitors Arrested in Margate" variety, of course, but *The Times* is clearly determined to inch its way into the story in an unspectacular way, by actually beginning at the beginning (or at least as near the beginning as was required for the story to be told at all). By

---

5. According to A. Aspinall, *Politics and the Press c.1780–1850*, London, 1949, 74–75, from January 1789 to "the summer of 1799", *The Times* received a Treasury subsidy of £300 a year: "In return for the allowance [John Walter, founder and editor] undertook to continue his general support of Government, and, in particular, to publish articles sent from the Treasury."

comparison the Opposition paper, *The Morning Post*, began the story with a more eye-catching statement: "The public attention was much engaged yesterday by circumstances of a very extraordinary nature." One of the tactics *The Times* employs to keep the reader at a distance is to use "person" and "persons" and pronouns instead of proper names which are reserved for a single sentence near the end of the piece: "Their names are *O'Connor, Binns, Fevey*, who assumed the name of Col. Morris, *Leary*, and *Alley*."[6]

That *The Times* is representing an official point of view is immediately evident in its reference to "treasonable correspondence", and its emphasis on the proper suspicion that the party aroused; while the statement towards the end that "In one of their great coats was found a most seditious paper, purporting to be an address from a secret Committee of United Irishmen to the Executive Directory of France" appears to seal this as a report phrased and framed by the Government. Readers that Friday were not to know how crucial that "most seditious paper" (but not "from a secret Committee of United Irishmen") was going to be in getting Coigly hanged (for the full text of this document from "The Secret Committee of England", see the Appendix). But naturally enough *The Morning Post*, in the Opposition camp, was rightly suspicious of the spin being given to the official yarn,[7] and immediately after its eye-catching opening sentence, prefaced its account of the arrests and the surrounding circumstances with a warning:

> Without making any observations of our own upon the subject, we shall lay before our readers as plain a narrative of facts as we are enabled to draw up from the information that has reached us, taken, as we believe, from the report of the Officers engaged in

---

6. In England Coigly called himself Fivey, which he says he believed "to be the English translation of Coigly" (*The Life of the Rev. James Coigly*, 22); in their first reports *The Times* and *The Morning Post* could not decide whether he called himself Favey or Fevey, which may be due to the Irish accents of Coigly and his companions. Allen's name appeared in the first newspaper accounts variously as Ally, Alley, Allay.

7. The information following the reference to the "seditious paper" that "Drawings and bearings of the English coast were also found on them; with a list of the houses where the Meetings of the Corresponding and other Democratic Societies are held in this country. On searching their luggage, the trunks were discovered to be made of such materials as to sink when put into the water" was obviously intended merely to blacken the characters of the Margate Five in the minds of the ministerially loyal readers of *The Times*: the information was never shown to be true or brought up at the Trials.

apprehending the persons herein after mentioned. — *The Public will, therefore, consider the following account as the Bow-street report.* We shall not attempt to prejudge the accused [italics as in the original].

As a "Bow-street report", *The Morning Post* advises its readers to regard it as inevitably one-sided, and therefore to be treated sceptically. Surprisingly, perhaps, it then proceeds to give a much longer account, from the beginning naming names and producing a very clear and exciting narrative:

[Last Thursday, BINNS, a well-known member of the London Corresponding Society, went to the coast of Kent, to provide a conveyance for certain persons desirous of going to France.] Government, we believe, had information of this proceeding. BINNS went to Canterbury in the stage, and from thence took a horse to review the coast. [He agreed with a fisherman at Whitstable, to take over a Gentleman and his Servants to Holland.] Whitstable is a small fishing town at the mouth of the Swale, and also at the mouth of a brook running from Canterbury, of which it may be considered as the sea-port. The bargain BINNS made was to give 150 guineas for conveying the persons to Holland, and to leave 300 guineas as security in case the vessel should be seized. This bargain being settled, the parties had advice of it, and on Sunday morning they sailed from London in the Whitstable hoy. They arrived on Sunday night, and being met by BINNS, they made immediate and eager inquiries respecting their departure. They at first represented that they wished to go to Holland; but then they observed, that being better known in France, they would rather go thither at once. This was the state of things on Sunday night; and here it will be proper to describe the parties that came down in the hoy:

JAMES JOHN FEVEY, said to have been a Roman Catholic Priest. He is a strong well made man, about five feet ten inches high, and about forty-five years of age. It is suspected that FEVEY is not his real name, and that he is a very different person from what he is represented. He is supposed to be a man of consequence.

JOHN ALLY, a young well made man, marked with the small pox, — Not the Gentleman at the Bar.

ARTHUR O'CONNOR, of whom the Public have already heard so much especting the affairs of Ireland.

—— LEARY, a young man, servant to O'CONNOR; and

BINNS, whom we have already mentioned. These are the five people accused. All of them except BINNS are Irishmen; we are not able to say whether he is from Ireland or not.

These four persons embarked on Sunday morning from London, in the character of Capt. JONES and servants. FEVEY was Capt. JONES, and all the others were his servants. [But when they landed at Whitstable, FEVEY gave himself out as Colonel MORRIS, and all their luggage, of which there was a considerable quantity, was marked "Colonel MORRIS." The parties were not however very eager to give themselves out for any thing; but at Whitstable inquiries being made, they with some reluctance and confusion gave out themselves as Colonel MORRIS and servants; and they did this, notwithstanding their previous account that they were Captain JONES and servants.]

This inconsistent account led to a suspicion at Whitstable.

[Another circumstance leading to suspicion was, their extreme anxiety to depart for France.

Early on Monday morning the Custom-house Officer examined their goods. They freely allowed him to inspect some packages of hams, biscuits, and sea-stores, trunks of clothes, &c. but certain very heavy small mahogany boxes they would not open, pretending the servant had not come forward with the keys. This was another circumstance that excited suspicion, and the Officers refused to allow them to depart till those boxes were examined. They now found that they were suspected, and resolved to seek for a more easy place of embarkation. For this purpose they, on Monday night, hired a cart to convey their trunks next morning. The carrier knew not whither he was bound; but he travelled along the sands on Tuesday forenoon from Whitstable to Margate. O'CONNOR, FEVEY, &c. walked all the way by the side of the cart; the distance is 25 miles. Binns had a map of the coast, and to the astonishment of the carrier seemed to know the roads better than him, tho' he had lived in the country many years.

The Party entered Margate on Tuesday afternoon, soon after day-light had expired. They desired to be conducted, not to one of the best inns, but to some small public-house. They were accordingly taken to the King's Head, close to the water side kept by Mrs. CRICKETTS. Here they took up their abode on Tuesday night, and made some inquiries about a fishing-boat to France, but the result not appearing to be very favourable to their views, they resolved to go to Deal next day, where there was a friend upon whom they could rely for providing them with a conveyance to France. Of this BINNS assured them, and he seemed to be the guide in all respects. On Tuesday night they slept at Margate, with the determination of setting off for Deal early next morning.]

REVETT and FUGION, two of the Bow-street Officers, were
the persons appointed by Government to apprehend them. It is
pretended that these officers were down in Kent, at Gravesend, on
other business; but we believe they were sent from London
specially on this business, and that Government had good
intelligence of the proceedings of the parties now in custody.
When the Bow-street officers found their men had passed
Gravesend, they followed them, desirous that they should first
commit themselves with regard to their design of going to France
before they were apprehended; and at the same time the officers
were prepared with a vessel to follow and seize them, had they
embarked. It was thought that the parties had sufficiently
committed themselves at Whitstable, with regard to their place of
distination [*sic*], and it was feared they would take a vessel under
pretence of going to Deal, Dover, or some other part of the coast,
and when they had it at sea, compel the crew to carry them to
France. These reasons made the officers resolve to seize them at
Margate; they saw that the parties might escape to the Continent
without embarking for that country, and they saw no prospect of
having better proof against them than they were actually possessed
of with respect to their object of going to France. The officers,
therefore, resolved to seize them next morning. On Tuesday night
they got hold of the Carter, and drew from him every information
possible. At first he was not at all communicative, the parties
having cautioned him to be silent respecting whatever he might
observe; but being urged by the officers, he told all he knew.

[On Wednesday morning about five o'clock, the Bow-street
Officers proceeded to the King's Head, at Margate, to arrest the
parties. The officers had previously consulted some Custom-house
Officers, whom they engaged in their cause, together with a party
of military. FEVEY was in the parlour at breakfast. They pounced
upon him, and took him by surprise. BINNS they apprehended
coming down stairs, and O'CONNOR and ALLY they took in their
bed-rooms. On BINNS were found a pair of pistols, and all the
others were provided with arms.

From FEVEY's person was taken a large, strong, sharp,
serpentine-shaped dagger. As the parties were taken separately,
they were easily secured. FEVEY submitted quietly, but O'CONNOR
stormed much.] Before the proper measures were taken at Margate
for securing their luggage, papers, the witnesses, &c. it was one
o'clock on Wednesday, when all the parties departed under a
military escort for Canterbury. As they travelled slowly, it was too
late when they arrived in Canterbury to hope to reach London the
same day in any reasonable time for business. They therefore
resolved to remain all night at the Red Lion. Several military
officers, among others Lord PAGET, came to see the prisoners.

FEVEY was civil, though reserved, but O'CONNOR and BINNS were very warm and indignant, speaking in language designedly offensive to their visitors. They remained on mattrasses all night, prisoners and officers in the same room, and a military guard in the inn. Early yesterday morning they departed from Canterbury, and arrived at the Public Office, Bow-street, under a guard of light horse, about half past three o'clock. They came in three post-chaises, besides a post-coach with the luggage and some of the witnesses, and the escort consisted of twelve horsemen. It was not the hours of business at the Public-office, Bow-street, when they arrived; but Mr. KING, Secretary to the Duke of PORTLAND, Mr. FORD, and other Magistrates, were instantly assembled before whom they underwent a slight examination. From the first of their arrest, FEVEY said he came down to the coast for his health, and was desirous of going to Ireland in a vessel. O'CONNOR and BINNS refused to answer all questions, and in this conduct they respectively persisted before the Magistrates. Mr. O'CONNOR avowed who he was, and BINNS was easily identified. On being taken, they owned such trunks as contained clothes, and packages as contained provisions; but they denied all knowledge of certain mahogany boxes, said to have been in their possession.] These boxes were uncommonly heavy; made so, it was supposed, for the purpose of sinking, had the vessel in which they were been seized by any English ship of war. These boxes had not been opened at seven o'clock last night; the contents of them are to be first examined by the Privy Council. It is reported that they may contain many important papers respecting a traitorous correspondence between Ireland and France, and England and France, such as assurances and declarations of the various societies and individuals. It would be improper to relate here all we have heard respecting the papers. They are represented as of the utmost importance, and likely to disclose the most interesting facts. In the pocket of a great coat hanging in the room where FEVEY was taken, a Declaration or Address to the Directory was found. This paper, it is said, proves the correspondence of the parties with the Directory.

FEVEY disowns the paper, and denies that the coat belongs to him; but the officers say, the coat must be his, as it is powdered on the neck, and he is the only person of the five who wore powder. It seems he did not wear powder till he set off on this journey. The paper, it is said, purposes to be an address from the Executive Directory of Britain (constituted of Members of the London Corresponding Society) to the Executive Directory of France, stating that a Delegate from each division were then sitting, and that the bearer was the worthy Citizen who had the honour of waiting on them once before.

The money found upon their persons was nearly as follows:
Fevey 20L. O'Connor 20L. Ally 10L. Leary 9L. Binns 1L.

Making in all about sixty guineas; but it is conjectured that in
the heavy boxes there were about five hundred guineas.

We have now given as ample and impartial an account of the
Reports respecting this extraordinary affair as the information of
Bow-street enables us to do; and we again repeat, that late trials
shew the innocent have nothing to dread in an English Court of
Justice. The parties were all sent to separate prisons: Mr.
O'CONNOR was sent to Tothill Fields. They are to be examined
this forenoon before the Privy Council. In a letter from Margate
will be found some further particulars on this subject.

There are many features about this long account which deserve
comment, the first concerning those sections of the report which I have
put between square brackets: the next day, Saturday 3 March, *The Times*
prefaced a further report with the explanation that "the following account
of the apprehension of *Arthur O'Connor*, and his companions *Favey,
Binns, Allen,* and *Leary*, contains some particulars which we had not an
opportunity of giving yesterday". This seems fair enough, for perhaps
The Times had to go to press earlier than *The Morning Post*, perhaps it
appeared on the streets earlier, perhaps there had not been enough space
the previous day to give the full story of the arrests. But when they begin
to fill in the details — "Last Thursday, *Binns*, a well-known member of
the London Corresponding Society, went to the coast of Kent, to provide
a conveyance for certain persons desirous of going to France ...." — one
finds oneself reading word for word, almost comma for comma, the
same narrative as had appeared the previous day in *The Morning Post*.
The passages given in square brackets in *The Morning Post* story for the
Friday are identical with what *The Times* was to print the following day.

One can hardly believe that *The Times*, admittedly not then a paper
with the eminence it was to achieve in the middle of the nineteenth
century, but still a paper in the pay of the Treasury, would simply lift the
particulars of the story, and more than the particulars the whole literal
account, from a Jacobin rival. The only alternative is that both papers
were in receipt of a written Government hand-out — it would have to be
written in order to explain the identical syntax and punctuation. Is it
possible that on the Friday *The Times* gave a summary account of the
information it had been given, and then on the Saturday faced with the
full story in *The Morning Post* felt obliged to follow suit? *The Times*'s
policy seems to have been to spread the story as a slow smear over two
or three days (Friday, Saturday and the following Monday), with a

weekend to allow the story as told so far to sink in;[8] whereas *The Morning Post* was determined to give it all as a dramatic straight narrative with obvious political implications.

Did *The Times* steal the story from *The Morning Post*, or did they both have in their possession identical Government statements? These questions cannot be answered, despite the evidence of the story which was to appear on Saturday in *The Morning Post* about the Editor's own encounter with the Privy Council, which suggests that *The Morning Post* had put together the full story themselves contrary to Ministerial intentions. But before coming to that, two further observations have to be made. Whether *The Times* blatantly reprinted *The Morning Post* story or whether they printed from a Government hand-out common to both, in two places *The Times*'s version shows evident deterioration as a text. *The Times*'s Saturday account says "Binns had a map of the coast, and seemed to know the roads as if he had lived in the country many years", which does not make much sense until one consults *The Morning Post* version: "Binns had a map of the coast, and to the astonishment of the carrier seemed to know the roads better than him, tho' he had lived in the country many years." Similarly in the next sentence — "The Party entered Margate on Tuesday afternoon, soon after day-light" — *The Times* also garbles *The Morning Post*'s version — "The Party entered Margate on Tuesday afternoon, soon after day-light had expired". Does this prove that *The Times* compositor was misreading the long and crammed *The Morning Post* story? (Perhaps it is not entirely accidental that these two significant mistakes in *The Times* version are in juxtaposed sentences.) However, it is equally possible that the compositor was simply misreading the shaky handwriting of the Government statement.[9]

---

8. Some information, such as the detail of Coigley's hair powder and the greatcoat in which the incriminating document was found, that had appeared in *The Morning Post* on Friday did not appear in *The Times* until Monday, and then in a somewhat oblique way: "This great coat has the marks of having been worn by a powdered head; and besides the above paper, there was a pocket-book in the great coat, in which was a certain instrument, containing a dispensation from a Roman Catholic Bishop to *Favey*. His name and profession are thus identified.

Favey is the only one of the five who wears hair-powder; but he denies that the great coat belongs to him."

9. It was later to emerge in the evidence of the Trials and in Binns's own much later account that neither the newspapers nor their source was accurate about the attractive graphic detail of Binns and his maps, since neither he nor O'Connor had walked from Whitstable to Margate. Binns had originally gone ahead alone to Whitstable to try "to procure O'Connor [and the rest of the party] a passage to

The second observation to be made is that apart from its openly editorial comments "that late trials shew the innocent have nothing to dread in an English Court of Justice", *The Morning Post*'s claim at the beginning that they will not be "making any observations of [their] own upon the subject" and in the last paragraph that they have "given as ample and impartial an account of the *Reports* respecting this extraordinary affair as the information of Bow-street enables [them] to do", is not quite true, nor would one expect it to be. *The Morning Post* deliberately intimates at various places that they were determined not to be taken in by aspects of the information with such phrases as "This paper, it is said" and "but the officers say, the coat must be his", such formulations as "It is pretended that ... but we believe", and carefully qualified statements such as the following:

> It is reported that they [the heavy mahogany boxes] may contain many important papers respecting a traitorous correspondence between Ireland and France, and England and France .... It would be improper to relate here all we have heard respecting the papers. They are represented as of the utmost importance, and likely to disclose the most interesting facts.

On the day after the story broke, *The Morning Post* had the following tale to tell:

> Yesterday forenoon Mr. O'CONNOR, BINNS, and the other persons apprehended at Margate, were taken to the Duke of PORTLAND's office, to be examined before the KING's Ministers. There were present,

Mr. PITT,	Lord CHATHAM,
Mr. DUNDAS,	ATTORNEY GENERAL
Duke of PORTLAND,	SOLICITOR GENERAL
Lord CHANCELLOR	&c.

France"; when he returned to London, he found O'Connor and the rest had already set off for Whitstable; Binns tried to catch them up, but failed, and went instead to Canterbury. As Binns himself later recalled, "Early the next morning [Monday, 26 February] I left Canterbury, on foot, for Whitstable .... On the road, about five miles from Canterbury, I met O'Connor on his way from Whitstable to Canterbury in search of me .... On our arrival in Canterbury, we ordered a post-chaise and posted to Deal, where we slept that night. The next morning we posted to Sandwich, where we discharged the post-chaise and walked a few miles across the country to the town of Margate, where we expected to meet, and did, a few hours after our arrival, meet Coigley, with whom were Allen and Leary, with a cart heavily laden with baggage" (*Recollections of the Life of John Binns*, Philadelphia, 1854, 88).

This information was shared with *The Times* on the same day, but *The Morning Post* also had some exclusive background information to offer its readers:

> There was a very considerable number of persons at the Treasury door, Whitehall, and along the passage, waiting to see the prisoners come out. The mahogany boxes were opened; but the circumstances we shall now state will shew the impropriety of publishing at present, any particulars that may have reached us upon report.
>
> A few minutes after the persons arrested arrived at Bow-street on Thursday, intelligence of the fact reached our Office. The Editor was immediately struck with the importance of the affair, and felt it his duty to give as accurate and circumstantial an account as possible. He would not trust in the common information sent by the person who usually gives the Bow-street intelligence, but he went himself to the Office to make inquiries.
>
> After some time spent very fruitlessly, FUGION, one of the officers who apprehended the prisoners, came in. Several persons who knew him, asked questions, and he answered most of them. To these the Editor listened, and put questions on points he thought material. When he had collected sufficient information for a connected narrative, he retired. FUGION knew him not.
>
> Yesterday forenoon a verbal message was left at this Office, that Mr. KING wished to see the Editor at the Duke of PORTLAND's Office. The editor went accordingly, and after some time, was introduced to a room in which were all the above Gentlemen excepting the Lord Chancellor, who had gone to the House of Lords. As the circumstance of the Editor's being examined will no doubt be generally known, to prevent misrepresentation, he thinks it proper, in his own defence to state what passed. The Editor feels that his examination is of the *greatest Public importance*; but from motives of delicacy he must leave it to the reader to discover wherein the importance consists. The following is very nearly the Editor's examination.
>
> *Mr. Dundas (with the Morning Post in his hand)* asked the Editor if he was Printer of the Morning Post? *Answer.* Yes. Looking at the account, Mr. DUNDAS asked how he obtained so particular an account? *Answer.* When first I heard the intelligence I went to Bow-street to learn as many particulars as possible, and from the information I obtained there wrote that account.
>
> *Mr. Dundas.* But how did you know that one of the persons at Whitstable went by the name of JONES?
>
> *Answer.* I heard it at the Bow-street office.
>
> *Mr. Dundas.* Who told you?

[*Here the Editor explained his motives for going to the Office, and the manner in which he obtained the information.*]

Mr. Pitt. But how came you to know that the unopened boxes contained a quantity of gold?

Editor. It is merely stated as a conjecture that they contained gold. This conjecture was publicly made in the Office, on account of the weight of the boxes.

Here the Gentlemen seemed to whisper as if they did not believe the Editor. Mr. PITT came forward into Mr. DUNDAS's place; Mr. DUNDAS retired to the fire; and Mr. PITT closely questioned the Editor, laying his finger on the beginning of the paragraph, and going all through it, asking at every dozen lines how the Editor came to know such and such fact? He particularly dwelt on that part of the paragraph, which mentioned the *reports* of the boxes containing many important papers respecting a traitorous correspondence with France, and asked how the Editor knew the boxes contained such papers? The Editor answered, that the parties denying the boxes belonged to them, induced the Bow-street Officers to suspect such papers were in them. The Editor said, it was merely stated in the *Morning Post* as the conjecture of the Officers.

(Fugion, the Officer, was called in).

Mr. Dundas to Fugion. Did you send this account to the Morning Post?

Fugion. I know nothing of the Morning Post.

Mr. Dundas. Did you not say to the Editor that the parties went down to Whitstable in the name of JONES?

Fugion. I don't know the Editor.

Editor (to Fugion). Don't you remember being in conversation with me last night at the Bow-street Office?

Fugion. Yes, I do.

Editor. Don't you remember telling me that FEVEY came down to Whitstable as Captain JONES, and then took the name of Col. MORRIS?

Fugion. Yes; I said so.

Mr. Dundas. But how could you, Mr. FUGION, tell such particulars?

Fugion. When I went into the Office, several persons I knew came about me asking questions, and I answered such as I thought there was no harm in answering.

Mr. Pitt (to Fugion). Did you say the boxes contained money and papers, addresses and declarations to the Directory?

Fugion. No; I did not.

The Editor made no remark upon this answer, as he had already stated that it was only said in the Paper, as *conjecture*, that the boxes contained papers and money. The reasons for making this conjecture were the weight of the boxes, and the denial of them by the Prisoners.

Mr. Pitt (to the Editor, reading the Morning Post). How do you know that a paper was seized in a great coat pocket, purporting to be an Address or Declaration to the Directory, &c.?

Editor. Mr. FUGION told me so.

Mr. DUNDAS and Mr. PITT looked towards FUGION, who seemed to assent, observing, at the same time, that it was the common conversation of the Bow-street Office.

Mr. Pitt (to the Editor, reading the Morning Post again). But how came you to know so very particularly the nature of this paper; that the boxes contained Declarations and Addresses from the Societies of Ireland to France, and in England to France?

Editor. These were the conjectures at the office, and as such they are stated.

Mr. Pitt. But how came you to know so many particulars respecting them?

Editor. Some of the particulars I heard my self in the office, and others were sent by the person who regularly supplies the Morning Post with the Bow-street intelligence *(pointing on the paper to Mr. Pitt.)* To this place I had written and finished my account when I received another account from that person, and from his statement it was, I added, "the paper purports to be an Address from the Executive Directory of Britain to the Directory of France, saying, a Delegate from each division is now sitting, and the bearer is the worthy citizen who had the honour of waiting on you once before."

Mr. Pitt. "Was the account you have inserted in the *Morning Post* entirely made up from what you heard in casual conversation at the Bow-street Office, and from the account sent to you by the person who regularly supplies the *Morning Post* with the Bow-street intelligence?"

Editor. Entirely.

Mr. Pitt. Entirely?

Editor. Yes, entirely.

Here Mr. PITT concluded his examination.

The Attorney General (to the Editor). Don't you know, Sir, that it is very improper to publish such accounts as this, tending to prejudice the public mind against men going to trial?

Editor. The practice of publishing such accounts is not peculiar to the Morning Post. There are no circumstances stated in that account which can be deemed prejudicial to the Prisoners, that are not published in every paper in London. Both at the beginning and the end of the account, you may observe, I stated the whole as *report*, and said the innocent had no reason to fear the decision of an English Jury. I guarded the account as much as possible against doing mischief to the prisoners; but, at the same time, I felt it my duty to gratify public curiosity, by giving as full a detail of circumstances as possible.

Attorney General. — I shall put a stop to such accounts from Bow-street in future. I shall prosecute any paper that publishes them, or any person that sends them.

Editor. I have no objection to their being stopped, but while other papers insert them, so must I. I have no desire to publish them, provided they are generally prohibited.

Attorney General. I mean generally.

Mr. Pitt. Certainly, it should be general.

Here it was signified to the Editor he might retire, and he accordingly did so. The Duke of PORTLAND and Lord CHATHAM sat in the room the whole time, but asked no questions. All the Gentlemen were very polite to the Editor.

The Editor again repeats, that he published the above account for no other purpose than to prevent misrepresentations of his examination. It appears the account he published yesterday was very accurate; so accurate, that Ministers suspected him to be of the party. This is not the first time persons connected with the *Morning Post* have been examined at the Duke of PORTLAND's Office for giving very accurate accounts of events, and probably will not be the last. Of late years the *Morning Post* has been distinguished for its early and accurate information, and the same exertions will still continue to be made.

The ATTORNEY GENERAL accused us of injuring the persons going to trial. How far is this reconcilable with the infamous charges daily made in the Treasury Journals, that we are partizans of France?

The ATTORNEY GENERAL also complained of publishing so accurate an account from Bow-street. To this we answer, it would be impossible to silence the Public Prints on such an important event; and surely, the more accurate the accounts are, the better do they answer the ends of public justice.

This interesting report not only gives a general insight into the relationship between Government sources of information and the Press in this period (and certainly indicates the existence of a far less "well regulated" Press, ready to give details about official interference), but also provokes speculations about who is playing with whom, and why and how? At face value it would seem to indicate that the story published in *The Morning Post* the day before, and in *The Times* that very day, was produced not from a Government hand-out but from notes taken at an informal press conference:

After some time spent very fruitlessly, FUGION, one of the officers who apprehended the prisoners, came in. Several persons who knew him, asked questions, and he answered most of them. To these the Editor listened, and put questions on points he thought material. When he had collected sufficient information for a connected narrative, he retired. FUGION knew him not.

This would seem to support the notion that *The Times*'s editor or reporter was not so alert, and therefore did after all have to borrow his account of the arrest from an Opposition newspaper. However, one has to be careful about this, since following the Editor's report of his interrogation by the Privy Council, including the Prime Minister, *The Morning Post* moves to the usual business of reporting public affairs with the statement, "The following particulars have reached the Editor from a friend". This statement would not have attracted any comment had it not appeared that this friend seems to have been equally friendly to *The Times* and to *The Morning Post*, since the same account of the examination of the contents of the prisoners' trunks as well as of the prisoners themselves appears in both newspapers, again in almost the same words with occasional slight variations.[10]

What the Editor's grilling by the Privy Council would seem to indicate is that they had not intended so much of the story to get out so fast, hence *The Times*'s comparative reticence the previous day. It would appear that Fugion spilt the beans too fast and too readily. On the other hand, that might be just the impression that the Government was trying to give — using the loose-tongued Bow-street runner, Fugion, as a means of misleading the Opposition, and putting the Government in the position, should they care to take advantage of it at any later politically advantageous stage of the case, to muzzle the Press on the grounds of justice to the prisoners.[11] Possibly the Government was willing to risk being made to look foolish, knowing that the Editor of *The Morning Post*, Daniel Stuart, would be only too eager to reveal the grounds of his earlier scepticism of some of the details of the story, and the motivation of the whole event. Inevitably, he does leap at the chance of getting in a few shots at the hypocrisy of the Ministerial law officers.

---

10. Is this friend perhaps the same person as appears in the exchange with Mr Pitt to whom the Editor refers as "the person who regularly supplies the Morning Post with the Bow-street intelligence"?

11. The fact that *The Times* itself published the story the next day would not have prevented the Government from blaming the Opposition Press for making the story public in the first place.

The State Trials: Monday and Tuesday 21–22 May 1798
The State Trials began before a Special Commission at Maidstone at 7
o'clock in the morning of Monday 21 May 1798; and the first day,
devoted to the case for the prosecution, adjourned just before midnight.
On Tuesday morning at 8 o'clock the defence opened its case, and the
Jury retired at ten-to-one the following morning, and returned thirty-five
minutes later with their verdict.[12] According to John Binns's
Recollections, while the court was sitting "the several parties never left
their places more than for a few minutes at a time; whatever they ate or
drunk, was eaten and drunk by the judges, the jury, the bar, and the
prisoners, in the several places where they were severally stationed".[13]

In their Wednesday editions the papers were able to make the
following announcement (I give the version as it appeared in *The Times*
— the main text in *The Morning Post* is identical):

TIMES OFFICE,
Wednesday Morning, 8 o'Clock
An Express is just arrived at our Office with information that
At two o'clock this morning, the Jury, after a consultation of
40 minutes, returned the following verdict,
JAMES O'COIGLEY, *Guilty*
ARTHUR O'CONNOR, John Binns, John Allen,
and Jeremiah Leary — *Not Guilty*.
Silence then being proclaimed in Court, Mr. Justice BULLER
observed, that there was no circumstance favourable to the
prisoner on which he should conceive the prisoner could expect
mercy. He then entered into a serious discourse on the enormity
of the prisoner's crime, and the nature of our Government, the
blessings we enjoyed, and the miseries that should follow if the
French should conquer this country, and then he passed the usual
sentence for high treason on Mr. O'Coigley.

---

12. According to Joseph Gurney, "The Jury withdrew at fifty minutes past
twelve o'clock at night, and returned into Court at twenty-five minutes past one,
with a Verdict" (*The Trial of James O'Coigly, otherwise James Quigley, otherwise
called James John Fivey, Arthur O'Connor, Esq., John Binns, John Allen, and
Jeremiah Leary, for High Treason, Under a Special Commission, at Maidstone, in
Kent*, London, 1798, 535); cf. the timing of the verdict given in *The Times* and the
other newspapers in their Wednesday editions.

13. *The Recollections*, 132: for some reason Binns says that the Trials began at
"eight o'clock in the morning" and that the first day's session lasted "sixteen
hours".

As far as Coigly was concerned the fatal outcome all depended on a scrap of paper found in the pocket of the greatcoat which he refused to accept as his own when he was arrested at the King's Head, Margate. Granting that it was his greatcoat, which is very likely though it is doubtful that this was ever proved, there are at least five questions that need to be considered respecting this scrap of paper: firstly, was Coigly carrying it, or was it planted on him? Secondly, even if he was carrying it, did he know that he was carrying it? Thirdly, if he knew he was carrying it, did he know what its contents were? Fourthly, were the contents of the document treasonable? And fifthly, even if Coigly knew what its contents were, and even if they were treasonable, was carrying such a document a treasonable action? Rightly or wrongly, the Jury was satisfied with the prosecution's contention that Coigly was carrying the paper, that he knew that he was carrying it and what its contents were, that the contents of the document were treasonable, and that he was therefore involved in a treasonable action.[14]

The execution: Thursday 7 June 1798

In the opening section of this article I quoted *The Times*'s account of Coigly's execution, a comparatively brief item, which hardly amounts to more than an announcement. This may be compared to the account in *The Morning Chronicle* on Friday 8 June; and the even more extended version in *The Morning Post*. These two versions are too long to be printed in full in this article, but we will look at a few details, and consider their overall characteristics.

Both *The Morning Post* and *The Morning Chronicle* clearly want to give greater prominence to the story than *The Times*, and this is evidently for political reasons, as the give-away word "Jacobin" ("one of the Jacobin Papers") in *The Times* report indicates. Since the British Government were embarrassed about Coigly, not because he was being executed but because it was he, Coigly, who was being executed and alone, the newspapers speaking for the Whig Opposition were determined to make sure that the execution of James Coigly should be given as much coverage as possible, and in such a manner as to highlight his dignity and calmness, his humanity, and to stress the inhumanity of what was being

---

14. A detailed consideration of the Trials and how they were reported will be included in an extended discussion of the arrest and trial of the "Margate Five", and the execution of James Coigly, which will be appearing in a book now in preparation on the year 1798; there too the newspaper accounts of the execution of James Coigly will be given in full.

done to him. Both reports in the Opposition papers accent the quiet way
that he received the news of his impending execution:

> Mr. O'COIGLEY, lately convicted of High Treason, having
> been informed yesterday, between four and five o'clock in the
> afternoon, he was to die this day, received the information without
> the least surprize or apparent emotion. He spent the evening
> comfortably.
>
> *(The Morning Chronicle)*

> This gentleman, since his conviction, had conducted himself
> with great piety, fortitude, resignation, and decorum; and by his
> behaviour he had obtained the respect of all his keepers .... It was
> announced to him by Mr. Watson, the Gaoler, on Wednesday,
> about five o'clock. Mr Watson, who it appears acted with great
> humanity, was very much agitated in communicating the dreadful
> intelligence. O'Coigley received it with composure.
>
> *(The Morning Post)*

Both place the incident of his eating of an orange in a dramatic spotlight:

> and then he read his prayers from a Roman Catholic prayer-book
> in Latin, which he performed with great fluency and ease; he sang
> a verse in the Psalms in English. He then took out an orange, and
> desired a gentleman who was near him to cut it. — "I will thank
> you, Sir," said he, "to cut an orange for me; here, take my knife
> (pulling out a pen-knife); it was said they were afraid to trust me
> with a knife, because I wished to cut my throat; but I could not
> deprive myself of the glory of dying in this manner."
>
> *(The Morning Chronicle)*

> He next read aloud a very long Latin prayer: After he had read
> about five minutes, he took an orange out of his pocket, and then
> took out a penknife; but his arms being bound behind, he could
> not cut the orange; upon which he beckoned to his friend who had
> attended him in the morning; the friend came close to him, and
> O'Coigley gave him the orange and penknife, saying ——
>
> "Open this orange with my penknife: it has been said they
> would not trust me with a penknife, lest I should cut my throat;
> but they little know that I would not deprive myself of the glory
> of dying in this way."
>
> He desired his friend to keep his penknife for his sake, and to

hold some of the pieces of orange, all of which he ate in the course of his devotions.

(The Morning Post)[15]

But in these two passages we already see a difference between the accounts in the two newspapers: *The Morning Post* account being even more circumstantial and detailed than *The Morning Chronicle* story, more self-conscious about what it is doing, more deliberate, more literary. The treatment of the execution itself might be taken as proof of this (although this could be qualified by saying that *The Morning Post* reporter is simply fonder of gory detail).

First, however, the question of the source of *The Times* account:

> After hanging near a quarter of an hour, *O'Coigley* was taken down, the head taken off by a Surgeon, and the Executioner held up the head to the populace, saying, "This is a head of a traitor!" Both the head and the body were then put into a shell, and buried at the foot of the gallows.
>
> *(The Times)*

> The Board was then dropped, as at Newgate, and he remained suspended for twelve or thirteen minutes; he was then taken down, the head taken off by a Surgeon, and the executioner held up the head to the populace, saying, "This is the head of a Traitor." Both head and body were then put into a shell, and buried at the foot of the gallows.
>
> *(The Morning Chronicle)*

The identical wording of the final paragraph of *The Times* announcement and the penultimate paragraph of *The Morning Chronicle* story seems to demonstrate that *The Times* did not have a reporter present, and that their version of Coigly's execution, which significantly appeared a day later than the reports in the Opposition Press, was plagiarized from *The Morning Chronicle* this time. The fact that *The Times* seems not to have had its own reporter there might in itself be construed as a political act, although again it seems to have been forced to make some gesture towards recording the events by the appearance of the story in dramatic fashion in the Opposition Press.

---

15. One cannot help but wonder whether in this almost ritualistic act of cutting and eating an orange before his execution, Coigly was not intending to convey a symbolic threat to the Orangemen who had destroyed his father's house in Dundalk and provoked him into rebellion.

But now for *The Morning Post*:

> After the body had hung about twelve minutes, it was lowered, the executioner holding it in his arms, till it was laid gently on the platform. A young man, a surgeon, put on a yellow linen dress, and prepared to cut off the head, the other part of the sentence being remitted. The coat, waistcoat, and shoes, were taken off, and the cap was taken from his face, which lately so comely (for he was a very handsome man, with a good complexion) was now the colour of lead. He appeared to be quite dead. The surgeon felt if there was any pulse, and took out a large knife, like a bill hook: the head was laid so as to hang over the edge of the platform, and the surgeon began to cut it off; he had considerable difficulty in cutting through the windpipe. When the head was severed from the body, the executioner held it up to the spectators, and turning round to shew it them all, said three times, *"This is the head of a Traitor."* At this time the blood was streaming from the head, which now began to change from blue to white. The head was laid down on the scaffold, and it, together with the body, were allowed to bleed about ten minutes, when the body was stripped quite naked, put into the coffin together with the head; the coffin was nailed up, and the whole was buried in a grave under the gallows, it being against the law on this occasion, to allow the friends to take the body away.

There seems to be no doubt about the presence of *The Morning Post* reporter at the scene, lapping up every horrible detail, keeping his eye on the head, without blanching or fainting away. He has a remarkable gift for presenting significant detail in precise declarative prose.

Both *The Morning Chronicle* and *The Morning Post* pieces have a clear narrative and dramatic structure, seen at its simplest in *The Morning Chronicle*:

    I. 1. The announcement (to Coigly that he will die).
       2. The final visits.

    II. 3. The procession.
       4. The arrival at the place of execution.

    III. 5. The prayers, the incident with the orange.

    IV. 6. The Last Speech.

    V. 7. The execution itself.

Epilogue: The reporter's final comment.

It is presented as a Five Act drama. The version in *The Morning Post* is made slightly more complicated, by the deliberate sensational use of the headline, which is in fact the first sentence of the report, foregrounded by the dramatic use of lay out and type size:

THE EXECUTION
OF
JOHN JAMES O'COIGLEY
FOR
HIGH TREASON,
Took place yesterday on Pennenden Heath,
near Maidstone

Furthermore, each Scene or Act of *The Morning Post* report is filled with significant and interesting detail: first a reference to Mr Derry who was to edit and have published *The Life of the Rev. James Coigly ... written by himself during his confinement in Maidstone Gaol* (was *The Morning Post* reporter in fact giving a pre-publication plug to this book?); then the two talkative gentlemen who shared Coigly's cell on his last night and disturbed his sleep; Coigly's attire ("At a quarter past eleven o'clock Mr. O'Coigley left the goal. He was dressed in a black coat, black kerseymere waistcoat and breeches and black worsted stockings; his hair was cropped and powdered"); and the weather and how he travelled to Pennenden Heath ("Whether it is usual to prepare for execution, or whether it was on account of the great heat of the day, his shirt collar was open, and he wore no neckcloth. His elbows were tied behind with ropes, and over his shoulder was the rope with which he was executed").

Despite its apparent naïveties, and gaucheries, this must be one of the most striking instances of accurate eye-witness journalism that has ever been published. Although we will never be able to check it, it certainly sounds like the authentic account of the event; for despite his obvious sympathy with Coigly, and the space he gives himself to pay tribute in an obviously subjective way (without, however, becoming sentimental), the reporter clearly feels duty-bound to record exactly what happened. Strangely, or perhaps not so strangely in view of the political and legal situation at the time, in no way does he indicate what he feels about the victim's guilt or innocence. In fact, neither of the two Opposition papers comment upon the justice of the case, although *The Times* is quite outspoken and suspiciously over-emphatic on the matter ("as great a traitor as ever was sent to the gallows", they say, in condemning the

Jacobin Press's apparent success in "draw[ing] forth the compassion of the public for the fate of [Coigly]").

While *The Times*'s account is designed (as it openly admits) to report the salient facts with as little involvement as possible and to keep the situation cool and the public basically unconcerned, *The Morning Chronicle* clearly wants to involve its readers emotionally in its account of Coigly's last hours and death. But that it also seems to be worried about legal repercussions is indicated by the many gaps in its more summary account of Coigly's speech. It is full of deliberately and carefully calculated lacunae, which the newspaper itself indicates, no doubt made for legal and political reasons. The question then arises, why was *The Morning Post* ready and willing to go so far beyond even *The Morning Chronicle* in its reporting of the speech and accumulation of other details? At first one might be inclined to agree with *The Times*, when it speaks about "the affected manner in which one of the Jacobin Papers [presumably, *The Morning Post*] records the dying moments of [Coigly]", and many reasonable, sympathetic people may feel that it could be accused of going over the top.

One notes the religious manner of *The Morning Post* account: it almost sounds like a version of the story of the Last Supper and the Crucifixion, and corresponds in some respects to Coigly's own memoir, in which "the biblical theme of the sacrificial victim laying down his life for his friends was invoked".[16] Undoubtedly lying behind these reports are literary models, a tradition of literature and subliterature, celebrating executions and preserving or inventing affecting final speeches.[17]

It may even be possible to identify *The Morning Post* reporter, or at least the source of the intimate information that he has access to. In his *Recollections* John Binns identifies the friend who "attended poor Coigley to the place of execution, and wrote and published an account of that sad spectacle" (46) as John Fenwick; and Fenwick's own record of Coigly's

---

16. Marianne Elliott, *Partners in Revolution: The United Irishmen and France*, New Haven and London, 1982, 184. Incidentally the variations in *The Morning Chronicle* and *The Morning Post* reports provide a revealing demonstration of the differences that may occur even in eye-witness accounts — *The Morning Chronicle* claiming that Coigly's hurdle was drawn by two horses, and *The Morning Post* by three.

17. Cf. for instance the penultimate chapter of Henry Fielding's *The History of the Life of the Late Mr Jonathan Wild the Great* — unfortunately, Wild does not have time for a final speech, having "just opportunity to cast his eyes around the crowd, and to give them a hearty curse, when immediately the horses moved on, and with universal applause our hero swung out of this world".

conversation with one of the "two gentlemen who had gone to Maidstone post, during the night, to attend his last moments ... [and] to receive his last wishes"[18] is filled with such detail that one must assume that the interviewer was Fenwick himself, who was also the "Gentleman from Mr. O'Coigley's Solicitor" in *The Morning Post*'s report.[19] Fenwick's account of the anonymous friend's attendance at the execution, and his involvement with the orange incident is so close to the newspaper account, the direct speech being identical (with the exception of one verb tense), that one might even be inclined to suppose that Fenwick himself was *The Morning Post* reporter.[20]

These speculations about how texts appear in print, who wrote what and why, might seem trivial to those who are properly interested in the dramatic and pathetic story of the Margate Five, their Trials, and Coigly's execution. But by examining the various texts and forms in which the narrative was given to the public, the more able are we to appreciate the rhetorical and stylistic qualities of the newspaper accounts, and later reports, reminiscences, observation, etc. The more we become aware of the political strategies and stances behind the way the stories are

---

18. John Fenwick, *Observations on the Trial of James Coigly, for High Treason: Together with an Account of His Death*, London, 1798, 112.

19. In his *Observations* Fenwick publishes a number of letters from Coigly's solicitor, Mr Foulkes, and his account of his attempt to intercede on Coigly's behalf (Appendix No. VII, 12-30). Samuel Simms in his pamphlet, *Rev. James O'Coigley, United Irishman*, Belfast, 1937, takes it for granted that the conversation Fenwick reports on Coigly's last morning was with Valentine Derry, and that he was also the friend who accompanied him to the gallows. But *The Morning Post* distinctly says that "The only relation, and that a distant one, who had visited him since his confinement was Mr. Derry ... Mr. Derry has not seen him for some days. We could not learn that any other friend had visited Mr. O'Coigley, but one who saw him yesterday" — which clearly suggests that the friend was not Mr Derry (and Binns, of course, says it was Fenwick).

20. With *The Morning Post* text, cf. Fenwick's: "In a few minutes, he took an orange from his pocket, and afterward a penknife, but his arms being bound he could not cut the orange, and beckoning to his friend he said, 'Open this orange with my penknife: it has been said they would not trust me with a penknife, lest I should cut my throat; but they little knew that I would not deprive myself of the glory of dying in this way.' His friend having quartered the orange and given him a piece of it, he desired him to keep the penknife for his sake" (*Observations*, 116). One presumes that this conversation was a fairly quiet and intimate one, unlikely to be heard by many bystanders. On the other hand, Fenwick might have given his story to *The Morning Post* reporter and a little while later when he came to write his own book reread the narrative in the newspaper.

told, the more tangible and more imminent become the painful and perplexing actualities that existed, and may be said still to exist, behind the public records. Drawing attention to the words and the structures of the narrative allows the real story to escape from its linguistic shackles. Of course, this is still something of an illusion, since without the words we have no story, and this is as true of a newspaper report as of a novel. But there is a crucial difference: once James Coigly did exist and did hang, and by resurrecting the texts that tell his story in a certain sense we bring him back from the dead, and by dissecting the texts that tell his story, or at least by investigating their purposes and their provenances, we free him from their designs, so that he can begin to have designs of his own, even posthumously.

Historians often attempt to create out of documents a seamless fabric of narrative and analysis,[21] reconstructing a simulacrum of true events, what really happened, and why they happened in the way they did. At the time of the arrest and trials of James Coigly, Arthur O'Connor, John Binns, John Allen and Jeremiah Leary in 1798, and afterwards, often many years afterwards, several participants and witnesses contributed strands of narrative to their story. What I have attempted to do in this article is to examine part of the story as it is related in some of the documents that accompanied or created it for a short time as a sequence of events of great current concern in public consciousness. Even if the full truth about the Margate Five and the Maidstone Trials can never be discovered, at least we can begin to appreciate the implications of the rhetorical and stylistic response to the events and the literary manner in which the actions were made public, mused on, commemorated and remembered. In this narrative, like many others, the telling is an essential part, and may even be the most important part, of the story.

---

21. As Marianne Elliott does so well in *Partners in Revolution*, ch. 6, "Rebellion".

APPENDIX

The paper said to have been found in a pocket-book in Coigly's great coat at the King's Head, Margate, 28 February 1798. Text as in Public Record Office copy (XC 3610 CL PC1/42/A143), with the following written on the outside of the packet: "Copy of Address from the Secret Committee of England to the Executive Directory of France." The text in Gurney (125–27) is the same, and from internal evidence would appear to have come either from this copy or the original that I have not seen (and may no longer exist). The version published in the newspapers is somewhat different, and will be discussed in a later article dealing with the reporting of the Trials:

The Secret Committee of England
to the Executive Directory of France

Health & Fraternity!

Citizen Directors

We are called together on the Wing of the Moment to communicate to you our sentiments, the Citizen who now presents them to you and who was the Bearer of them before having but a few hours to remain in Town expect not a laboured Address from Us but Plainness is the great Characteristic of Republicans.

Affairs are now drawing to a great & awful Crisis; Tyranny shaken to its' Basis seems about to be buried in its own Ruins. With the Tyranny of England that of all Europe must fall. Haste then great Nation! Pour forth thy gigantic Force! Let the base Despot feel thine avenging Stroke and let one oppressed Nation carol forth the Praises of France at the Altar of Liberty

We saw with Rapture your Proclamations they met our warmest Wishes and removed Doubts from the Minds of Millions. Go on! Englishmen will be ready to second your Efforts.

The System of borrowing which has hitherto enabled our Tyrants to disturb the Peace of our whole World is at an end; they have tried to raise a kind of Forced Loan — it has failed! Every tax diminishes that Revenue it was intended to augment and the Voluntary Contributions produce almost nothing — The Aristocracy pay their Taxes under that Mask; — the poor Workmen in large Manufactories have [*sic*: Gurney, p. 125, adds the obviously necessary "been"] forced to contribute under Threat of being turned out of Employ even the Army have been called upon to give a Portion of their Pay to carry on the War; by far the greatest Part have peremptorily refused to contribute to so base a purpose and the few that have complied have in general been cajoled or reluctantly compelled to it

Englishmen are no longer blind to their most sacred Claims; no longer are they Dupes of an imaginary Constitution; every day they see themselves bereft of some part of the poor Fragment of Democracy they have hitherto enjoyed And they find that in order to possess a Constitution they must make one

Parliament Declaimers have been the Bane of our Freedom. National Plunder was the Object of every Faction and it was the Interest of each to keep the People in the dark: But the delusion is past! The Government has pulled off it's Disguise & the very Men who under the Semblance of moderate Reform only wish to climb into Power are now glad to fall into the Ranks of the People. Yes! They have fallen into the Ranks and there they must for ever remain for Englishmen can never place Confidence in them

Already have the English fraternized with the Irish and Scots and a Delegate from each now sits with Us. The sacred Flame of Liberty is rekindled holy Obligation of Brotherhood is received with Enthusiasm even in the Fleets & the Armies it makes some Progress — Disaffection prevails in both & united Britain burns to break her Chains

Fortunately We have no Leader; Avarice & Cowardice have pervaded the Rich but We are not therefore less united. Some few of the opulent have indeed by Speeches professed themselves the Friends of Democracy but they have not acted, they have considered themselves as distinct from the People — and the People will in its' Turn consider their Claims to its Favour as unjust & frivolous. They wish perhaps to place us in the Front of the Battle that unsupported by the Wealth they enjoy We may perish when they may hope to rise upon our Ruin. But let them be told though We may fall through their Criminal Neglect — they can never hope to rule and that Englishmen once free will not submit to a few political Impostors

United as We are We now only wait with Impatience to see the Hero of Italy & and the brave Veterans of the French Nation. Myriads will hail their Arrival with Shouts of Joy; they will soon finish the glorious Campaign! Tyranny will vanish from the Face of the Earth & crowned with Laurel the invincible Army of France will return to its' Native Country there long [*sic* — an omission recorded but not filled by Gurney] to well earn't Praise of a grateful World whose Freedom they have purchased with their Blood.

L.S.

6th Pluviose
A.R.P.G.6

A NOTE ON THE MUSIC MANUSCRIPT OF ANNA CORRI

PETER DAVIDSON

This essay offers a few and necessarily very simple reflections on a topic which appears to have been neglected in the debate on politics and the arts which this volume carries on: the process of the late eighteenth and early nineteenth centuries which might be called the colonization of music — the process whereby the indigenous music of Scotland and Ireland was assimilated, for purposes of publication, to an approximation of the style of the European mainstream.[1]

These few reflections stem from a music manuscript in my possession: it was copied in Edinburgh, in the years around 1805, for Anna Corri, who appears to have been one of a family of professional musicians of Italian origin, active in Scotland for at least two generations. They had varying success as musicians, reflecting the abrupt rise and equally abrupt fall of serious musical activity in eighteenth-century Edinburgh. They moved at least on the fringes of circles which included Burns, Walter Scott and Burns's friend and publisher George Thomson. Their central position in the half-flourishing of a "classical" musical tradition in Scotland, in the development of which the Scots vernacular style was blended with surprisingly avant-garde aspects of Continental composed music, is well attested.[2] In the previous generation, a Domenica Corri

---

1. The following may be found useful as general background reading: Iain Fenlon, *The Fitzwilliam Virginal Book*, London, 1981; Roger Fiske, *Scotland in Music*, Cambridge, 1983; David Johnson, *Music and Society in Lowland Scotland in the Eighteenth Century*, Oxford, 1976.

2. Examples of this would be the Corellian Cantatas and Sonatas of the early eighteenth-century composer and jurist Sir John Clerk of Penicuik (1676–1755) and the mixture of vernacular elements with "Mannheim" techniques in the violin solos and trio sonatas of Thomas Erskine, Sixth Earl of Kellie (1732–81), particularly in the *Largo in Bb*, which exists in an unpublished edition by Dr David Johnson from the manuscript in the National Library of Scotland. The unavailability of this particular work, prompts a general observation concerning the references in this paper and its lack of conventional footnotes: so much of the material is derived from

had been the first professional singer to sing Scots Airs in the context of a formal concert, in this case at meetings of the Edinburgh Musical Society. She did so with enormous success, causing something of a fashion for classically-accompanied folk-songs and, as a long-term effect, causing Burns's friend and publisher George Thomson to conceive his idea of *A Select Collection of National Airs*, an ambitious collection of accompanied traditional songs which appeared spasmodically from the 1790s until the early 1840s. If they are remembered at all today, it is for Burns's contributions to the first volume and for Haydn's and Beethoven's contributions to the later ones. This apparently unlikely assertion is the sober truth: due to a combination of rampant inflation in Austria with his own unshaken confidence in his somewhat quixotic enterprise, Thomson succeeded in extracting a considerable number of arrangements of Scottish, Welsh and Irish airs from the Viennese composers. This produced those *Schottische und Irische Lieder* which look rather lost in the catalogues of Beethoven's and Haydn's works, as well as the curious belief, shared by Beethoven with his subsequent learned editors, that the Massacre of Glencoe took place in Ireland.

The contents of Anna Corri's music book are much what one might expect from a musically-informed inhabitant of Edinburgh at the turn of the nineteenth century. There is some "mainstream" classical piano music of variable quality, there is a very comprehensive range of local military and dance music: marches and reels preserving the names of disbanded regiments and forgotten patrons of the Assembly Rooms. What makes the collection rather more interesting is the presence of some high-quality Scottish material, scrupulously presented: some pieces by the impeccably authentic Perthshire folk-composer Neil Gow, some Scots songs. There are Burns songs, copied, I suspect, from no more exciting source than the earliest volumes of Thomson's *Collection* although there is one song which appears to be an unrecorded Burns variant. All of this so far is much what one might expect. There is an Ossianic fragment copied from

---

privately communicated information from Professor D.A. Low and Dr David Johnson that continual citation of oral indebtedness would prove irritating. The bibliographical chaos which surrounds the publishing histories of both Thomson's *Select Collection* and Moore's *Irish Melodies* renders precise citations within these volumes at best injudicious and at worst impossible. (Thomas Moore, *Irish Melodies*, London, 1808; expanded edition with introductory "Letter to the Marchioness Dowager of Donegal", 1811; many subsequent editions in various forms. *A Select Collection of Original Scottish Airs*, ed. George Thomson, 1793–1841; many states and issues of all volumes. The Oxford D.Phil. thesis of Ms Kirsteen McCue, currently approaching completion, will address these problems in detail.)

the first song-book in which Burns played a significant part, *The Scottish Musical Museum*, published in Edinburgh by James Johnson between 1787 and 1803.[3] All the Scottish material in the collection gives the impression of being valued and used and that care has been devoted to its presentation. It is therefore a surprise to find *An Irish Air* in such company, not because it is Irish, but because its words are a random redeployment of virtually every racist stereotype of the Irish to have accumulated over the unhappy centuries: pigs, nakedness, bogs, pipers, grandiloquence and potatoes. The music is little better, although the accompaniment has a sort of irrelevant insouciance, being apparently a distant and rather dissolute relative of Carolan's *Planxty Ridlon*. Here are the words (the music appears as Fig. 1).

An Irish Air.
Sung by Mr Johnstone

I

When I was a boy in my father's mud edifice,
Tender and bare as a pig in a stye,
Out at the door — a I looked with a steady phiz,
Who but Pat Murphy the piper came by!
Says Paddy, but few play this music; can you play?
Says I, I can't tell for I never did try:
He told me that he had a charm
To make the pipes prettily speak,
So he squeez'd a bag under his arm,
And sweetly they set up a squeak:
With a faralla laralla loo;
Och hone, how he handled the drone
And then such sweet music he blew
'Twould have melted the heart of a stone.

II

Your pipe, says I, Paddy, so neatly comes over me
Naked, I'll wander wherever it blows;
And if my father should try and recover me
Sure it won't be by describing my cloaths:
The music I hear now, takes hold of my ear now,
And leads me all over the world by the nose,

---

3. J. Johnson and Robert Burns, eds, *The Scottish Musical Museum*, Edinburgh, 1787–1803.

So I followed the bagpipe so sweet,
And sung, as I leaped like a frog,
Adieu, to my family seat
So pleasantly placed in a bog.
With my faralla laralla loo;
How sweetly he handled the drone,
And then such sweet music he blew,
'Twould have melted the heart of a stone.

III

Full five years I followed him, nothing could sunder us
Till he one morning had taken a sup,
And slipped from a bridge in a river just under us
Souse to the bottom just like a blind pup:
I roar'd and I bawl'd out, and hastily called out,
O Paddy my friend don't you mean to come up?
He was dead as a nail in a door,
Poor Paddy was laid on the shelf,
So I took up his pipes on the shore,
And now I've set up for myself.
With my faralla laralla loo,
To be shure I have not got the knack,
To play faralla laralla loo,
And Bubaroo didaroo whack.[4]

The glossolalia of the last line are apparently meant for comic Gaelic. Perhaps this exhibit is harmless at such a distance, but still it cannot help but give rise to certain thoughts. Little needs to be said concerning the obviously unacceptable words, except perhaps that the rebellious Ireland of the 1790s was not a pleasant vision for a Scotland in which the 1707 Act of Union was at last having a delayed cultural effect under the unitive pressure of the Napoleonic Wars. We are still left with the obvious problem that the cultivated Scots apparently found this song funny, presumably forgetting that Scottish uncouthness and Scottish susceptibility to minor if embarrassing venereal diseases had one generation before been the comic staple of the Scotch Songs of the London theatres. This failure of sensibility, this failure to put Scottish and Irish music on the kind of equal footing which their closely interwoven histories might suggest, has given rise to the enquiry which

---

4. From musical manuscript with ownership stamp "Anna Corri" copied in Edinburgh *c.* 1805–15. In the possession of Dr Peter Davidson, University of Warwick, England.

Fig. 1: *An Irish Air*

Tender and bare as a Pig in a stye, Out at the door-a I looked with steady phiz Who but Pat Morphy the
a
Piper came by! Says Paddy, but few play this music can you play Says I, I can't tell for I
never did try: He told me that he had a charm To make the pipes prettily speak, So he squeazed a under his
bag
sfz sfz

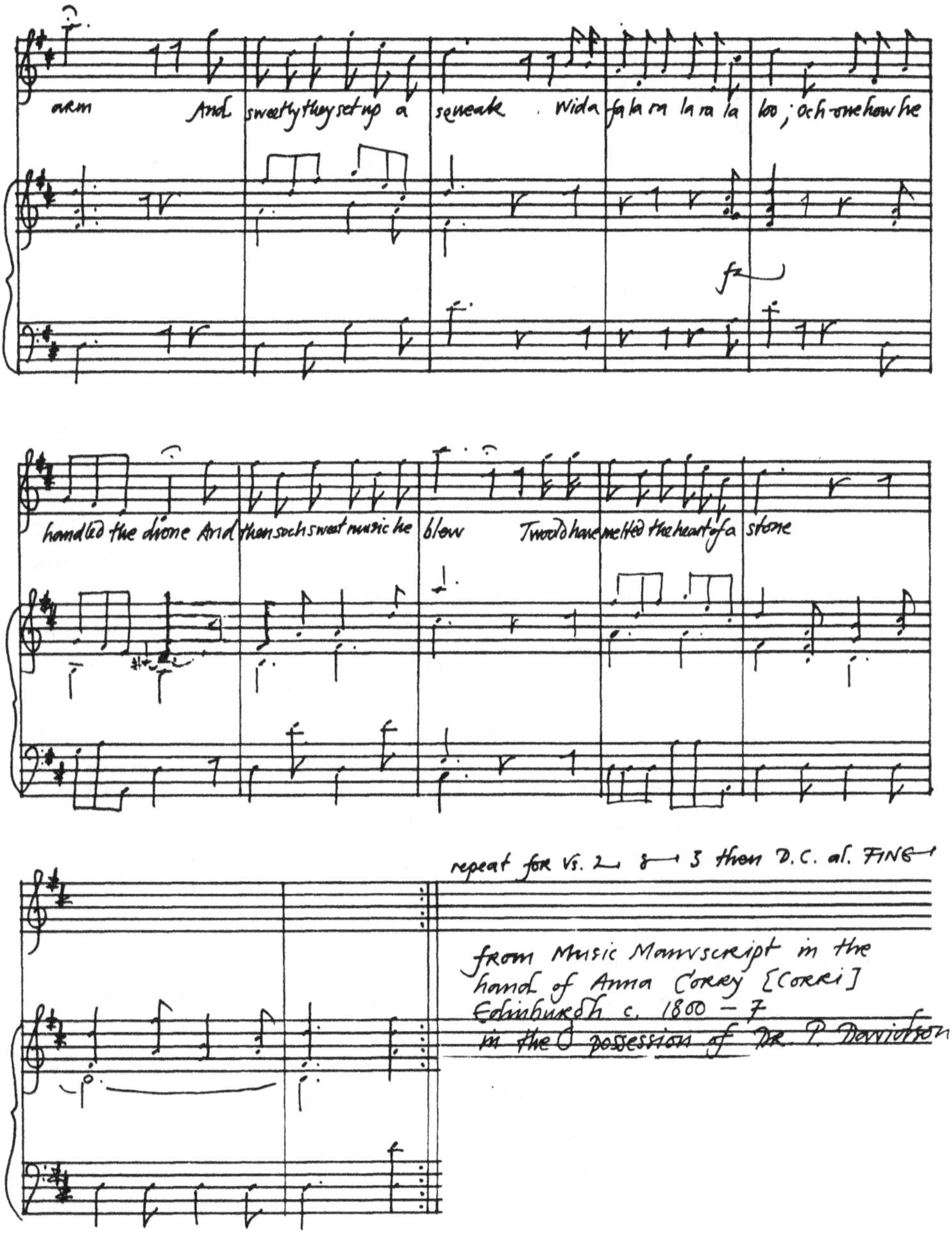
arm And sweetly they set up a squeak . Wid a fa la ra la ra la loo ; och-one how he
fz
handled the drone And then such sweet music he blew 'Twould have melted the heart of a stone
repeat for Vs. 2 & 3 then D.C. al. FINE
from Music Manuscript in the
hand of Anna Corry [Corri]
Edinburgh c. 1800 – 7
in the possession of Dr. P. Davidson

is the subject of this brief paper: an attempt to establish what the Corris might have known about Irish music and, more importantly, what was the likely state of knowledge of their friend Thomson, which led him to treat the Irish material in the *Select Collection* in a manner which might be described as simultaneously patronizing and cavalier.

When in doubt about the state of knowledge on any musical question in the late eighteenth century, it is invariably instructive to begin with Charles Burney, *A General History of Music: From the Earliest Ages to the Present Period*, which was published in London in 1789. It does not take long to discover what Burney knew about Irish music. He knew nothing whatsoever. His index has entries for Coloured Lines, Iceland, Orang-Ootangs, Swans and Dilettanti, but of Ireland there is no mention whatsoever. His text does venture far enough into Celtic territory to suggest that, while the Druid Bards may well have been eunuchs, there is no evidence to suggest that they were Irish eunuchs. Scots music is indeed present, but as part of the formal analysis of primitive and ancient music. He has a pioneering and surprisingly full account of Welsh Harp music, he has found, and substantially understood, Geraldus Cambrensis on the vocal music of the early-medieval Britons. It is possible that the notable absence of Ireland owes something to prevailing eighteenth-century antiquarian theory in which Scotland and Wales exist and existed, Druids are a shadowy but indisputably British presence, and innovations came from Scandinavia. It would be possible, given leisure, to trace the roots of these theories which appear, taken together, to imply that a Celtic culture is only a safe object for Metropolitan contemplation when that culture has ceased to be a present threat.

There is one other, extremely simple, reason for the absence of Ireland from Burney's work: there was almost nothing for him to work from. Two Irish pieces of some antiquity, the *Irish Ho Hone* and *Calino Casturame,* are present in what is now called the Fitzwilliam Virginal Book, which manuscript was known to musical London in the eighteenth century.[5] So far as I have discovered, only a very few books of Irish airs and dances were in print, J. and W. Neal's *A Collection of the Most Celebrated Irish Tunes* (Dublin, *c.* 1726) and W. Jackson's *Jackson's Celebrated Irish Tunes* (Dublin, *c.* 1780) are two survivors. There was also *A Favourite Collection of the so Much Admired Old Irish Tunes*

---

5. This manuscript, originally copied by the Elizabethan recusant Francis Tregian, passed into the collection of the Viscount Fitzwilliam in 1783, having belonged for a time to a central figure of eighteenth-century Scottish musical life, the publisher and composer Robert Bremner.

published at Dublin in 1780 by John Lee.[6] In contrast, there was a diversity of Scottish material available in late eighteenth-century London: there was one serious collection of traditional song (*Orpheus Caledonius*, 1725) and so great was the demand for Scottish dance music that at least two Edinburgh publishers (Bremner was one of them) found it worthwhile to move their offices to London. Scotland had at least one composer of modest international status, Thomas Erskine, Sixth Earl of Kellie, who is noted approvingly by Burney. Sccts songs of varying degrees of authenticity are a long-lived fashion in the London theatre, whereas Irish music is represented by a few tunes contrafacted in ballad-operas and a number of denigratory pseudo-Irish songs on the comic stage.

In the same year as Burney's resounding silence on the subject of Irish music, there appeared at Dublin a first attempt at least to reclaim and publish the words of Irish traditional song. This was Charlotte Brooke's *Reliques of Irish Poetry*,[7] a serious and extensive collection in parallel texts, Irish and English. For our purposes it is essential to note that she did not print music (any more than Bunting was to print words) and that her splendid Preface tells us by its tone alone that the status which her material is expected to enjoy with the Anglophone public is, to put it mildly, low. She is eloquent, moving and, inevitably, defensive, providing a sharp contrast to the confident dedications of the volumes of *The Scottish Musical Museum*, as they ran through the 1790s, inscribed to the Society of Antiquaries of Scotland, a learned body drawing many of its members from the ruling class:

> The productions of our Irish Bards exhibit a glow of cultivated genius — a spirit of elevated heroism — sentiments of pure honour, instances of disinterested patriotism, and manners of a degree of refinement totally astonishing, at a period when Europe was nearly sunk in barbarism: And is not all this very honourable to our countrymen? Will they not be benefitted, will they not be

---

6. Cf. *The Complete Works of O'Carolan: Irish Harper and Composer (1670–1738)*, Dublin, 1984. This volume also cites a work, which I have been hitherto unable to trace, which might place the questions advanced in this paper in a very different light: Dan. Wright, *Aria da Camera: Being a Choice Collection of Scotch, Irish and Welsh Airs for the German Flute by the Following Masters: Mr Alex. Urquahart, of Edinburgh; Mr Dermt. O'Connor, of Limerick; Mr Hugh Edwards, of Camarthen*, London, *c.* 1730.

7. Charlotte Brooke, *Reliques of Irish Poetry: Consisting of Heroic Poems, Odes, Elegies and Songs, Translated into English Verse: With Notes Explanatory and Historical, and the Originals in the Irish Character*, Dublin, 1789.

gratified, at the lustre reflected on them by ancestors so very different from what modern prejudice has been so studious to represent them .... There are many Irish songs now in common use, that contain, in scattered passages, the most exquisite thoughts, though on the whole much too unequal for translation .... But the beauties of the musick of this country are at present almost as little known as those of its poetry. And yet there is no other musick in the world so calculated to make its way directly to the heart.

[She goes on to tell the story of "one Maguire, a vintner residing near Charing cross":] His house was very much frequented and his uncommon skill in playing on the harp was an additional incentive. He was one night called upon to play some Irish tunes; he did so; they were plaintive and solemn. His guests demanded the reason; and he told them, that the native composers were too deeply distressed at the situation of their country, and her gallant sons, to be able to compose otherwise ... offense was taken at these warm effusions; his house became gradually neglected, and he died soon after of a broken heart.

This preface speaks for itself in its dignity and its passion for its subject. Charlotte Brooke is obviously a serious collector, taking her material absolutely seriously. Assuming that it will meet with hostility, misunderstanding or indifference, she publishes no music. As well as a tentative beginning, her book is a lament for the paradoxical inarticulacy of those who are supremely articulate in the wrong language: the linguistically-isolated "mere-Irish".

No stronger contrast could be imagined than that of the status enjoyed in the 1790s by Scottish traditional song. The volumes of the *Scottish Musical Museum* were appearing with an increasing number of contributors of all classes offering material to further what was clearly perceived as a source of national pride. Scottish songs had acquired accompaniments by Geminiani, the English Bach, Pietro Urbani, and by the growing number of native composers brought into being by the flourishing of a musical tradition combining vernacular elements with the style of the continental mainstream. There can be no doubt that the material of the song-books was in circulation amongst all classes of society, as was a vast quantity of new dance-music.[8]

---

8. There are shadows of this *status quo* even today: in many ranks of contemporary Scottish society, to be a good dancer is considered as virile an accomplishment as is, in the Netherlands, the suave management of a small boat.

It is this social difference which is immediately apparent: traditional music in Scotland is still in use throughout what is just beginning to break up as a homogeneous society. In Ireland traditional music is exclusively the preserve of that part of society marginalized by status, religion and language. This finds purely musical reflection: whereas Scotland is united (this happens seldom except in time of peace) in respecting pentatonic scales, tunes with a double tonic centre and the other "deviations" of Celtic music, Irish music (when at last it reaches print) is ruthlessly musically normalized to the harmonic standards of the metropolis, so that, for example, cadences are smoothed out by the use of that quintessentially "mainstream" progression, the dominant seventh.

These features can be noted in the first serious collection of Irish music to appear: this was Edward Bunting's *A General Collection of the Ancient Irish Music*, which appeared in Dublin and London in 1796. This volume consists of piano transcriptions of harp music which Bunting had been employed to notate at the Belfast Harp Festival of 1792, an enterprise which represented something of a concerted effort to preserve what was essentially perceived as a dying art. (Joseph Cooper Walker's *Historical Recollections of the Irish Bards*, which had appeared in 1786, seems in its title tacitly to admit that it concerns itself with a moribund school.) Bunting's approach is tentative: he appears to normalize and simplify relatively liberally. He publishes no words, though apparently he did collect them. His subsequent career appears to have been one of growing enthusiasm for Irish traditional music, answered by relatively little support or encouragement.

This leads us to those who made use of the tunes which Bunting had collected: George Thomson and Thomas Moore. Before giving their publications brief consideration it is necessary to note one slender collection which offered the words and music of a dozen Irish airs. This was produced by Sydney Owenson [Lady Morgan], the author of *The Wild Irish Girl,* who broke ground in 1805 by printing both the words and the music of *Twelve Original Hibernian Melodies,*[9] thus anticipating Moore's celebrated work by two years. She does not seem, however, to have particularly influenced Moore in the methodology which he adopted in presenting his material. The same problem attends Irish traditional song as attends that of the Scottish Highlands: the Gaelic language defies transference, demanding translation instead. Here is another central contrast with the Scottish experience: Scots or Scottish English is a language to which the majority have easy access, whatever variety of

---

9. Sydney Owenson [Lady Morgan], *Twelve Original Hibernian Melodies,* Dublin, 1805.

English they employ in daily life; Gaelic and Irish on the other hand remain hermetically sealed to the English speaker, and the incidence of bilinguals is not notably high in either country. It is perhaps worth noting in passing that Sydney Owenson, the first to bridge this particular gap in Ireland, comes of a mixed background. It seems possible that the kind of social grey area from which she emerged, comparable to that which produced the anachronistically tolerant Archbishop Ussher in an earlier century, provides the only kind of fructifying crack in a divided society from which such works can emerge. She was the product of a mixed marriage, her father had risen by the backstairs to the ambiguous eminence of the successful actor. Even after she had published the *Hibernian Melodies*, her father appeared as the stage-Irishman singing "An Irishman all the World Over" and continuing in his stock-roles as the caricature of what he had been in his early life.

It seems likely, at least on the evidence of Moore's "Letter to the Marchioness Dowager of Donegal", prefaced to the 1811 edition of the *Melodies*, that Moore was modelling his enterprise on the Scottish collections which have been discussed above. The form in which the songs appeared, provided with "Symphonies and accompaniments" by Sir John Stevenson, is reminiscent of the form of George Thomson's *A Select Collection of Original Scottish Airs* which is itself a more elaborate version of the simpler style of accompaniment in *The Scots Musical Museum*. It is worth noting that Burns warmly approved the accompanied versions in which his songs appeared: his origins rendered him immune to worry about "authenticity", and in any case the accompanied Scots song has, by the 1790s, more than half a century of tradition behind it.[10] The *Select Collection* began to appear in the 1790s, and it raises a beguiling question of theory: it appeared to be established at the beginning of the nineteenth century that the obvious form in which to present traditional song was with accompaniments which assimilated it to the classical mainstream. This theory is, in fact perfectly reasonable, but only in the light of the tradition of the intermixture of the modes which had established itself during Edinburgh's brief musical flowering. With the decline of the Edinburgh Musical Society, and the radical Anglicization in Scottish manners which was in full swing at the turn of the century, this solution appears at once dubious. Whether it ever had any real relevance outside Scotland is obviously open to question, even if "Carolan's Concerto", with its blending of Irish traditional form with the classical manner of Geminiani, appears to offer a shadow of a

---

10. Cf. my appendix "Burns Accompanied" in *The Songs of Robert Burns*, ed. D.A. Low, London, 1993.

parallel development which might have occurred had the Irish society of the time been less divided.

Moore's introductory "Letter to the Marchioness Dowager of Donegal", which appeared in the 1811 edition of the *Irish Melodies*, makes a number of points which appear to suggest that Moore did take the activities of the Edinburgh publishers as a kind of precedent. In other matters, he is paradoxically learned and symptomatically confused.

Although he makes surprisingly strong remarks about the social misery from which the music emerges, he is in no doubt for whom he is writing :

> It is not through that gross and inflammable region of society that a work of this nature is intended to circulate — it looks much higher for its audience and readers — it is found upon the piano-fortes of the rich and the educated — of those who can afford to have their national zeal a little stimulated, without exciting much dread of the excesses into which it may hurry them.

He is oddly inconsistent in his defence of the accompaniments provided by Stevenson: on the one hand he dismisses "Carolan's Concerto" as essentially an isolated incongruity: the styles do not mix and there is an end of the matter. In the next paragraph, he is justifying the accompaniments, with their mixture of styles, by claiming as precedent precisely that "incongrous" Edinburgh tradition and its logical issue, the Scots songs arranged by Haydn for George Thomson:

> We might cite the example of the admirable Haydn, who has sported through all the mazes of musical science, in his arrangement of the simplest Scottish melodies.

While there is not the place to go further into the stances which Moore's "Letter" adopts, it is worthy of note that he has clearly read Burney on Celtic music, and responds to it by stating the claim that much Scottish music is of Irish origin and has been unjustly stolen as has the credit for many of Ireland's early saints. He cannot resist a *tu quoque* of a familiar scholarly kind:

> They had formerly the same passion for robbing us of our Saints, and the learned Dempster was, for this offence called "The Saint Stealer." I suppose it was an Irishman, who, by way of reprisal, stole Dempster's beautiful wife from him at Pisa.

The subsequent history of Moore's *Melodies* is one of consistent success, so much so that the publication overtook and surpassed Thomson's collection which failed increasingly, with each volume that appeared, to catch the public taste. The latter history of the *Select Collection* is a melancholy one and only two points need detain us here: when Thomson expanded his range to include Irish material, he was clearly untroubled by any consideration that his material demanded even the respect which he allowed to the Scottish songs in his later volumes. There are no attempts at translation: words are contrafacted at random to tunes which are dispatched to Vienna for harmonization with no indication of their context. The only result of the process is to provide us with an instance of Beethoven setting the word "potato" and to indicate that, with the Edinburgh tastes of his youth now thoroughly obsolete, Thomson's enterprise was in his lifetime an anachronism, whose public had pre-deceased it.

From this point onwards, the fates of Irish and Scottish traditional music are almost reversed: the Irish material was increasingly collected and respected, where the Scottish material lost prestige. The Scots material was presented in increasingly anglicized form, diluted and tidied as Thomson ranged ever lower in the literary world to find someone prepared to fit words, any words, to his unsold stocks of Beethoven arrangements. Only the enormous personal prestige which Burns's contribution had lent to the first volume could be said to have kept the enterprise even minimally afloat. In Ireland, in contrast, George Petrie's *Ancient Music of Ireland* (1853–55, 1882), a collection which transcends Thomsonian origins, achieved print and Forde and Pigot set about collecting from source in Munster and Leitrim. The process continued without interruption into the twentieth century with traditional culture and language enjoying an increasing status. In Scotland, one might almost say that the opposite happened (although the real collection of Gaelic material is a nineteenth-century phenomenon): Lowland Scotland suffered a sharp dislocation, not least in the influence of the dazzling and ambiguous Walter Scott who made his Scottish heritage the rage of Europe while simultaneously asserting at home that it was a dead letter, irrelevant to the progressive modern country in which he held his Union Baronetcy.

The process of the metamorphosis of the Scottish musical heritage from a common property to the preserve of the less sophisticated is not by any means a simple one: but it may be asserted with some confidence that the common possession of that tradition was what was lost and that the brilliant fieldwork of the late nineteenth century was just that, fieldwork in the modern sense. Burns's prestige remained and remains unassailable, but the shifty hagiographies which tried to render his life fit for the consumption of a genteel nation, continued throughout the century and provide in themselves an index of loss, the history of a failure of cultural nerve.

If we have apprehended some reasons why a musically-cultivated family at the end of the period of Edinburgh's musical prosperity, should have, for all their sensitivity to Scottish traditional music, been able to produce no response to an Irish air finer than to find it matter for racist mockery, perhaps we have also seen the extent to which Scotland provided the precedent for an assimilation of traditional music into a classical idiom. What the family who copied the little manuscript from which we began could hardly have anticipated was that the idioms of Enlightenment Edinburgh would have a short lifespan, and that in the course of the nineteenth century the positions of Scottish and Irish traditional song would be very nearly reversed.

POLITICS AND LANGUAGE IN ANGLO-IRISH LITERATURE

RICHARD WALL

Hiberno-English is a contact vernacular which has its genesis in the prolonged interaction of two cultures, Irish and English. The basic impulse which led to and sustained this interaction was political: the determination of England, especially after 1541 when King Henry VIII assumed the title King of Ireland, to establish and maintain hegemony over all of Ireland. This paper will examine, within the context of Anglo-Irish literature, part of the legacy in Hiberno-English of the political impulse which led to its genesis by focusing on some idioms deriving from English efforts to conquer, control and assimilate Ireland.

Irish resistance to English hegemony necessitated repeated, extensive and expensive military campaigns in Ireland, the cost of which was borne by both English and Irish. The cost to the English is reflected in Shakespeare's *King Richard II*, when Richard seizes the property of his deceased uncle, John of Gaunt, to finance his campaign to "supplant those rough, rug-headed kerns"[1] (< Ir. *ceithirn*), the lightly-armed and highly mobile, Irish foot-soldiers, who proved so troublesome to the English. Richard's adjective, "rug-headed", describes their hair, which was worn in a glib (< Ir. *glib*), a thick matted mass on the forehead and over the eyes. In *A View of the Present State of Ireland*, written about 1596, Edmund Spenser condemns the "savage brutishness and loathly filthiness" of glibs, which were proscribed under various English statutes. They evidently served two useful functions, mask and helmet, which, understandably for a planter, he did not appreciate: "Irish glibs ... are fit masks as a mantle is for a thief ...." The Irish, he later adds, "battle without armour on their bodies or heads, but trusting only to the thickness of their glibs, the which they say will sometimes bear off a

---

1. William Shakespeare, *King Richard II*, ed. Peter Ure, The New Arden Shakespeare, London, 1978, 60.

---

good stroke ...".[2] The latter function of the glib is also mentioned by William Allingham in the description of kerns in his poem *Laurence Bloomfield in Ireland* (1864): "With axe and sling, their feet and bosoms bare,/No helmet but their matted glibbs of hair ...."[3] In his poem "A Vision of Glendalough" (c.1930), Joseph Campbell mentions kerns and their glibs in his evocation of the tenacity of the ordinary Irish who managed to survive the massacres and plantations of the sixteenth and seventeenth centuries: "But, most,/Trooped in the country folk: poor kerns,/Wild in shag rugs ... with glibs of matted hair ...."[4]

The campaigns resulted, among other things, in military impositions on and exactions from the population, called cesses. The various kinds of cesses, such as billeting troops in people's houses, and their politically negative consequences are described in detail by Spenser, and condemned along with other "evil customs ... in Ireland".[5] These practices, which were, naturally, hateful to the Irish may have given rise to a very common curse: "bad cess to". When the Da, in Hugh Leonard's play *Da* (1973), burns his hand on the handle of the teapot, he exclaims: "Bad cess to it for an anti-Christ of a teapot."[6]

The massacres of civilians which were an integral part of Oliver Cromwell's campaigns in the mid sevententh century resulted in another curse, once common, now relatively rare: the curse of Cromwell, used by William Butler Yeats as a title for one of his poems. Explaining the force of this curse to an Italian audience, James Joyce said that for the Irish, "the great Protector of civil rights is a savage beast who came to Ireland to propagate his faith by fire and sword".[7] In the "Cyclops" episode of Joyce's *Ulysses* (1922), the angry, chauvinistic Citizen invokes "the curse of Cromwell on" Leopold Bloom,[8] and in *Finnegans Wake* (1939) the Prankquean "punched the curses of cromcruwell with the nail

2. Edmund Spenser, *A View of the Present State of Ireland*, ed. W.L. Renwick, Oxford, 1970, 53, 57.

3. William Allingham, *Laurence Bloomfield in Ireland*, London, 1864, 128.

4. Joseph Campbell, *Poems*, ed. Austin Clarke, Dublin, 1963, 215.

5. Spenser, 81.

6. Hugh Leonard, *Da: A Life and Time Was*, Penguin, 1981, 20.

7. James Joyce, *The Critical Writings of James Joyce*, eds Ellsworth Mason and Richard Ellmann, New York, 1959, 168.

8. James Joyce, *Ulysses*, London, 1986, 280.

of a top into jiminy ...".[9] If one reads the latter with the requisite "aural eyeness" (623.18) and thereby grasps its "sound sense" (612.29), one hears and sees the curses of Cromwell, Cromwell's crew, cruel Cromwell, Crom, a plague which afflicted Ireland in ancient times, and Crom Cruach, the Bloody Croucher, an ancient idol overthrown by St. Patrick. The subtle linking of the ancient curse of Crom and the modern curse of Cromwell is clearly part of the cyclic theory of history that operates in the work. It is repeated in the phrase "crow cru cramwells" (53.36), and bluntly made in the juxtaposed slogans in Irish and English towards the end of the work: " — Crum abu! Cromwell to victory!" (500.06).[10]

Resistance to English rule by Irish standing armies ended formally on October 3, 1691, with the signing of the Treaty of Limerick, following which the Irish commander, Patrick Sarsfield, withdrew to France with about 12,000 men, who became known by that most persistent and romantic of metaphors, the wild geese. Its best known expression is in Yeats's occasional poem "September 1913". In his bitter attack on the petty politics of modern Ireland, he asks rhetorically: "Was it for this the wild geese spread/The grey wing upon every tide ....".[11] Joyce, however, makes much more extensive and complex use of the metaphor than Yeats. In *A Portrait of the Artist as a Young Man* (1914–15) there is an ironic play on it. When Stephen Dedalus calls his timid university classmates "the tame geese",[12] he implicitly links himself with the wild geese, who were forced into exile. The link between the artist and the wild geese is continued in *Ulysses* and *Finnegans Wake*. Leopold Bloom calls his attempt to catch up with Stephen in the "Circe" episode of *Ulysses* a "Wildgoose chase" (452). Shem, in one of at least seven allusions to the wild geese in *Finnegans Wake*, "winged away on a wildgoup's chase across the kathartic ocean" (185.06). The metaphor is rather popular in titles: "The Wild Geese" is a poem by William Drennan (1745–1820) and a novel (1938) by Bridget Boland; *With the Wild Geese* (1902) is a volume of poems by Emily Lawless; "The Wild Goose" (1903) is a short story by George Moore and a play (1936) by

---

9. James Joyce, *Finnegans Wake*, New York, 1975, 22.13.

10. Since *Crum Abu!* (God to Victory!) is the motto of the Fitzgerald family, there are obviously other levels of meaning in the juxtaposition of the two slogans.

11. W.B. Yeats, *Collected Poems*, London, 1963, 120.

12. James Joyce, *A Portrait of the Artist as a Young Man*, New York, 1964, 181.

Teresa Deevy; and *The Wild Geese* (1973) by Maurice Hennessy is a study of the Irish soldier in exile.

Exile to Europe was not the only option open to the dispossessed Irish. Many became internal exiles and formed fugitive bands called tories (< Ir. *tóraidheacht*, the act of hunting or searching), or rapparees (< Ir. *rapaire*, a rapier, a short pike).[13] So many Irish over the years became fugitives that Hiberno-English has a special phrase for someone on the run: "on his keeping", recorded as early as 1668, and found in works ranging from William Carleton's *The Black Prophet* (1847) to Joyce's *Finnegans Wake*. A character in the former was "on his keeping, for the truth was, he had been reported to Government, and there was a warrant out for him".[14] Consistent with Joyce's refusal to make concessions to his reader, there is no contextual clue to the meaning of the term in the latter: "There grew up beside you ... [an] oaf, outofwork, one remove from an unwashed savage, on his keeping and in yours ..." (191.09–12). Later in the work it appears, lightly disguised, as "on whosekeeping" (422.14).

The wild geese metaphor is part of an extensive code language. Given the realities of English rule, Irish writers, for very practical reasons, had to develop a code with which to make patriotic references to Ireland and hostile references to England and its supporters. In Brendan Behan's play in Irish, *An Giall* (1958), and in the early version of its English adaptation, *The Hostage* (1958), a hornpipe called "The Blackbird" is heard on the radio just before the hero, Leslie, appears on stage for the first time.[15] At the precise moment of his appearance its title is announced, and it is clearly an oblique comment on Leslie: the Irish word for blackbird, *londubh*, is also a metaphor for hero. An early use of this metaphor in Hiberno-English is in the anonymous Jacobite song "The Blackbird". It also appears in "The Blackbirds", Frances Ledwidge's allegorical poem on the executed leaders of the Easter Rising of 1916: "I heard the Poor Old Woman say:/'At break of day the fowler came,/And took my blackbirds from their songs/Who loved me well thro' shame and blame.'"[16] The "Poor Old Woman" (< Ir. *Sean Bhean Bhocht*), a common metaphor for Ireland, combined with the metaphor

13. These terms are recorded respectively as early as 1646 and 1690.

14. William Carleton, *The Black Prophet*, Shannon, 1972, 379.

15. Brendan Behan, *An Giall*, tr. and ed. Richard Wall, and *The Hostage*, ed. Richard Wall, Washington, D.C., and Gerrards Cross, 1987, 48.

16. Francis Ledwidge, "The Blackbirds", in *The Penguin Book of Irish Verse*, ed. Brendan Kennelly, Penguin, 1970, 306.

in the title of the poem, makes the identity of the fowler quite clear. James Clarence Mangan (1803–1849) uses a much more hostile term than fowler for England or an Englishman in his poem "The Captivity of the Gaels". He complains bitterly: "Yea, even our Princes ... themselves must bow low/Before the vile Shane Bwee!"; and, he predicts: "Freedom's Bell will ... ere long time toll/The deep death-knell of Shane Bwee."[17] The term Shane Bwee (< Ir. *Seán Buidhe*, Yellow [Dirty] John [Bull]) is used to conclude each of the five stanzas of the poem.

As might be expected, this characteristic of Hiberno-English did not escape the somewhat jaundiced eye of James Joyce. In *Ulysses*, the Citizen uses the English form of Shane Bwee as he denounces the economic and social consequences of English rule: "What do the yellowjohns of Anglia owe us for our ruined trade and our ruined hearths?" (268). He also uses two code names for Ireland, Kathleen ni Houlihan and Granuaile, when he predicts that Irish exiles in America will return as liberators: "those that came to the land of the free remember the land of bondage. And they will come again and with a vengeance, no cravens, the sons of Granuaile, the champions of Kathleen ni Houlihan" (270). Earlier, in the National Library episode, there is a complete sentence in the code: "Gaptoothed Kathleen, her four beautiful green fields, the stranger in her house" (152). Kathleen, four green fields and the stranger are, respectively, code terms for Ireland, the four provinces of Ireland and the English. Since Kathleen is usually seen as a beautiful woman, Joyce makes his attitude towards Irish nationalism clear with the initial adjective. Granuaile is an Anglicized form of *Gráinne Uí Máille* (Grace O'Malley, *c.* 1530–1603), who was a powerful and colourful leader and sea captain in Co. Mayo and along the west coast. In Lady Gregory's play *The Rising of the Moon* (1904), the fugitive Fenian organizer, who pretends to be a ballad singer, sings a patriotic song about Granuaile and later invokes her in his successful attempt to subvert the police sergeant's loyalty to the Crown: "Maybe, sergeant, it comes into your head sometimes, in spite of your belt and tunic, that it might have been as well for you to have followed Granuaile." The sergeant accedes to his plea: "You won't betray me ... the friend of Granuaile", and helps him to escape.[18] *Ulysses* also

---

17. James Clarence Mangan, *Poems of James Clarence Mangan*, ed. D.J. O'Donoghue, Dublin, 1922, 52, 54.

18. Lady Gregory, *Lady Gregory: Selected Plays*, ed. Elizabeth Coxhead, London, 1962, 28, 29.

contains other code terms for Ireland: "Silk of the kine" (12, < Ir. *síoda na mbó*), and "Dark Rosaleen" (244, < Ir. *Róisín Dubh*).

Róisín Dubh, by Seán Clárach Mac Domhnaill (1691–1754), is probably Ireland's most famous patriotic poem. It has been translated into English by Mangan as "Dark Rosaleen", by Joseph Campbell as "O Beautiful Dark Woman" and by Thomas Kinsella as "Little Dark Rose". Instead of Dark Rose, Ireland is sometimes called the Dark Cow, as in the last stanza of Ledwidge's elegy for Thomas MacDonagh, one of the executed leaders of the 1916 Rising: "when the Dark Cow leaves the moor,/And pastures poor with greedy weeds,/Perhaps he'll hear her low at morn/Lifting her horn in pleasant meads."[19] The name is used, ironically, for a pub by Benedict Kiely in his short story "A Ball of Malt and Madame Butterfly" (1973).[20]

The most unusual use of the code in its history occurred during World War II: Plan Kathleen was the code name adopted for a German invasion of Ireland proposed by the Irish Republican Army.[21] The code, like Hiberno-English itself, is not static. Since the partition of Ireland in 1921, the phrase "lost green field" has come into use in nationalist circles as a term for the North of Ireland state, because it is under British rule. Commenting on one of his distant relations in *After the Wake*, Behan remarks: "When he was bent in thought it wasn't the declining Gaeltacht [Irish-speaking area] was knotting his brow nor the lost green field ...."[22]

Many pejorative terms were coined for those, like the sergeant in Lady Gregory's play, who overtly supported English rule in Ireland. Members of the para-military Royal Irish Constabulary were nicknamed Peelers, after Robert Peel, founder of the force. The widespread contempt for the force in rural Ireland is best expressed in the popular satiric song "The Peeler and the Goat" by Jeremiah O'Ryan (d.1855). The song is a dialogue between an officious drunken Peeler and a goat he has arrested at bayonet point for being out after dark, and, *ipso facto*, engaged in what the authorities called "agrarian outrages". A character in Gerald Griffin's novel *The Rivals* (1829) prefaces his singing of the

---

19. Francis Ledwidge, "Thomas MacDonagh", in *The Penguin Book of Irish Verse*, 305.

20. Benedict Kiely, "A Ball of Malt and Madame Butterfly", in *Modern Irish Short Stories*, ed. Ben Forkner, Penguin, 1980, 426.

21. *A Dictionary of Irish History*, eds D.J. Hickey and J.E. Doherty, Dublin, 1987, 477.

22. Brendan Behan, *After the Wake*, Dublin, 1987, 140.

song with sarcastic remarks, which, incidentally, reveal the role of the force as an effective set of eyes and ears for the government:

> I'll sing you a song ... about a set o' people that's very well desarvin' for industhry, an' that's the Peelers. For what would the country do at all if it was'nt for 'em? 'Tis they that airn their money well. There isn't a mouse can squeak; there isn't a calf can blate; there isn't a hen can clock a-near 'em but they must know what raison! ... [I]'m ... sure there's nobody ... but will allow that there was no ho [equal in mischief] with the pigs until the Peelers come into the barony.[23]

The malicious glee with which the song was sung, its enduring popularity, and its capacity to enrage the police, is evident in the "Cat 'n Cage" pub episode of Sean O'Casey's autobiography *Pictures in the Hallway*, published well over a hundred years after the song. When two members of the Royal Irish Constabulary enter the pub, Johnny's brother, Mick, sings it, "knowing that this song was the song they hated and dreaded above all others ...".[24] The song precipitates a brawl between the police on the one hand, and Johnny's brothers and a group of nationalist hurlers on the other.

Among the terms for those who supported or were suspected of supporting British rule and the Anglicization of Ireland are "West Briton" and "Shoneen". The former, which originally meant a Protestant loyalist, was eventually applied to anyone considered pro-British. In Joyce's short story "The Dead", the nationalist Miss Ivors accuses Gabriel Conroy of being a West Briton on the rather slender evidence of book reviews he published in *The Daily Express*, a pro-British Dublin newspaper. Gabriel is astonished by her accusation: "that," he muses, "did not make him a West Briton surely".[25] The emotive force of the term is suggested in Gabriel's unspoken response when she repeats the accusation: "she had no right to call him a West Briton before people, even in a joke" (190). Shoneen (< Ir. *Seoinín*, Little John [Bull]) is a term for a would-be gentleman, particularly an Irishman who attempts to improve his social status by rejecting his own heritage and aping English ways. The political and social implications of the term are evident in Joyce's most overtly political short story, "Ivy Day in the Committee

---

23. Gerald Griffin, *The Rivals and Tracy's Ambition*, ed. John Cronin, Lille, n.d., 111.

24. Sean O'Casey, *Autobiographies I*, London, 1963, 230.

25. James Joyce, *Dubliners*, New York, 1969, 188.

Room". Mr Hynes asks rhetorically: "Hasn't the working-man as good a right to be in the Corporation as anyone else — ay, and a better right than those shoneens that are always hat in hand before any fellow with a handle to his name?" (121).

Ireland was ruled from Dublin Castle, which gave its name to a number of pejorative terms: "in the pay of the Castle", an informer; "Castle hack", a petty informer or police tout; and "Castle Catholic", a Catholic loyalist. The first two appear in Joyce's "Ivy Day". According to Mr Henchy, half of the "hillsiders and fenians" are "in the pay of the Castle", and when Old Jack, the caretaker, demurs, he asserts that they are "Castle hacks" (125). Both terms appear also in Thomas Flanagan's novel *The Tenants of Time* (1988).[26] In Behan's play *The Hostage*, Meg shouts at Miss Gilchrist: "Get off the stage, you Castle Catholic bitch" (157).

The incompatibility of Catholicism and loyalty to Britain in the eyes of some people, which is implied by the phrase "Castle Catholic", is still a critical question in the North of Ireland. Religion and politics became inextricably linked in Ireland following the Reformation, when attempts to Anglicize the country were invariably accompanied by attempts to Protestantize it. There is evidence of this link in Irish and Hiberno-English. The Irish word *Sasanach* means an Englishman and a Protestant, and Hiberno-English is rich in pejorative terms for adherents of the two religions. In the mouth of a Nationalist, the word Fenian (< Ir. *Fianna*, a band of heroic warriors in Irish mythology) used by Mr Henchy, is a term of approbation, but in the mouth of a Protestant Unionist, such as Mr Deasy in the "Nestor" episode of *Ulysses*, it is a pejorative term for a Catholic and, by implication, a Nationalist: "You fenians", he tells Stephen Dedalus, "forget some things" (31). The continuing emotive force of this term in the North of Ireland is conveyed bluntly in Eugene McCabe's short story, "Cancer" (1978), in which a Catholic reads a Lisnaskea District Development Association public notice of rewards for the extermination of vermin, ranging from one shilling for a magpie to one pound for a fox. At the bottom of the notice someone had added: "For every Fenian fucker: one old penny."[27] As Mr Deasy rambles on about Irish history, Stephen recalls another pejorative term for Catholics in a popular Protestant slogan and song title, "Croppies lie down". The croppies were the Irish insurgents of 1798, who wore close-cropped hair as a sign of their sympathy with the

---

26. Thomas Flanagan, *The Tenants of Time*, New York, 1989, 544, 615.

27. Eugene McCabe, "Cancer", in *Modern Irish Short Stories*, 534.

French Revolution. Synonymous with Fenian is "Teague" or "Taig" (<
Ir. *Tadhg*), the once-common, first name of the Irish servant in George
Farquhar's play *The Twin Rivals* (1702), which has served as a pejorative
term for Catholic and native Irishman or Nationalist for centuries. It is
used in the first line of "Lili Burlero", a seventeenth-century,
anti-Catholic song: "Ho! broder Teague, dost hear de decree?";[28] and
in the contemporary short story, "Some Surrender", by the Belfast writer
Bernard MacLaverty: "Roman Catholics. There's something spooky
about them. Taigs."[29] In Daniel Magee's play *Horseman Pass By*
(1983), set in Belfast, the term is used in an illustration of that venerable
game of discovering an individual's religious affiliation: "what's the
difference between 'Our Father *who* art in Heaven', and 'Our Father
which art in Heaven' ... you are a taig if you say the first. One of the
ways of separating the goats from the sheep in this little 'kingdom' of
ours." Magee's play also contains a fourth pejorative term for Catholic,
"Mick", in the British Army sergeant's threat to Paddy Quinn: "I'll ram
this fucking rifle down your Mick throat so far you'll think you have a
hard on ...."[30]

The equivalent Catholic lexicon is more extensive and discriminating.
This appears to be a reflection of two facts: Protestantism was not
monolithic, and Catholics were subjected to the persistent attentions of
what one Protestant novelist called "missionary misses and proselytising
peeresses".[31] Catholics discriminated between the three major Protestant
denominations in Ireland: Church of Ireland (Anglican), Presbyterian and
Methodist. Members of the Church of Ireland, who formed the
Anglo-Irish Ascendancy, were called horse Protestants. They are the
hard-riding country gentlemen, celebrated in the poetry of Yeats and in
the novels and stories of Somerville and Ross. When Meg in Behan's
play *The Hostage* asks what in the name of God is an Anglo-Irishman,
Pat responds: "A Protestant with a horse" (93). Presbyterians were called
"black-mouths". An example in one of Carleton's stories provides a hint
that the religious question was inseparable from the land question:
"Yellow Sam ... put him out of his comfortable farm and slipped a *black*

28. Thomas Percy, *Reliques of Ancient Poetry II*, London, 1844, 388.

29. Bernard MacLaverty, "Some Surrender", *The Irish Times*, 8 Aug. 1987,
"Weekend" supplement, 1.

30. Daniel Magee, *Horseman Pass By*, *Theatre Ireland*, Belfast, April/June
1984, 131, 141.

31. Lady Morgan (Sydney Owenson), *The O'Briens and the O'Flahertys*,
London, 1988, xv.

mouth into it." Carleton reveals that the term was also applied to Orangemen: "these black-mouthed Presbytarians or Orangemen ...."[32] "Black" is the usual adjective used by Catholics to describe extreme Protestants. The best-known example is in Dante's complaint during the Christmas dinner in *A Portrait of the Artist*: "The blackest Protestant in the land would not speak the language I have heard this evening" (35). This usage may have been influenced by the name of the Grand Black Orange Lodge of Ireland, founded in 1802, and its successor, the Imperial Grand Black Chapter of the Orange Order, members of which are known as the Blackmen.[33] Methodists were called "swaddlers", a term for which there are two Protestant and one Catholic explanations.[34] According to the main Protestant account, an ignorant Dublin Catholic priest, hearing one of the early Methodist preachers speak on Christmas Day of the "babe in swaddling clothes", dubbed the new sect "swaddlers". According to the Catholic account, it is one of several pejorative terms for Catholics who converted for material rewards such as clothing or food. All accounts agree on the fact that the term has its origin in a negative response to Protestant missionary activity. Originally applied to Methodists only, it was later applied to all Protestants. In Samuel Lover's *Legends and Stories of Ireland* (1831), it is used in what is obviously a heartfelt complaint against Methodists: "[T]hem dirty swaddlers knocked ... [the pub] down and built a meetin'-house ...."[35] In Joyce's short story "An Encounter", the term is used in a verbal attack on the narrator and his friend by some working-class boys to whom they appear to be middle-class Protestants: "[W]e walked on, the ragged troop screaming after us: *Swaddlers! Swaddlers!* thinking we were Protestants ..." (22).

The rather common Protestant practice (with the notable exception of the Quakers) of combining proselytizing with the distribution of food and clothing in times of famine aroused bitter hostility,[36] and Catholics who converted as a result of material inducements were especially despised.

---

32. William Carleton, *Stories from Carleton*. ed. W.B. Yeats, London, n.d., 9, 15.

33. Tony Gray, *The Orange Order*, London, 1972, 19, 212.

34. The origin of the term was the subject of lively exchanges in *Notes and Queries*, March and April 1868.

35. Samuel Lover, *Legends and Stories of Ireland*, Boston, 1902, 150.

36. See D. Bowen, *Souperism: Myth or Reality*, Cork, 1970; E.M. Forster pokes fun at this practice in his novel *A Passage to India*.

Swaddlers may, originally, have been a term for such Catholics. The most common term, "souper", is used by Tim Casey in Lady Gregory's play *Spreading the News* (1904), in his question about Bartley Fallon, a married man, who is apparently involved with another man's wife: "Sure you don't think he'd turn souper and marry her in a Protestant church?" (41). The term is used for Protestant missionaries on placards carried during a demonstration in Dublin outside a Protestant institution for the poor in "All to Nothing" (1980), a short story by Nial Quinn: "No soupers here ... No Proselytising here."[37] In *Ulysses,* Bloom recalls the origin of the term: "They say they used to give pauper children soup to become protestants in the time of the potato blight" (180). Dualta in Walter Macken's famine novel, *The Silent People* (1962) repeats a Catholic boast: "We didn't take soup. And", he continues bitterly, "we are stricken. We are being wiped out."[38]

The most striking of these religious (?) terms may, indeed, be the most striking of all Hiberno-English idioms. It is found in the description of a meal in *Finnegans Wake*, which includes a dish called "boiled protestants" (456.03): boiled potatoes. This term clearly has its origin in the practice of combining proselytizing with food distribution, but the fact that it may also be a bilingual pun (the Irish word for potatoes, *prátaí*, sounds rather like the first half of Protestants) would make it especially attractive to Joyce.

Amid this welter of pejorative terms, there is one polite euphemism for individuals of a different religion: they are said to "dig with the other foot". This curious euphemism has its origin in the fact that in Protestant districts in the north-east of Ireland the left foot is normally the digging foot.[39] The euphemism can, of course, be used pejoratively. During a discussion of Irish names in Flann O'Brien's novel *The Hard Life* (1961), Mrs Crotty snaps: "I always heard that St Finbarr was a Protestant .... Dug with the other foot."[40] Reilly, in O'Brien's play *Faustus Kelly* (1943), asks Captain Shaw: "Are you an R.C. still or did you learn to dig with the wrong foot?"[41]

As the illustration of the term "black mouth" suggests, the religious and land questions in Ireland became inseparable. By the end of the

---

37. Nial Quinn, *Voyovic and Other Stories*, Dublin, 1980, 34.

38. Walter Macken, *The Silent People*, London, 1982, 307.

39. E. Estyn Evans, *Irish Folk Ways*, London, 1976, 131.

40. Flann O'Brien, *The Hard Life*, London, 1976, 16.

41. Flann O'Brien, *Stories and Plays*, London, 1973, 170.

eighteenth century, Protestants, who formed about twenty-five percent of the population, owned about ninety-five percent of the land. Most of the land was in the hands of the mainly Church of Ireland, Anglo-Irish Ascendancy, and tenanted by Catholics. This situation has given many English terms particular connotations in Hiberno-English. From the time of Spenser on, landlords or their agents subjected their tenants to rack-rents.[42] The practice was so widespread that it is reflected in the title of the first Anglo-Irish novel, Maria Edgeworth's *Castle Rackrent* (1800). Many landlords were absentees, who lived in London and left the operation of their estates to agents, a practice which gave Edgeworth the title for her novel *The Absentee* (1812), adapted for the stage in 1939 by Lady Longford. The Hiberno-English connotations of the term Ascendancy are evident in the title of Lord Longford's play, *The Ascendancy* (1935). The usual term for the home of a member of the Ascendancy in rural areas was the "Big House", and the Big House is a recurrent theme in Anglo-Irish literature since the publication of *Castle Rackrent. The Big House* (1926) is the title of a play by Lennox Robinson, a radio play (1957) by Behan, a poem by Padraic Colum, and part of the title of the Somerville and Ross novel, *The Big House of Inver* (1925).

There are a number of terms for individuals on the fringes of the Ascendancy. In addition to "shoneen", discussed above, there are the three common synonymous terms "squireen" (< squire + H. E. dim. suf. -*een* < Ir *ín*), "half sir", "half-mounted (gentle) man", and "tally woman". References to them suggest that such people were held in particular contempt, probably because of their role as agents or supporters of the Ascendancy. Dion Boucicault's play *The Colleen Bawn* (1860) contains the following terse definition: "Genus, squireen — half sir, and a whole scoundrel."[43] In Flanagan's *Tenants of Time*, a Land League organizer outlines his plan of campaign: "Bloody little squireens .... Half-mounted gentlemen .... The ragtag and bobtail of Cromwell's crew. We'll clear out that scruff to begin with ... and then ... we can turn our attention to the absentees and the great estates" (415). The contempt in which the class was held is best illustrated in P. W. Joyce's *English as We Speak It in Ireland* (1910). The definition of squireen concludes with a bitter comment: "The class of squireen is nearly extinct:

---

42. Spenser, 81.

43. Dion Boucicault, *The Dolmen Boucicault* ed. David Krause, Dublin, 1964, 53.

'Joy be with them.'"[44] The class was not, however, universally despised. Yeats invites one of them to join him in "The Tower": "Come old, necessitous, half-mounted man" (221), and Flurry Knox, the half-sir in the Somerville and Ross *Irish R. M.* stories, is an engaging character. As might be expected, the terms appear in titles: *The Squireen* (1903) is a novel by Shan F. Bullock, and "The Half-Sir" (1829) is a story by Griffin.

Frequently, members of the Ascendancy exercised the *droit du seigneur* and took mistresses, known as tally-women, from among their Catholic tenants. Such a woman lived in the Big House and enjoyed its privileges until she became pregnant, or no longer desirable, at which time she was married off by her master to one of his tenants or given a cash settlement. The term is, however, not as common in literature as one might expect. There is a possible explanation for this in Flanagan's *Tenants of Time*: among "things unmentionable" in nineteenth-century rural Ireland were "squireens with their tally women ..." (358).

A widespread response of the tenant class to injustices, such as rack-rents and evictions, particularly in the period of the land war (1879-1903), was to engage in attacks on the persons or property of landlords and their agents, or on "grabbers", those individuals who had the temerity to replace the evicted. Since written threats usually bore the signature "Captain Moonlight", the participants in these attacks were popularly called "moonlighters". A typical threat appears in Flanagan's *Tenants of Time*: "Grabbers Beware. Let John Fallin give up the farm he has grabbed from his neighbour lest harm befall himself and his sons. Signed, Captain Moonlight" (501). *The Moonlighters* is a play (never produced) by George Fitzmaurice (1877-1953).

The majority of the idioms discussed in this paper are now rare or obsolete, or are rapidly on their way to becoming so. However, as long as the age-old "Irish Question" remains unresolved, idioms such as Fenian, Taig, shoneen and West Briton will remain current and retain their emotive force.

---

44. P.W. Joyce, *English as We Speak It in Ireland*, Dublin, 1910, 333.

LANGUAGE REVIVALISM BEFORE THE TWILIGHT

JOEP LEERSSEN

Many accounts have been written of the vicissitudes of the Irish language. Less attention has been paid to the history of Irish language interest among non-native speakers — if we disregard, that is, the immensely important phenomenon of Gaelic League revivalism over the last hundred years, which is well documented.[1]

The Gaelic League was established towards the end of the last century, and is usually seen as a manifestation of cultural nationalism: the Gaelic counterpart of Yeats's Anglo-Irish literary revivalism, part of that disenchantment with parliamentary activism which followed the fall of Parnell. But, rather than seeing the Gaelic League in synchronic context — in the context of late-nineteenth-century developments, that is — I wish here to trace its antecedents in the earlier parts of the nineteenth century, and to consider the nineteenth-century tradition of Irish language interest with regard to cultural attitudes generally and the image of Irish identity in particular. What emerges in such a perspective is a process of translation rather than of survival: the Gaelic language survived, not so much because the community of its native speakers survived and maintained the language, but rather because an English-speaking urban middle class in Ireland became sensitized to a Gaelic cultural heritage and adopted a Gaelic cultural identity as their own.

My starting-point in tracing the nineteenth-century tradition of Irish language interest lies in the Patriot heyday of late-eighteenth-century Anglo-Ireland. The decades following the publication of Macpherson's Ossian in 1760 have been called, and not without reason, the first Celtic

---

1. See Reg Hindley, *The Death of the Irish Language: A Qualified Obituary*, London, 1990, and the bibliography on 297–324. Desmond Ryan's *The Sword of Light: From the Four Masters to Douglas Hyde, 1638–1938*, London, 1938 has described Gaelic revivalism before the Gaelic League, but has done so from an old-fashioned nationalist viewpoint and with a strongly Gaelic-League-oriented teleology. The centenary of the Gaelic League in 1993 has attracted a number of commemorative surveys of its activities.

revival.[2] There are some striking parallels between the two revivals, a century apart: in both cases (albeit to a different extent) a marginalized Gaelic heritage was eagerly seized upon for a contemporary national purpose, in order to emphasize Ireland's inherent non-Britishness; plays, poems and translations dealt with the glories of Gaelic antiquity; and in both cases, the wave of cultural interest foundered in a climate of political violence, leading to anguished soul-searchings and a transient awareness that cultural interest cannot be divorced from political practice. Yeats's musing whether that play of his sent out certain men the English shot was prefigured, a century previously, in the correspondence of antiquarians who wondered whether their Patriotic researches had contributed to the anti-English climate in which the 1798 rebellion took place.[3]

These parallels are not without importance; but at the same time they should not be overemphasized. Whereas the first Celtic revival was essentially one of antiquarian interest, concerned with conservation and the scholarly investigation of the national past, the second revival was precisely that: an attempt to revive. The notion of awakening the national culture from its death-sleep was central to the cultural climate of the time and perhaps explains the unusually intense occurrence, in the Anglo-Irish Literary Revival, of the rising of supposedly dead people. The Tim Finnegan of "Finnegan's Wake" and *Finnegans Wake*, the patriarchal characters in *The Shadow of the Glen* and *The Playboy of the Western World* are part of this literary-political imagination as much as the fact that a visionary like Patrick Pearse should stage his Rising on the Feast of Easter.

The overall picture, then, is this: a surge of interest in the late eighteenth century, and a surge of interest in the late nineteenth century. What happened in between?

Interest in the Irish language around 1800 was inextricably bound up with an antiquarian interest. The language was studied as a cultural relic or as a vehicle for the understanding of the monuments of Gaelic antiquity. Most importantly, the language was that of the old poets and annals.

---

2. Cf. generally Edward Snyder, *The Celtic Revival in English Literature, 1760–1800*, Cambridge: Mass., 1932.

3. Cf. my *Mere Irish & Fíor-Ghael*, Amsterdam and Philadelphia, 1986 (hereinafter referred to as MIFG), 434–36; Donal MacCartney, "The Writing of History in Ireland 1800–30", *Irish Historical Studies*, X, 40 (September 1957), 347–62.

As a result of the 1798 rebellion, a backlash took place on the intellectual scene which placed the entire practice of Gaelic antiquarianism under a cloud. The old symbiosis of Anglo-Irish Patriot politics, Ascendancy antiquarians and Gaelic assistants was now by definition suspect, and Patriot-style antiquarianism petered out in the nineteenth century.[4] Yet this decline was neither immediate nor absolute. A continuation of the antiquarian tradition can be registered across the divide of 1798–1800, for instance in the ongoing if increasingly eccentric work of General Charles Vallancey, or the reprinting of eighteenth-century antiquarians like Charles Ledwich or Joseph Cooper Walker. Similarly, the important Gaelic scholars Theophilus O'Flanagan, Peter O'Connell, Edward O'Reilly and (in his early career) Owen Connellan essentially continued the older practice of conducting Gaelic scholarship under the patronage of Ascendancy scholars. Although the Royal Irish Academy for a number of years after 1798 drastically curtailed its activities in the field of Irish antiquity, other scholarly associations sprang up.[5] A *Dublin Gaelic Society* published the sole volume of its *Transactions* in 1808, edited by O'Flanagan and containing, among other things, the first adaptation of the Deirdre story in English.[6] The work of the Dublin Gaelic Society was taken over by the *Iberno-Celtic Society* — there was a good deal of membership overlap between the two[7] — which published its *Transactions* (likewise a once-off venture) in 1820. Some members of this society (including George Petrie, James Hardiman and Edward O'Reilly) became involved in the Royal Irish Academy and were responsible for the fact that the Academy's transactions from the mid-1820s onwards once again began to include matters of Irish language and antiquity. An *Ulster Gaelic Society* was set up in Belfast in 1830.[8] In

---

4. Cf. my "On the Edge of Europe: Ireland in Search of Oriental Roots, 1650–1850", *Comparative Criticism*, 8 (1986), 91–122.

5. MIFG, 434–37.

6. I discount the heavily distorted Ossianic version by Macpherson, "Darthula". The importance of the Gaelic Society's *Transactions* in Anglo-Irish literary history is very high; not only is it the fountainhead for all subsequent renderings of the Deirdre story; material contained in this volume also inspired Thomas Moore's "Avenging and Bright" and "Silent O Moyle". Desmond Ryan quotes Moore's appreciative comments on O'Flanagan's work (68).

7. Barron in 1835 even conflated the two societies altogether and spoke of "the Gaelic or Hiberno-Celtic [sic] Society" (*Ancient Ireland*, 4, 52).

8. For the activities of its members (Mcdonnell, Bryce, McAdam, O Fiannachta *et al.*) cf. O Buachalla, *I mBéal Feirste Cois Cuan*, Dublin, 1968.

1840, James Henthorn Todd founded an *Irish Archaeological Society*, dedicated to the printing of important ancient texts; in 1845, a *Celtic Society* was founded, and the latter two fused in 1853 to form the *Irish Archaeological and Celtic Society*. In that same year 1853 the *Ossianic Society* was founded. These mid-century societies all benefited from the work of Eugene O'Curry and John O'Donovan. Later on, societies of a more specifically linguistic interest were founded, such as the *Society for the Preservation of the Irish Language* (1877) and the *Gaelic Union* (1880). This last-mentioned body published an important review, the *Gaelic Journal* or *Irisleabhar na Gaedhilge*, from 1882 onwards, and among the contributors to that journal we encounter the name of Douglas Hyde.

Among all the listed societies and bodies we find continuities, even though they were (the Royal Irish Academy excepted) ephemeral and their productive life-span limited to some five or ten years at best. We notice from case to case, from one society to the next, an overlap of membership which indicates that throughout the century there was an ongoing albeit variably composed community of Irish intellectuals with a Gaelic antiquarian interest, who periodically undertook to incorporate into some form of society. There is, then, an institutional tradition which links the Gaelic League (established 1893) back to the days of Charles Vallancey and Theophilus O'Flanagan; but it is a tenuous tradition at best, and one which was marked and transformed by many intervening crises in Irish society, culture and politics.[9]

Many members of these societies also published in their own right. The Rev. Paul O'Brien, Professor of Irish at Maynooth and member both of the Dublin Gaelic Society and of the Iberno-Celtic Society, published an important primer of the Irish language in 1810. A Protestant scholar, the Rev. William Neilson, also a member of the Dublin Gaelic Society, had likewise published a primer, in 1808; this book, remarkably enough, stood under the patronage of two consecutive Lords Lieutenant of Ireland, the Earl Hardwicke and the Duke of Bedford. Other primers were published by men like William Halliday and Patrick Lynch (both members of the erstwhile Gaelic Society of Dublin). Later on, in 1844,

---

9. Mention should also be made of that language interest which was expressed through the establishment, throughout the century, of various journals — short-lived ones, but none the less remarkable. Among these should be mentioned *Ancient Ireland*, set up in 1835 by one Philip Barron, MRIA, and *An Fíor-Éirionnach*, set up in 1867 by one Richard D'Alton. Cf. S. Ua Casaide, "An Fíor-Éirionnach, A Scarce Tipperary Journal", *Journal of the Waterford and South-East of Ireland Archaeological Society*, 13 (1910), 107–111.

Owen Connellan, Historiographer Royal and Professor of Irish in the newly established Queen's Colleges of Cork and Dublin, and member of the Ossianic Society, published a *Practical Grammar* of Irish. And throughout the early-to-mid-century there was a constant activity in language teaching conducted on behalf of Protestant evangelistic societies, who believed that the Catholic population of Ireland could best be approached through the medium of Irish. A particularly active body in this respect was the *Irish Society for Promoting the Education of the Native Irish through the Medium of their own Language*, a Bible-teaching mission. The extreme evangelism of such bodies made them odious to those whose interest in Irish was of a more national or philological nature, and their standing with nationalist historians is a poor one indeed. Even so the Irish Society did employ a fair number of native scholars and offered one possible channel at least for Irish texts to get into print. Owen Connellan was marginally connected with it, and his namesake Thaddeus Connellan managed to publish, not only pious proselytizing works but also poetic anthologies based on the model of Charlotte Brooke.[10]

This thumbnail inventory may show that there was a fair amount of language interest in nineteenth-century Ireland. The question now arises — in what relation did this language interest stand to other literary and cultural activities at the time?

One thing which is striking is the deliberate respectability and aloofness from politics which all these ventures strove for. The tone was set by the Dublin Gaelic Society — understandably so, for it was established less than a decade after the 1798 civil war and at a time of great political mistrust. Thus the rules of the Society stipulated that "no religious or political Debates whatever shall be permitted, such being foreign to the Object and Principles of the Society". The Iberno-Celtic Society adopted a similarly-phrased rule, and the Ossianic Society in 1853 still had the rule "That all matters relating to the Religious and Political Differences prevailing in this country be strictly excluded from the meetings and publications of the Society". This rule was given special

10. Owen Connellan, *The Gospel according to St. John, in Irish* ..., Dublin, etc., 1830. Thaddeus Connellan published prolifically under the aegis of the Irish Society; cf. Donal O'Sullivan, "Thaddeus Connellan and his Books of Irish Poetry", *Éigse*, III/4 (1942), 278–304; Pádraig de Brún, "The Irish Society's Bible Teachers, 1818–27", *Éigse*, XIX/2 (1983), 281–332 and sqq.; Desmond Bowen, *The Protestant Crusade in Ireland 1800–1870*, Dublin & Montreal, 1978. The proselytizing use of Irish continued a long pre-Union tradition; cf. MIFG, 326–32.

emphasis in the Second Annual Report, which pointed out that this stipulation vouchsafed that the scholarly and cultural aims of the society could be pursued without anyone needing to "fear violence to his private opinion".[11] Again, Philip Barron's magazine *Ancient Ireland* canvassed a wide readership by pointing out, again and again, "that this Magazine is to be *solely and altogether* a *literary* publication. *Politics and polemics are totally excluded from its pages*".[12] The dissociation of language from politics was made as a matter of course by Richard D'Alton, who in his magazine *An Fíor-Éirionnach* wrote, "My object being the restoration of the Irish language, *therefore* I wish to avoid all those political topics on which Irishmen differ so much" (no. 2, 17, my emphasis); and in 1884 the Gaelic Union still adopted the following position:

> While the Council of the Gaelic Union is thoroughly Irish there is nothing sectarian or political in its aims — its members, while retaining their own private religious or political opinions, do not obtrude them on others .... Their only opponents are the Philistines and Vandals, who would annihilate the Irish language, regardless of its antiquity, beauty and literature, and because of its close connection with Irish nationality.[13]

This is very close to the position that Douglas Hyde took when he formulated the ideals of the Gaelic League. From his initial speech on *The Necessity for De-Anglicising Ireland* (1892) onwards, he never ceased to emphasize the non-partizan and indeed a-political nature of Irish language revivalism; it was this which eventually made his position untenable as the movement became more and more nationalistically politicized after 1900. As late as 1914, Hyde reiterated this view strenuously in his pamphlet *The Gaelic League and Politics*:

> Of course the Gaelic League has always kept politics out of its councils, but each individual Gaelic Leaguer has a perfect right

---

11. *Transactions of the Ossianic Society*, 1 (1854), 4; 2 (1855), 10.

12. Thus in the Prospectus (bound with the actual instalments of the magazine in the copy at the National Library of Ireland, Dublin). A similar statement was later placed on the cover of each number. Barron plied the clergy of all religious persuasions (Roman Catholic, Anglican and Presbyterian) for letters of approbation.

13. "Proceedings of the Gaelic Union", *Irisleabhar na Gaedhilge*, II/13 (January 1884), 223.

outside of the Gaelic League to take part in any politics he wishes ... (3–4).

> I will never attach myself nor allow myself to be attached to any body of men which I might think wished to use the Irish language as a cloak for politics, I don't care what kind of politics, or which might try to grab for political ends an apparent monopoly of the Irish language ... (5).

Hyde's position seems contradiction-ridden and untenable to us nowadays. We no longer see the cultivation of national individuality as an a-political activity and it is hard for us to appreciate the nineteenth-century notion that such cultural and *national* pursuits transcend "politics". That is not merely because nowadays we have a less rarefied notion of what is "culture" and a less restrictive notion of what is "politics" — even when taking such terminological pitfalls into account, the type of discourse cited above seems uneasy and contradictory. Throughout the century from O'Flanagan to Hyde, the exclusion of politics is constant, but seems to mean two things: an ascertainment that the activities of the body in question should not be seen as seditious or dangerous to the political status quo, and a recognition that the common pursuit of linguistic interest can only take place in an atmosphere where all members suspend their political antagonism.

If "politics" is so emphatically excluded from linguistic and antiquarian interest, that in itself is a sure sign that people at the time felt the need for such an exorcism; the very interdict on politics is a recognition of the potentially political nature of cultural nationalism — something which to us a century and a half later seems so obvious. The phraseology in the rules of the Kilkenny Archaeological Society (1849) is significant in this respect: it bans all matters "connected with the religious and political differences which exist in our country" as being, not only "foreign to the objects of this Society", but also "calculated to disturb the harmony which is essential to its success".[14] Such formulae both predicted and tried to block out the spectre of a combination between political agitation and Ireland's cultural and linguistic heritage. It was precisely that combination which had begun to germinate in the closing decades of the eighteenth century. It was precisely that combination which Hyde, eventually, failed to suppress; it was to become

---

14. The Kilkenny Archaeological Society later (in 1872) became the Royal Historical and Archaeological Association of Ireland and was called, as of 1892, the Royal Society of Antiquaries of Ireland.

Patrick Pearse's call for an Ireland, not only Gaelic, but free as well, not only free, but Gaelic as well.

We have, then, a tradition in the nineteenth century which draws on the cultural distinctness of Ireland whilst denying the political nature of such an act. It was the "respectable" side of an Irish programme of cultural nationality. Its respectability increased throughout the century. As we can gather from the various membership lists in these societies' Proceedings or Transactions, peers, members of parliament, ministers in the Church of Ireland and academics came to dominate these linguistic and antiquarian activities.

This tradition is the obverse of that important literary development traced by Malcolm Brown.[15] Anglo-Irish literature does, in the course of the century, prepare a mixture of culture and politics. Although Brown only begins his survey with Thomas Davis, we can trace that preoccupation back to the novels which began to be written immediately after the Act of Union, such as those of Lady Morgan, Charles Maturin or the Banim brothers. Like the novels of Lady Morgan, the poetry of the *Nation* is imbued with the quaint appeal of a distinctly Irish local colour and combines strong anti-English resentment with a language peppered with Gaelic names and phrases. *The Nation* makes it a matter of policy to render proper names of persons and places only in their Irish form, and even in the Irish typography, and adds a liberal dose of mavrones, machrees, aboos and similar interjections. In the middle of the most rousing battle songs of the *Nation*, the reader invariably stumbles across asterisks and footnotes informing him as to the meaning of certain Gaelic words and phrases or their pronunciation. That, too, is a language interest of sorts (and one which frequently relies on some of the grammars and primers mentioned above). However, what *The Nation* does is not to spread a knowledge of Irish for purposes of communication or philology; rather, it invokes the aural flavour of Ireland's Other language for the purpose of fostering a sense of non-English cultural identity.[16] Thomas Davis aimed almost explicitly at "imagining a

---

15. Malcolm Brown, *The Politics of Irish Literature: From Thomas Davis to W.B. Yeats*, London, 1972.

16. This occasionally leads to solecisms that are every pedant's delight — such as the fact that the Irish form of the place-name Tara (Teamhair) is made to rhyme with "defamer" (in Edward Walsh's "The Songs of the Nation", in *The Spirit of the Nation. Ballads and Songs by the Writers of "The Nation"*, Dublin, 1882, 137–38).

community" — to use Benedict Anderson's phrase.[17] In his essays, he furnishes pages-long lists of suitable topics for Irish painting, creates a gallery of key texts for Irish literature, Irish history. Davis hammers out, from the trials of the past, a tradition, selects those cultural manifestations which define Irish nationality. These invariably combine a strong sense of Ireland's biculturalism with an equally strident anti-English nationalism. This, in turn, leads Davis to contradictions peculiarly his own. His sense of nationality is ethnic at some times (where only Celts are the stuff that Irish nationality is made of) and at other times voluntaristic, relying on people's commitment rather than on their ethnicity. Be that as it may, Davis's invocation of Irish is just that, an invocation, a form of tokenism. Davis resents the imposition of the English language of Ireland but his notion of Irish does not get beyond Stage-Irishisms of the begorrah mode. Irish as used in *The Nation* is high on symbolism but low on denotation, high on significance but low on signification. Davis (and most of the *Nation* poets with him) performs a divorce between language and politics not unlike that of the linguistic enthusiasts: while realizing the political importance of creating a sense of cultural identity, of inventing a tradition and a diachronic community, he only dabbles in the language, sees it merely as an evocative abracadabra with which to conjure up the national spirit. To make such a stricture is not merely an *ex post facto* cavil: Davis's tokenism was discernable to critical nineteenth-century eyes as well. Witness the sarcasm heaped by Charles Gavan Duffy upon the *Nation* poems and their invocation of Irish orthography and toponymy:

> The text of the ballads is to be larded with a Celtic nomenclature furnished by John O'Donovan, which sometimes consists of an aggregate meeting of the consonants with scarcely a vowel to take the chair .... You will stare with all your eyes to see what has become of all your old acquaintances. What do you say to the Lee becoming the Laoi, and the Shannon the Sionann, Limerick Luimneach, and Slieve Donard Sliab Domangart?[18]

---

17. Benedict Anderson, *Imagined Communities: Reflections on the Origins and Spread of Nationalism*, London, 1986.

18. Quoted in Ryan, 147. This sarcasm applied to place-names in Duffy's own contributions to *The Nation*: "Sliabh Domhanghart" appears in his "The Men of the North" (*Spirit of the Nation*, 80). Evidently the orthography was imposed against Duffy's wishes.

Non-native speakers *need* the native Gaelic connection in order to authenticate their cultural nationalism as truly Irish. This seems to be a fundamental trait of revivalism: urban and (upper-)middle-class as it is, it constantly seeks to validate its pursuit by invoking the *Idealtypus* of an authentic Ireland, the Ireland of the place names, of the Native Speaker, the *Gaeilgeoir*. Hence the great symbolical emphasis placed on the existence of the *Gaeltacht*, the areas where Irish is still the community's native, first language. That desire to hark back to native authenticity in linguistic matters echoes a similar literary desire: the desire, as evinced by Yeats, Synge and Lady Gregory, to let their literary efforts sparkle with the authentic life of the Irish peasant. That search for self-authentication I have described elsewhere as one of "auto-exoticism", and in terms of a quest for reinvigoration: as an escape from what was felt to be a declining, decadent "mainstream" European civilization.[19]

It appears that romantic language revivalism is motivated by similar desires. The allure of the Native Speaker is not so much that he should speak Irish, but rather that he speaks no English. The ignorance of English is idealized as a lost state of pristine purity, of virginal, unsullied authenticity. The title of Hyde's trail-blazing lecture, which sparked off the Gaelic League, betrays much: "On the Necessity for De-Anglicising Ireland." English cultural influence should be washed away like an unsightly stain, so as to return to a pristine state of unadulterated Gaelophone purity.

That such a programme should be conceived and propagated by an English-speaking middle class is, in an ironically twisted form, a re-enactment of earlier forms of hegemonism. The issue of Gaelic culture is conjured up in a deliberately, strenuously de-politicized form so as to screen the possibility that social and economic tensions might be lurking behind Ireland's diglossia. The tension is glimpsed in this exercise dialogue from *An Fíor-Éironnach* (1862) between "An Old Gentleman and a Labourer":[20]

> G. — I know there is great distress among the labourers and small
>   farmers
> L. — We must all leave old Ireland

---

19. Cf. my "On the Treatment of Irishness in Romantic Anglo-Irish Fiction", *Irish University Review*, XX (1990), 251–63, and my "Europese literatuur en nationale beeldvorming: Het geval John Synge", *De Gids*, CLVI, 1 (January 1993), 68–79.

20. I here quote the English translation of the Irish dialogue between "An seanduine agus an sglabhaidh", as given in the original on facing pages (100–103).

G. — Ireland for ever Paddy.

L. — We'll go where the rich man does not reap what the poor man sow's [*sic*]

G. — Ireland for ever Paddy.

L. — Bread for ever for me, sir.

G. — Well, bread for ever for me, too; come with me and I'll give you work.

L. — Long life to your honour, and Ireland for ever.

This time the Gaelic peasant is commandeered for nationalist rather than colonialist purposes, by patriotic Dubliners rather than by conquering Cockneys, but he is once again subdued as a passive and subordinate partner in the scheme. The peasant is to provide symbolical goods this time, rather than rent, tithes, produce or cheap labour: he is asked to furnish a native knowledge of the language and a correspondingly picturesque lifestyle; he is asked to provide that authenticity and that unbroken link with past traditions which the revivalists by definition do not have, and cannot do without; and he is asked to acquiesce in the role of provider of rustic continuity and cultural authenticity. Occasionally his stories or poems are written down and published (usually in bowdlerized form); and he can win medals and diplomas by dancing and playing and reciting at *Oireachtas* or *Feis*; but that is all he gets out of the bargain.

While language revivalism defines itself as a transpolitically "national" concern, it follows a generally current, romantic image of Ireland as a country split along class- and regional lines. The rural peasant is held to embody authentic, Gaelic Ireland, but his role in national developments and politics is a passive, submissive one; the urban bourgeoisie holds an active, leading position in the socio-economic and political sphere but by the same token lacks cultural authenticity. It is in these terms that a pattern of cultural trade-off (some might say, exploitation) emerges.[21] The pattern is operative in various spheres of cultural life: in language, in literature, and in the interaction between such spheres.

Irish literary history of the nineteenth century, in order to be more fully comprehended in its ideological developments, should be placed in the context of other areas of cultural history, e.g. linguistic history. To do so may yield interesting topics for future research.

---

21. Cf. also Alf Mac Lochlainn, "Gael and Peasant: A Case of Mistaken Identity?", in *Views of the Irish Peasantry 1800–1916*, eds D.J. Casey and E. Rhodes, Hamden: Conn., 1977, 17-36.

Anglo-Irish literature announces its national intent by means of an insistent use of *couleur locale*.[22] That local colour is often antiquarian in nature, in that it draws on materials and events from Ireland's history or mythology. However, there is also a linguistic, phraseological mode of self-authentication: the use of Hiberno-English and, more importantly, the use of those macushlas, machrees and mavrones which pepper Anglo-Irish poetry from Mangan to the *Nation* poets to the early Yeats and Alfred Perceval Graves.

These two modes of local colour, antiquarian and phraseological, are difficult to combine. One harks back to the past, the other remains in the present; one goes for high culture and important figures, the other emphasizes the Plain People living in their rustic cottages; one tends to opt for a tragic mode (the drooping Celticism common to Macpherson and young Yeats), the other is more comic and vitalistic to the point of rubbing shoulders with "Stage Irishness".

It is obvious that the contemporaneity, rusticity and vitalism of the "phraseological" mode of local colour is much closer to the aim and attitudes of the language revivalists than the antiquarian mode. As the highly interesting case of the relations between the Gaelic League and the Abbey Theatre makes clear, language enthusiasts and literary aficionados may come to confrontation over the issue of local colour.[23] Such confrontations between various strains of cultural nationalism deserve closer study. Another topic which by the same token suggests itself is that of the position of academic Gaelic philology in the culture-political landscape of those decades.

These are as yet mere pointers to future work; I offer them here, in lieu of a formal conclusion, and as an illustration of the interest in studying Anglo-Irish literature in the context of Irish cultural history.

---

22. On the notion of *couleur locale*, cf. generally J. Kamerbeek, *Tenants et aboutissants de la notion "Couleur locale"*, Utrecht, 1962.

23. Cf. also Declan Kiberd, *Synge and the Irish Language*, London, 1979.

HOMAGE TO HESLINGA

ARTHUR GREEN

Marcus Heslinga wrote about the common society of the British Isles, and about Ireland as part of that society. He wrote as geographer and historian, and his conclusions are based on the objective power of detached observation. This is wonderfully refreshing. Irish issues have been too much discussed in emotional terms. Because it is inconvenient, the concept of the British Isles has almost disappeared from public language, or is veiled by meaningless references to "these islands". It took a Dutch scholar to demonstrate what should be a basic presupposition for everyone in Great Britain and Ireland. Heslinga is neglected because bi-insular realities are nemesis for Little Englander and Irish separatist alike. This paper sketches Heslinga's views, and contrasts them with the Irish insularism which is damagingly conventional among some influential historians and critics.

Marcus Heslinga taught at the Free University of Amsterdam, and visited Ireland extensively in 1959, 1960, and 1961. Later he was Professor of Geography at the Free University. We owe him homage because he wrote the best social and historical account of Ireland within the British Isles in his *The Irish Border as a Cultural Divide*.[1] It was first published in 1962 and reprinted without amendment in 1971. It is a scarce and valuable item in secondhand bookshops in the UK, although it is in print in the Netherlands.

There are only about 200 pages in *The Irish Border as a Cultural Divide*, but it is written with elegant concision and great intellectual drive. Since it is in itself a short summary of Irish history within the British Isles there is a risk of distortion in reducing it to a paragraph. But I shall try to do so as a starting point and then use its general approach as a touchstone for some of today's literary and historical themes.

Heslinga's subject is the Irish border between the United Kingdom and the Republic of Ireland. By this he means both the sea and the land

---

1. M.W. Heslinga, *The Irish Border as a Cultural Divide* (1962), Assen, 1971.

borders, both, in his view, problematic. Historically, sea has allowed easier communication than land. There are, and always have been, great barriers and contrasts within Ireland. On the other hand, there are and always have been great linkages and similarities between the two parts of Ireland and Great Britain. Heslinga explains the separation of the Irish state from the United Kingdom mainly by Catholic religious considerations, and the separation of Northern Ireland from the Irish Free State mainly by Protestant religious considerations. In his opinion the Irish land boundary could be interpreted as a cross-Channel extension of the Scottish Border, marking off, in a very arbitrary way, the "scoticized" part of Ireland from the most anglicized part. He finds the separatism of the Republic harder to explain than the Unionism of Northern Ireland.

Heslinga writes as a physical as well as a human geographer. He sees Ireland as historically without a political focus, and with the central Ulster Lowlands and the Foyle valley standing apart. Physiographic conditions favoured separate communities rather than any form of central authority. Great Britain and Ireland are both extensions of the European mainland, rather than oceanic islands, and he quotes a geographer who says that "the physical geography of Ireland is so closely related to that of Great Britain that to the imaginative eye the intervening seas exist only as a geological creation of yesterday". There is a case, Heslinga says, for thinking of the British Isles as a major natural region standing on its own. "From Snaefell the peak which rises from the Irish Sea to form the highest summit of the Isle of Man the mountains on all four sides of the sea are visible." The uniqueness of Ireland's position is that, though an island, it has in fact only one neighbour. Thus Heslinga rejects the traditional nationalist proposition that because Ireland is an island it must be a separate political entity. In terms of human geography Heslinga argues that Ulsterism is a form of nationalism, but a nationalism which, like Scottish and Welsh nationalism, is fulfilled not by political independence but by the maintenance of the constitutional link with the British Crown.

Heslinga's book is a model academic exercise. The tone is courteous but the investigation is razor-edged. Under his inspection the major tradition of Irish historiography melts away. He provides a sharp analysis of the historical divisions within Ireland and the historical connections between Ireland and Highland Britain. This includes an account of the movements between Ulster and Scotland and back; the Viking incursion as a phenomenon of the British Isles; the to- and fro-ing between Wales and Ireland. Over the whole medieval period he shows that the area called Ulster fluctuated in extent but the links between Ulster and

Scotland remained close. The English king was accepted as a kind of high king in most of Ireland and there was far more warfare between the English and the Scots, than between the English and the Irish. What did, however, survive until the Tudors in the sixteenth century was an archaic Gaelic civilization in both Ireland and the Scottish Highlands.

Next he describes the "regional contrasts and contacts of post-Reformation Ireland". This includes a striking account of population movements in seventeenth-century Ulster. Government plantation was relatively unimportant. In essence he sees the continuation of a population movement from Scotland into Ulster which had been going on for a much longer time. Some of the settlers from Galloway were Gaelic speakers. The Lagan valley first began to be cultivated by English settlers. There was a shift from Irish chief to Scottish or English landlord. The Act of Union with Great Britain was initially supported by Catholics and opposed by Protestants. The failure to respond fairly to Catholic demands was the essential cause of later separatism. Heslinga notes the absence of racial divisions between people living in the different parts of the British Isles.

Heslinga's cool approach resembles that of Marie Therese Flanagan or Robin Frame writing today on the medieval history of the British Isles;[2] and the idea of the British Isles as linked societies is the basis of Hugh Kearney's recent book.[3] Others have made comparative studies between Ireland, Wales and Scotland. But it takes a bold scholar like Heslinga to deal freshly with relationships and their interpretation over such a great stretch of time and space, and probably it takes the detached outsider to produce the credibility and authority he possessed. The book does not deal with the twentieth-century American hegemony, and it is slightly outdated now by the arrival of the European Community and its effect on British/Irish relationships. The European Community remains an economic rather than a cultural force, however, whereas American influence is both political and cultural.

In his introduction Estyn Evans, the most distinguished geographer of the last generation in Ireland, praises Heslinga's objectivity, and excuses the fact that Irish scholars, north and south, had neglected the subject of the border because of its political sensitivity. Evans refers to the myth of

---

2. M.T. Flanagan, *Irish Society, Anglo-Norman Settlers, Angevin Kingship*, Oxford, 1989; R. Frame, *The Political Development of the British Isles*, Oxford, 1990.

3. Hugh Kearney, *The British Isles: A History of Four Nations*, Cambridge, 1989.

Ireland as a "natural geographic unit", the superficial view that the
Ulster problem was created by English politicians and militarists, and
also to the myth of "the historic Irish nation", commenting that it is a
myth Irish scholars have long ceased to defend. Finally Evans remarks
on the paradox that essentially religious frontiers came into existence,
even though the nineteenth-century Catholic church stood for established
law and authority and was, by definition, "the antithesis of nationalistic
faith".

Evans and Heslinga were writing during the peace of the early sixties.
Their precision and breadth are badly needed today. Irish liberalism is in
retreat and distinguished scholars lend themselves to racism and reaction.
Yet in doing so such writers also indicate their own despair: Ireland and
Irish people, they feel, are not prepared to fulfil their unique cultural
destiny: instead most Irish people seem prepared to lead Anglo-American
lives and have Anglo-American attitudes. You and I might say that by
this route Ireland may discover it has at last a common culture, and that
Irish cultural separatism, an example of early twentieth-century
micro-nationalism, belongs in the dust bins of history. But so far that
vision is left to Irish Unionists and has nothing to support it but the
strength of reason and the appeal of broader sensibility.

Such strictures may seem harsh. But consider Professor Lee's *Ireland
1912-1985*.[4] It ends with 175 pages on "perspectives". Here Lee's
history becomes a personal manifesto, not only for the social sciences in
Ireland but for Irish cultural separatism. He says that Ireland once had
an identity forged by "an obtrusive imperial presence, ... a national
revival, ... a struggle for independence". He concludes that "as
circumstances normalize only the husk of identity is left without the
language" (663), so he goes so far as to advocate Gaelic revival "if only
to create a bi-lingual society ..." and adds "Despite all the mundane
pressures to the contrary, despite the apparently imminent and inevitable
victory of the big battalions," (meaning, I insert, the United Kingdom
and the United States of America) "even cultural history may still have
many futures" (674). The book criticizes at extraordinary length an
article in the *Irish Independent*, claiming that the unknown author's
pragmatism turns out to be "that jaded alternative to an Irish identity, an
English identity in Ireland" (661). But it is only cultural nationalists who
talk in this way about alternatives. Professor Lee is so obsessed with
Ireland versus England that he cannot grasp the reality and attractiveness
of the British Isles as related communities. Instead he reckons that if only

---

4. J.J. Lee, *Ireland 1912-1985*, Cambridge, 1989.

Ireland were Gaelic speaking it would produce intellectual innovation of greater distinction. How many million Gaelic speakers would be needed to produce the equivalent of, say, one Swedish speaking Myrdal, is not disclosed. Yet a small country which can claim one Conor Cruise O'Brien might be said to be doing pretty well.

Another well-known cultural nationalist is Denis Donoghue. In his autobiography *Warrenpoint*,[5] he too clings to themes of Irish cultural separatism. Against such revisionists as Roy Foster,[6] he insists on the traditional version of Irish nationalist history, from Devorguilla to the 1916 GPO, as taught fifty years ago by the Christian Brothers in Newry. Also he still adheres to the Roman Catholic Church of his youth. It is as though on these topics he has never grown up. The book is wonderfully candid about his own predispositions, including as they do his wartime neutralism vis-à-vis Nazi Germany, his inability to speak the word "Chorister" because it has Protestant associations, or the fact that he cannot enjoy oratorios because most of them are Protestant. There is more, and much, much worse, about Ulster society.

Warrenpoint may be compared with Max Wright's *Told in Gath*,[7] another autobiography which came out at about the same time. *Told in Gath* relates the self-emancipation of a member of the Plymouth Brethren in Ulster. It does not whine. It is very funny. It moves from the local world of the sect to the universal world of the professional philosopher. There is great naturalness about Wright's spells of teaching in Canada, Australia, and Belfast. He takes for granted Ulster's place in an English speaking world. It is a book which enlightens and which will live.

Warrenpoint, however, is the work of a pure critic, elegant but crippled. If anyone wishes to explore the stunting effect of hibernianism it is a classic case study. Denis Donoghue, like Professor Lee, recognizes that his causes may be moribund, but sees that the unthinkable alternative would diminish Irish uniqueness. "Unfortunately Ireland without its story is merely a member of the EC, the begging bowl our symbol" (172). So the story, however unhistorical, must be adhered to.

Lurking behind both Lee's history and Donoghue's *Warrenpoint* there is the belief that Ireland has a unique destiny, which is obtainable if only Irish people would be faithful. This is not a purely Catholic Irish tradition. The last paragraph of Terence Brown's *Social and Cultural*

5. D. Donoghue, *Warrenpoint*, London, 1991.

6. R.F. Foster, *Modern Ireland 1600–1972*, Penguin, 1989.

7. M. Wright, *Told in Gath*, Belfast, 1990.

History[8] also derives from early twentieth-century fantasy when he advocates an "Irish humanism":

> The change in consciousness of Irish identity that such studies represent might, one hopes, have some effect over time in contributing to an ideological shift in Irish society as a whole as the humanistic values that currently govern intellectual activity in the country achieve a wider currency. At present of course such a nascent humanism is a fragile dyke against the cultural and social depredations of a rampant commercialism in an Ireland which could lose, before long, any distinctive identity it may once have possessed. But without it one could have little hope that the tides of commercialism could be resisted or that in future a new humanely comprehensive imperative be defined for Irish society — one which would take account of the material and social gains of modernization but which would also allow a sustaining and challenging role for the products of the imagination and of the mind.

Terence Brown seems to mean that ordinary western society can and should be resisted in the name of something called Irish humanism, which seems to be an update of "Holy Ireland", where, unlike lesser places, there is a role for the imagination and the mind. From here it is only a short step to Yeats and his rejection of the "filthy modern tide". There is no reason to follow Terence Brown into this hibernian dreamtime.

Separatist Irish thinkers are inhibited from facing up to their part in the society of the British Isles. When Richard Kearney writes about Ireland in the Nineties and explores its post-national dimension,[9] he feels it necessary to explain specifically that he is not anti-national, and when he develops the theme of Irish links with Europe he concentrates entirely on the Continent, merely saying that Irish links with Britain "are so intimate as to require no further mention". This is a very remarkable cop out. No Irish nationalist has attempted to trace at length Ireland's permanent involvement with British society, although Desmond Fennell, quoted by Heslinga, did say many years ago:

> Though the life of the people in Ireland — and in particular the Republic of Ireland — has characteristics of its own, these

8. T. Brown, *Ireland: A Social and Cultural History 1922–1979*, London, 1981.

9. Richard Kearney, *The Irish Mind*, Dublin, 1985; *Across the Frontiers*, Dublin, 1988.

characteristics do not make Irish life more than a regional variant of life within the British Isles. The flavour of Yorkshire life is very different from that of the Scottish Highlands or the English South-East: the "local flavour" of Irish life is not any greater in degree.

Characteristic of the emotional blockages at work outside Ireland, is the conclusion of Barbara Solow's study of the Irish land issue,[10] where the author, having demolished the historicity of an oppressive landlord system, goes out of her way to say that this does not put Irish separatism in question. It is as if Irish separatism were a sacred faith, and the historian is seeking to avoid blasphemy.

Deliberate insularity has so far not been conventional in Northern Ireland. But it is very remarkable that United Kingdom cultural policies now concentrate on narrowing its broader perspectives. Local history and local studies are heavily supported. Above all the core school history syllabus will not deal, for example, with the indispensable themes of British constitutional development, the Industrial Revolution, or British Isles expansion overseas but will focus in the nineteenth century on the Irish Home Rule controversy and the emergence of a separate Northern Ireland. As for the twentieth century the core focus will be on "Northern Ireland and its neighbours", a non-topic since Northern Ireland is not a constitutional, economic, or cultural entity. Still more striking perhaps is that there will be no core study of European history before the twentieth century, while for the twentieth century there will be some core study of European history, but there will not be any core study of American history. The programme is anti-educational because it derives from the mindset of Irish localism.

These examples suggest that Irish cultural separatism is still very much alive among scholars and governments, however much it is threatened by popular indifference and common sense. As you read professors Lee or Donoghue or study the proposed Northern Ireland history syllabus you recognize echoes of excited old scholarly nationalisms. When Benda wrote his denunciation of Barres, Maurras and the rest for their willingness to sacrifice their intellects to French nationalism,[11] there was a live tradition of cultural nationalism throughout Europe. In Northwest Europe that tide has probably ebbed. We tend to see our governments as more like local authorities than as a

<hr>

10. B. Solow, *The Land Question and the Irish Economy 1870–1903*, Cambridge: Mass., 1971.

11. J. Benda, *The Great Betrayal*, tr. Richard Aldington, London, 1928.

complete focus for loyalty. But in Ireland cultural nationalism remains important. The Dublin state has nothing to rely on except cultural nationalism, since without it, and without a separate Irish language, the whole enterprise of Irish separatism becomes a will o' the wisp.

Historians are free to impose their own preferred patterns on the past. It is possible to write, as Sir Francis Hill did, an immense history of the single small city of Lincoln,[12] and Thoreau made it clear, once for all, that someone who had travelled a great deal — in Concord — could be a citizen of the world. That may be the hope of Irish scholars. But local history is mindless without the perspective which Hill or Thoreau possessed, and it is, no doubt, the day-by-day boundaries set by social communication that determine what is an intelligible field of study. The proposition Heslinga suggests is that the British Isles forms such an intelligible field of study, both now and in the past.

On this basis it is a system dominated from Southeast England, but in continuous interaction. In early times the system was less structured, but at no stage, past or present, are the various localities of the British Isles free standing. It is true that the British Isles itself is not free standing either. Movements of ideas, economic change, and external power politics are woven into its history. But when Scottish, Welsh and Irish nationalists insist on Scotland in Europe, Wales in Europe, and Ireland in Europe, they really mean that they wish to leapfrog the actual hegemony of Southeast England. It is a backhanded tribute to the present reality of the British Isles as a cultural, economic and political system.

From the perspective of the 1990s we may say that the movement for peasant land ownership had been the economic engine for political change in the later nineteenth century but was ultimately satisfied and neutralized by the Wyndham Act of 1903. So it has become clear that the Irish separatism which finally triumphed was the product of pressure generated from Catholic loyalties and the Gaelic League. The impulse was carried forward (and anyone interested should read Garvin's *Irish Nationalist Revolutionaries*)[13] by people who narrowed their vision to Ireland, who were petit bourgeois to the marrow, and who left a legacy to Ireland of anti-intellectualism, puritanism, and xenophobia, as well as unquestioned Catholic mores and Gaelic cultural tyranny. It is not surprising that their state was disowned by Yeats, Joyce and AE, not to mention Beckett, nor that a large proportion of the Protestants there left,

---

12. Sir J.W. Francis Hill, *Medieval Lincoln*, Cambridge, 1948; *Tudor and Stuart Lincoln*, Cambridge, 1956; *Georgian Lincoln*, Cambridge, 1966.

13. T. Garvin, *Nationalist Revolutionaries in Ireland 1858–1928*, Oxford, 1987.

or were forced to leave. Northern Ireland's semi-detached devolution was a by-product of the post 1918 Irish settlement. This too was a disaster because, although Northern Ireland was saved from the full ill effects of separatism, it was unsuited in principle to devolution. Meantime the economic linkages and population movement between the islands continued. And in very modern times the whole of Ireland shares de facto in the Northwest Atlantic cultural world. The de-Anglicizing dreams of Hyde and Pearse have been mercifully by-passed, yet because those dreams led to a separate Irish state there is perpetual unease that its cultural basis has gone. Hence our intellectual Luddites, the Lees, the Donoghues, and (I fear) the drafters of the Ulster history syllabus.

There has been one very remarkable modern re-interpretation of Irish history. It is that historically Ireland is best seen as a colony. This concept is now used by some good historians and has become almost a cliché among literary critics. It would provide a more solid basis for Irish separatism than alleged cultural differences, were it well founded, and no one doubts that there were colonial aspects to Irish society in the sixteenth, seventeenth and eighteenth centuries. But after 1801, with Irish representation in Westminster, with free trade, with common citizenship, with better social communication, the idea becomes far-fetched. Certainly the colonial world described by Memmi or Fanon with its absolute racial distinctions and economic exploitation, is utterly different from nineteenth-century Irish experience. By the early twentieth century Ireland was even a net gainer from the United Kingdom Exchequer.

But the basic objection to the colonialist interpretation is that it ratifies an ill-founded Irish racism. It suggests that there were Irish people in Ireland — implicitly Catholic, Gaelic and poor, set against British people in Ireland — Protestant and relatively rich: and that Ireland, and truly native Irish people, were predestined for separatism. This is historicism with a vengeance. Besides, the model is not valid at all in Ulster, where it is obvious that today's "two communities" are not racially distinct, and where there is great economic overlap. Nor does it apply satisfactorily to the Pale or to many Irish towns. It is certainly relevant to major Protestant landlords and their Catholic tenants, although not for racial reasons. Besides, the traditional view of George O'Brien, that Ireland after 1801 could have become another contented Scotland, if Catholics had been treated better,[14] has much more to recommend it. Comparisons could also be made between nationalist Ireland and one or other of the minority nationalities in the Austro-Hungarian Empire,

14. G. O'Brien, *The Four Green Fields*, Dublin, 1936.

although it is true that Central European differences based on language have more intrinsic justification than Irish separatism ever had. The fact that Irish historians rely so much on the colonial model says more about their urge to justify being non-British than about fair judgment of historical reality. When J.J. Lee describes Unionist attitudes as those of a "Herrenvolk" he seems to overlook the Irish isolationism, racism and ecclesiasticism to which Unionists were opposed. From a broader perspective Irish separatism and xenophobia have colluded to produce a perverse cultural deprivation.

Irish revisionist historians are inhibited from being so critical. Even Roy Foster, who regrets the separatist consequences of 1916, writes with caution, and even if he is close to being an intellectual unionist himself he reserves particular scorn for the actual Unionists of Northern Ireland. Courage should be taken from the tremendous shifts in historical climates of opinion elsewhere. In nineteenth and early twentieth century Britain there was endless celebration of the Glorious Revolution of 1689, the electoral Reform Acts, and generally our splendid national past. This was the so-called Whig Interpretation of history. During more recent times there has been a British school of left-wing historiography, in which the seventeenth-century Civil War embodied a failed working class struggle, where the Glorious Revolution substituted oligarchy for the Crown, where the eighteenth century was a time of bourgeois scepticism and Lockean social theory, and an appalling Industrial Revolution occurred. After that time, it was suggested, a live working class movement came into existence.

But today, certainly in the United Kingdom, there is revived intellectual conservatism. Instead of revolutions we have rebellions. In the eighteenth century we have persistent Anglicanism and Jacobitism. The Industrial Revolution is transformed into a mainly nineteenth-century change and democratic influences are not seen to become important until about 1830. These are the views of Jonathan Clark,[15] who deals only with British history; but more widely there are the revisionists who see the French Revolution as a delayer of social progress, the Russian Revolution as a social and economic disaster, the Habsburg Empire as a bulwark of stability against narrow micro-nationalism. Looking back on the postwar world we see how misplaced may be faith in democratic collectivism.

Yet so far the essence of Ireland's version of Whig history remains untouched. Separatism is still assumed to have been a worthwhile goal.

---

15. J.C.D. Clark, *English Society 1688–1832*, Cambridge, 1985; *Revolution and Rebellion*, Cambridge, 1986.

However, Jonathan Clark is apparently making a study of seventeenth- and eighteenth-century history, of which one theme will be that mainstream United Kingdom history is unintelligible without a British Isles focus. *A fortiori* the histories of Ireland, Scotland and Wales are unintelligible on their own. Yet so far there has been no full-scale history with the conservative theme that the political fragmentation of the British Isles was a disaster for both parts of Ireland, and that the United Kingdom, a kind of mini-Habsburg Empire, an unreconstructed *ancien régime* of great diversity, was more tolerant of difference and more progressive in substance than any successor state could possibly be. Heslinga does not draw this conclusion either, but his book starts a train of thought that ends with some such point of view.

It is a consequence of political fragmentation that scholars follow the new boundaries too obediently. There have apparently been 7000 studies of Northern Ireland during the past twenty years. The late John Whyte wrote a full analysis of the points of view they suggested.[16] The results are diverse and inconclusive, partly because the British Isles subsystem is downplayed in the interest of localism. Even more striking are the multitude of studies which relate to Ireland on its own. By definition they cannot deal with the bi-insular dimension where that is relevant. F.S.L. Lyons's *Culture and Anarchy in Ireland*[17] dealt with a variety of Irish traditions, but did not attempt to deal with the Anglo-American influences which Lyons himself said were dominant in Ireland. This fatal limitation may have been caused by the scholarly imperative to find manageable topics. But because political frontiers do not reflect cultural reality there is endless confusion about Irish identities among Irish writers. It is objectively true that without a British Isles dimension it is not possible to understand the values of either nationalists or unionists. Yet the British Isles dimension suffers a silence by default, encouraged by the conscious insularity of Dublin, and the less consistent insularity of London.

Ireland on its own cannot sustain massive cultural significance. In philosophy it is eccentric to suppose that there is a non-verbal Irish double vision which is an alternative to the entire world of Western reflection. In arguing this case Richard Kearney was bewitched by cultural insularity, and one wonders for instance whether he had thought about Christian mysticism, not least in the Low Countries, or about traditional Protestant double vision, expressed memorably in this century

---

16. J. Whyte, *Interpreting Northern Ireland*, Oxford, 1990.

17. F.S.L. Lyons, *Culture and Anarchy in Ireland 1890–1939*, Oxford, 1979.

by Reinhold Niebuhr. But similarly no valuable essence of Irishness was disclosed in the Irish Literary Renaissance. The imaginative talents of that generation are not in question, but their ideas are. It is not rational to treat Irish primitivism, localism and xenophobia with respect, not to speak of table-rapping or fairies or theosophy or sentimental Anglo-Irishry.

Wales provides an interesting comparison. Half a million native Welsh speakers survive, as against the 10,000 native Gaelic speakers in Ireland. Yet Gwyn Williams, historian and elegist of Wales, is more openly pessimistic about Welsh cultural survival than his Irish counterparts. He ends his book *When Was Wales* with a quotation from Yeats:

> I made my song a coat
> Covered with embroideries
> Out of old mythologies
> From heel to throat;
> But the fools caught it,
> Wore it in the world's eyes
> As though they'd wrought it.
> Song, let them take it,
> For there's more enterprise
> In walking naked.

Then Williams says:

> One thing I am sure of. Some kind of human society, though God knows what kind, will no doubt go on occupying these two western peninsulas of Britain, but that people, who are my people and no mean people, who have for a millennium and a half lived in them as a Welsh people, are now nothing but a naked people under an acid rain.[18]

This pessimism comes very strikingly from a polymath who has written on medieval London, on Gramsci, on Goya, and on popular movements in Britain and France during the French Revolution. His melancholy convinces because he knows his family's working class, Welsh speaking world has gone for ever. J.J. Lee is also melancholy but he cannot bring himself to face the facts.

Such Welsh and Irish melancholy results from defeat for a unique cultural identity. Cultural pluralists, even those with a strong Irish cultural identification, are in a position to be more buoyant. George

---

18. G. Williams, *When Was Wales: A History of the Welsh*, Penguin, 1985.

Watson, son, like poor Denis Donoghue, of a Catholic policeman in Northern Ireland, put it like this:

> Cannot an admiration for Irish cultural traditions co-exist with an admission of the relevance of the modern world? I learnt many useful things from my encounter with "Englishness": and, on balance, I would say the benefits outweighed the very real drawbacks: ethnic political resentment is a fact but so is a sense of cultural enlargement.[19]

But if we go further and accept, as rationally we must, that our environment is the entire British Isles, the Irish reader is free to think of Ireland as a region like the others. This releases him from the dreary limits of the Irish territorial imagination. The Dorset reader, for example, is free to like or dislike the work of William Barnes, the county's nineteenth-century poet; or he may be more attracted (say) to Ettrick's James Hogg or the Potteries' Arnold Bennett, or for that matter to Wexford's John Banville. In turn the bi-insular Irish reader is in no way obliged to follow ethnic or collective prescriptions. He too is free to value Barnes, Hogg, Bennett or Banville or Bloomsbury, or New England's Literary Renaissance or Dublin's or eighteenth-century Scotland's. He can accept or reject at will from a galaxy of minds across the English speaking world, including minds only accessible in translation. It is masochism to suppose that our intelligences and our imaginations are uniquely fed by people with Irish birth certificates; and even more self-destructive to treat the rest of the British Isles as alien.

Heslinga had an enviable gift for making rationality attractive to objectors. It would be in his spirit to sketch the broader perspectives which are available.

There is no imaginative compulsion to focus on Ireland. We live in a multi-cultural world and can choose our own identities. In Heslinga's spirit I have suggested that the most immediate environment in Ireland is the entire British Isles, whose newspapers we read, whose television we watch, and which we understand and share in more intimately than anywhere else. We cannot help belonging to the English speaking world and most of us must encounter other worlds in translation. Beyond the British Isles the same facts of social communication involve us in North America. United States hegemony is cultural as well as political, and everyone in the British Isles is under its umbrella.

---

19. G. Watson, "Cultural Imperialism: An Irish View", *Yale Review*, 1986.

It is true that there are large sub-cultures within the English speaking world. Canada and Australia are examples. But Australians do not need an ideology to justify having independent government. To some extent Canada does, in its resistance to the United States, but the larger justification for Canadianism is the size of the country, the distinctive lives of its provinces, and its more collective governmental mode than that of the USA.

Nationalist Ireland's problem is that it is trying to invent a full-scale culture to shore up political separatism. In today's world that is a ridiculous ambition. To solve the problem by stressing European-ness is unreal for a monoglot English speaking island. The enlivening alternative is to face up, after all this time, to being varieties of Briton, and within that not English, Scottish, Welsh, but varieties of Irish, although Irish as minor variants rather than as isolated societies. Before Garret FitzGerald succumbed to the coerciveness and insularism of the Anglo-Irish Agreement he used to hint that his preferred model would be a confederal Ireland, with two heads of state, evidently the Queen and the President of Ireland. The notion was fanciful but it had imaginative power.

This enrichment is understood by some modern writers who bridge the two islands. Among modern novelists I think of William Trevor, J.G.Farrell, Patrick O'Brian, Anthony Powell and of course Iris Murdoch. With luck the historian Jonathan Clark may soon give us a right-wing update of Macaulay, the classic historian of the British Isles.

One theorist about these broader perspectives of British history is J.G.A. Pocock,[20] a New Zealander who taught at Christchurch, but is now in the United States. Metaphors are needed for the interrelationships of the British Isles, and Pocock's background is a reminder that you can take one from the South Island of New Zealand. Naturally the New Zealand archipelago had been discovered and named by Tasman and the Dutch East India Company but there is a River Avon at Christchurch, whose name is Celtic and English. There are St Asaph Streets, Gloucester Streets, and Hereford Streets, Armagh Streets and Cashel Streets, which speak for Wales, England and Ireland. Beside the river there is an Oxford Terrace and a Cambridge Terrace. The city is named after Christchurch College, Oxford, which was attended by the initiator of the city, J.R. Godley, an Anglican from Killegar, County Leitrim. It was at Christchurch that the Viennese Karl Popper wrote his *Open Society and Its Enemies*, which so greatly influenced an intellectual

---

20. J.G.A. Pocock, *The Scope and Limits of British History*, Institute for the Study of Public Policy, University of Strathclyde, 1979.

generation. Further south there is Dunedin, which originates from Presbyterian Scotland. In Queenstown there is, very properly, an Antrim Arms Hotel. At one point in the nineteenth century there were proposals to call South Island New Leinster. In its origins South Island settlement reflected the reality of the British Isles as a society. That society is as alive as ever but in a more multicultural North West Atlantic form.

Professor Marcus Heslinga lifts us to these broader perspectives by his cool empirical survey. His book must be a classic of Dutch scholarship, penetration and integrity. It is also a dazzling linguistic feat to have written such beautiful academic English. Anyone interested in the tangled relationships of the British Isles is deeply in his debt.

AN ENGLISH ORIENTALIST IN IRELAND:
CHARLES VALLANCEY (1726–1812)

CLARE O'HALLORAN

Irish historical writing in the late eighteenth century is renowned for its romanticism and its concern for traditional accounts of the Irish past, and particularly the pre-colonial period. It is seldom if ever noted for its contribution to historical scholarship, but rather seen as one of the major influences on the Irish novel from Edgeworth on. In accounts of the influence of this material, Charles Vallancey often figures as a colourful representative of this "inventive" school of writing.[1] This article is taken from a larger study which examines eighteenth-century Irish antiquarian and historical writing in terms not only of its Irish political context, but also the wider European cultural debates which informed it.[2] From these vantage points, Charles Vallancey can be shown to be a more complex and ambiguous figure than the traditional characterization allows. Reassessment of Vallancey began over ten years ago with Norman Vance's seminal article "Celts, Carthaginians and Constitutions", and was significantly advanced by Joep Leerssen in a major and, in Ireland at least, too-little-known essay on Irish origin myths which appeared in *Comparative Criticism* in 1986.[3] What follows is a further contribution to that reassessment, and also a commentary on the picture drawn thus far.

1. J.C. Beckett, "Introduction", *New History of Ireland*, eds T.W. Moody and W.E. Vaughan, Oxford, 1986, IV, lxii.

2. Clare O'Halloran, "Golden Ages and Barbarous Nations: Antiquarian Debate on the Celtic Past in Ireland and Scotland in the Eighteenth Century" (unpublished PhD thesis, University of Cambridge, 1991).

3. Norman Vance, "Celts, Carthaginians and Constitutions: Anglo-Irish Literary Relations, 1780–1820", *Irish Historical Studies*, XXII (1981), 216–38; J.Th. Leerssen, "On the Edge of Europe: Ireland in Search of Oriental Roots, 1650–1850", *Comparative Criticism*, VIII (1986), 91–112.

Charles Vallancey was born in Flanders in 1726 to French Huguenot parents who moved to England when he was a child. Educated at Eton and the Royal Military Academy, he was commissioned as an ensign in the Tenth Regiment in 1747 and came to Ireland in 1750 as an officer of the Engineers, eventually attaining the rank of general and the position of Chief Engineer in Ireland. His military survey work resulted in an ambitious, but unfinished, one-inch map of the whole kingdom, but he was also responsible for designing the fortifications in Cork harbour in the 1780s and for drawing up a scheme for the defence of Dublin in 1798.[4] In the tumultuous 1790s he was commander of the forts in Cork harbour and, following the arrival of the French forces at Bantry Bay, was able to claim that his defences had deterred them from attempting to land at Cork. Similarly, J.H. Andrews speculates that Vallancey's one-inch map was probably the main cartographical aid used by the army commander-in-chief when news of the 1798 French landing reached Dublin.[5] The nature and importance of his military work needs to be kept clearly in view when Vallancey's antiquarian endeavours are considered.

Indeed, his interest in the language and antiquities of Ireland was first stimulated by his survey work, which caused him to visit "the most unfrequented recesses of Ireland", although many of the place names which featured on his maps show that his grasp of the Irish language was poor.[6] In spite of this, in 1772 Vallancey wrote in great excitement to the acclaimed Gaelic scholar and antiquary, Charles O'Conor, of an "extraordinary discovery" he had just made, involving the allegedly Carthaginian speech in Plautus' comedy, *Poenulus*, which he alleged, "was as good Irish as can possibly be written in my humble opinion, spoken by an illiterate Carthaginian, transcribed by an ignorant soldier (such is the Interpreter Plautus introduces) and on Classic Ground".[7] The Carthaginian or Punic speech in this play had fascinated scholars and philologists on the continent since the time of Scaliger. In *Geographiae sacrae*, published in 1646, the French scholar, Samuel Bochart, had

---

4. J.H. Andrews, "Charles Vallancey and the Map of Ireland", *Geographical Journal*, CXXXII (1966), 48-50; *Dictionary of National Biography* s.n.

5. Andrews, "Charles Vallancey and the Map of Ireland", 58-59.

6. John Warburton *et al.*, *History of the City of Dublin from the Earliest Accounts to the Present Time*, 2 vols, London, 1818, II, 918-19; Andrews, "Charles Vallancey and the Map of Ireland", 56.

7. Charles Vallancey to Charles O'Conor, 25 Apr. 1772, Dublin, Royal Irish Academy (RIA), ms. B1.2.

argued that the speech was closely related to Hebrew.[8] Vallancey called Bochart a "great orientalist", but believed he had missed a vital link in the development of primitive languages through his ignorance of Irish.[9] Vallancey was not the first to see parallels between Gaelic and this speech from Plautus. The scholar Tadhg Ó Neachtáin had made an Irish rendition, known to the late eighteenth-century scribe, Theophilus O'Flanagan, who wrote a description on the inside cover of Ó Neachtáin's manuscript, giving the Punic translation special mention and dating it to 1739.[10] Since O'Flanagan was engaged by Vallancey to copy and translate manuscripts, it is probable that the latter was also aware of Ó Neachtáin's work and claimed it as his own discovery.

Much of the existing analysis of Vallancey concentrates on his first publication, the *Essay on the Irish Language* published in 1772, which announced his discovery of Irish–Phoenician links. The *Essay* argued for the "strongest Affinity, (nay a perfect Identity in very many Words)" between Gaelic and "the Celtic, Punic, Phoenician and Hebrew Languages" and declared it to be "a Punic-Celtic Compound" and "the most copious language extant". Thus, Gaelic was "a Language of the utmost Importance, and most desirable to be acquired by all Antiquarians and Etymologists".[11] Vallancey's claims for the eastern origin of Gaelic placed him with native Irish historians, such as Charles O'Conor and Sylvester O'Halloran, who sought to uphold the traditional account of a colonization by a people, known as Milesians, who journeyed to Ireland via Egypt and Spain and who introduced a glorious civilization into Ireland which lasted from about 1000 BC until the Anglo-Norman invasion in the twelfth century.[12] Vallancey also actively sought to identify with this group by denying his English origins in the preface to the *Essay*, referring to himself in an offhand way as "an Irish man but little skilled in Hebrew".[13] Although the *Essay* came out anonymously,

---

8. For the history of this scholarship, see Maurice Sznycer, *Les passages puniques et transcription latine dans le "Poenulus" de Plaute*, Paris, 1967, 11–14.

9. Vallancey to O'Conor, 14 May 1772, RIA, ms. B1.2.

10. Dublin, National Library of Ireland, ms. G135, 39–40.

11. Charles Vallancey, *An Essay on the Antiquity of the Irish Language: Being a Collation of Irish with the Punic Language*, Dublin, 1772, 1–2.

12. Charles O'Conor, *Dissertations on the History of Ireland*, Dublin, 1766; Sylvester O'Halloran, *Introduction to the Study of the History and Antiquities of Ireland*, London, 1772.

13. Vallancey, *Essay*, viii.

he signed the preface with his initials, which hardly indicated a serious desire to hide his true identity.

The result of Vallancey's self-presentation was that he was perceived to be an adherent of the native Irish or Catholic viewpoint. The English antiquary, Michael Lort, writing in 1784 to Thomas Percy, then Bishop of Dromore in Co. Down, linked Vallancey's antiquarian and philological work with hopes for greater political freedom:

> In my travels on the continent last year, I fell in with many Irish officers, ecclesiastics and others, who seemed big with expectation of their island recovering that independence and pre-eminence which it once had, as they supposed, over its sister island. To what do Vallancey's researches tend, but to prove [Ireland] is the elder sister?[14]

More recent commentators, Norman Vance and Joep Leerssen, have seen a similar political programme behind Vallancey's eccentric theories. In his article on what he terms the "Gaelo–Phoenicianism" of which Vallancey was the leading proponent, Leerssen points to its "undeniable political dimension" and focuses on a striking short passage in Vallancey's *Essay* for proof. Writing of the scarcity of manuscript materials for Irish history, Vallancey made a parallel between the Irish and Carthaginians, following the sacking of Carthage by the Romans:

> Almost all the Carthaginian Manuscripts were committed to the flames, and the History of this brave and learned People, has been written by their most bitter Enemies, the Greeks and Romans; in this too they resemble the Irish ....[15]

Leerssen rightly points to what he terms "The explosiveness of an equation between Irish–English and Carthaginian–Roman relations [which] could be lost on no one", and he places Vallancey and his theories squarely on the "Patriot" side of the Irish political spectrum, represented by Grattan and other opposition politicians who campaigned for an independent Irish parliament, and, with varying degrees of enthusiasm, for a relaxation of the penal laws against Catholics.[16] For

---

14. Michael Lort to Thomas Percy, 19 Aug. 1784, in John Nichols, *Illustrations of the Literary History of the Eighteenth Century*, 8 vols, London, 1817–58, VII, 465–66.

15. Vallancey, *Essay*, 3.

16. Leerssen, "On the Edge of Europe", 100–102.

Norman Vance, however, Vallancey had "an oddly touching romantic patriotism for a country not his own", and was spellbound by the Celtic past. Vallancey, according to this characterization, was "quite unconscious of any tension between his official position with the army which supported the English domination of Ireland and his imaginative sympathy with the old Ireland before the coming of the invader".[17] Both of these somewhat contradictory positions echo the contemporary perceptions of Vallancey as, on the one hand, champion of the Catholic Irish but also as Celtomaniac or dreamer. At the same time, Leerssen has broadened our understanding of Vallancey by showing that, far from being an idiosyncratic fantasist, his ideas were representative of an important strand of early linguistic speculation in Europe. Similarly, an examination of Vallancey's politics reveals ambiguities and evasions which undermine the notion of him as defender of Catholic liberties, but also helps to explain the development of his research and writing.

References to Carthage and Carthaginians also occur in three later works by Vallancey, but are not employed in a consistent way. In an essay published in 1783, he made brief allusion to the Nemedians, one of older tribes on the island, suffering "the yoke of the Carthaginians".[18] In the following year in a work entitled *Vindication of the Ancient History of Ireland*, he wrote of the sufferings of the inhabitants of Ireland while under "the Carthaginian yoke of slavery".[19] Thus, some twelve to fourteen years after he first made the first analogy between Carthage and Ireland under imperial domination, Vallancey was actively undermining it by linking the Carthaginians with the same tyrannical practices as the Romans. Twenty years later, he again used the Carthaginian–Irish trope, in the *Prospectus of a Dictionary of the Language of the Aire Coti: Or, Ancient Irish, Compared with the Language of the Cuti, or Ancient Persians* (1802), giving it a similar political meaning as the first time he used it.[20] The reasons for Vallancey's temporary abandonment of the Carthaginian–Irish analogy in the fraught political atmosphere of the 1780s may lie precisely in its explosive nature and his consequent unease at its use. Moreover, even in his early work, he openly expressed political views which were much

---

17. Vance, "Celts, Carthaginians and Constitutions", 226.

18. Vallancey, Preface, *Collectanea de Rebus Hibernicis*, III/12 [1783], lxxi.

19. Vallancey, *A Vindication of the Ancient History of Ireland*, Dublin, 1786, reprinted in *Collectanea de Rebus Hibernicis*, IV/14 [1786], xi–xii.

20. Vallancey, *Prospectus of a Dictionary of the Language of the Aire Coti*, Dublin, 1802, lii–liii.

closer to orthodox Protestant opinion than Catholic. This was particularly apparent in his second book, the *Grammar of the Iberno-Celtic, or Irish Language*, which came out in 1773, and for which he received much assistance from Charles O'Conor, and the scribe Maurice O'Gorman, who was later employed by the Royal Irish Academy. Their influence and the technical nature of the project, meant that Vallancey had less space to indulge in his theories, and the result was the most useful of the books which came out under his name.[21]

Leerssen sees Vallancey's *Grammar* as "the first ... by a member of the Ascendancy to be published without being inspired by motives of proselytization".[22] But in the preface, Vallancey censured the Protestant clergy for "their neglect of learning of the Irish tongue, which is the only language understood by one half of their parishioners, and the only language in which they will receive instruction". Alluding to the efforts of Ussher, Bedell and Robert Boyle in the previous century to provide Irish language versions of the Old and New Testaments, which might "induce the Irish, to consider a little better of the old and true way, from whence they have hitherto been misled", Vallancey launched an impassioned and pious appeal for a new Protestant crusade with the rhetorical questions: "Shall one million inhabitants of this unhappy country be deprived of reading the scriptures, and judging for themselves? Is there no bishop Bedell, no Robert Boyle left among us?"[23] This call for a renewed campaign of proselytization through Irish may be interpreted as a cynical attempt to ensure the sale of the *Grammar* to the widest possible market. However, there is some evidence that Vallancey did actually support such a campaign, and did not hold to the idea of even limited religious toleration for Catholics. Among the papers of Thomas Orde, chief secretary in Dublin Castle from 1784 to 1787, who formulated a proposal for a national education scheme, there is a note by Vallancey on the education of Irish Catholics, advocating a government strategy to deny them access, ultimately, to

---

21. Brian O Cuív, "Irish Language and Literature, 1691–1845", *New History of Ireland*, IV/416.

22. Leerssen, *Mere Irish and Fíor-Ghael*, Amsterdam and Philadelphia, 1986, 427. See also Id., "Antiquarian Research: Patriotism to Nationalism", in *Talamh an Eisc: Canadian and Irish Essays*, eds C. Byrne and M. Harry, Halifax, Nova Scotia, 1986, 79.

23. Vallancey, *A Grammar of the Iberno-Celtic, or Irish Language*, Dublin, 1773, xxix–xxxi (*recte* xxi–xxiii).

any, unless they converted to the Established Church.[24] Thus, Vallancey's sentimental attachment to a country not his own, did not, evidently, extend to its majority religious community. This was by no means uncommon in Ireland, where elite interest in the surviving Gaelic culture, one of the stages in the rediscovery of popular culture which Peter Burke has identified, was severely limited and usually confined to past rather than contemporary manifestations.[25]

At one level, Vallancey's antiquarian work in the 1780s can be seen as an intensification of the strain of fanciful speculation which was evident in the earlier *Essay* and *Grammar*, and which, it may be argued, by accident rather than design, led him far from the concerns of Catholic writers such as O'Conor. However, that is to ignore some evidence that he made a conscious attempt to distance himself from those writers; he insisted that he was "of no party", and that his researches had nothing to do with Catholic antiquarian projects.[26] In essays written in 1782 and 1783 and published in his own journal, the *Collectanea de Rebus Hibernicis*, he himself raised the charge that in seeking connections between Irish and the languages of the Orient, he had been "yielding too much to the ancient historians of Ireland", commenting that "It is now the general voice to condemn these writings as fabulous, and to deprive the Irish of ... their favourite Asiatick origin". However, in defence of his origin theories he quoted copiously, not from Irish sources, but rather from the English orientalist, John Richardson's *Dissertation on the Languages, Literature, and Manners of Eastern Nations* (1777), which, among other things, made Tartary the "great *Officina gentium*, whence such myriads of barbarians have at different periods poured into the more cultivated regions of the Earth". He also cited Anquetil-Duperron's *Legislation orientale* (1778), and Sir William Jones's *The Mohammedan Law* (1782), and commented:

> Had these gentlemen studied to have given the picture of the Irish Brehon Laws, they could not have done it to greater perfection; and the pains they have taken to free the eastern nations from *barbarism* and *despotism*, by proving these people to have had a

---

24. Vallancey, note, n.s, n.d., c. 1787, NLI ms. 15,883 (15).

25. Peter Burke, *Popular Culture in Early Modern Europe*, London, 1978, 3–22.

26. Vallancey, "Preface", *Collectanea de Rebus Hibernicis*, III/12 [1783], cxxxvii–cxxxviii; Vallancey to Joseph C. Walker, 12 Apr. [?1800], Trinity College Dublin, ms. 1461(4), fol. 186.

written law, time immemorial, reflects honour on their humanity.[27]

Vallancey was visibly aligning himself with both the scholarly and political concerns of the major figures of what Raymond Schwab has called "the Oriental Renaissance" who in this period worked to recover and understand the Persian and Sanskrit languages from ancient manuscripts.[28] An awareness of the political liabilities associated with work on Irish antiquities, which were increasing in this decade of agrarian and political unrest,[29] made Vallancey anxious to relocate his topic, which he did by pushing the ostensible roots of Gaelic culture and pre-Christian religion further into the Orient, until his work bore virtually no relation to that of Charles O'Conor or earlier Irish writers, and was thus also distanced from their political agenda of civil rights for Catholics.

One of the main characteristics of Vallancey's often chaotic approach was a jackdaw-like appropriation of orientalist theories, and their application in an ill-digested way to Irish history. This is particularly true of the *Vindication of the Ancient History of Ireland*, published in 1786. In this, his longest and most ambitious work, the structure of the text collapsed, as he failed to control either his material or his thoughts, and information spilled over into vast notes, with annotations even to items in the index.[30] But the resultant literary mess should not blind us to the fact that behind it lay a great deal of reading and an awareness of the progress of scholarship in Europe and India, which few other Irish writers displayed. Furthermore, some of these theories came from respected sources, most notably from Sir William Jones who speculated in a loose way about the relationship between Celtic and the Persian and Sanskrit languages, in one instance noting a resemblance between Celtic ogham script and Persian runes.[31] Vallancey took this several stages further, as was his wont, and extrapolated from it definite racial and

---

27. Vallancey, "A Continuation of the Brehon Laws of Ireland", *Collectanea de Rebus Hibernicis*, III/10 [1782], vi–xii. In 1783 he also wrote, "I am of no party, have no system to support, but write for information", *ibid.*, 12 [1783], cxxxvii.

28. Schwab, *Oriental Renaissance*, New York, 1984, 11–20.

29. James Kelly, "The Genesis of 'Protestant Ascendancy': The Rightboy Disturbances of the 1780s and their Impact upon Protestant Opinion" in *Parliament, People and Politics*, ed. Gerard O'Brien, Dublin, 1989, 93–127.

30. Vallancey, *Vindication*, 462 ff. (not paginated).

31. Sir William Jones, *Works*, 13 vols, London, 1807, III, 123–24, 134–35.

cultural links between Ireland and India, citing "the great affinity of the old Irish with the Sanscrite or Hindostan language" as "a strong proof ... of the Brahmins deriving their origin from the Tuatha Dadann of Irish history ...".[32]

Vallancey sent a copy of the *Vindication* to Jones, who responded in a diplomatic vein, deeming it a "learned work" which he had read with pleasure, but added: "We shall soon I hope see faithful translations of Irish histories and poems. I shall be happy in comparing them with the Sanskrit, with which the ancient language of Ireland had certainly had an affinity."[33] The phrase "faithful translations" was a coded critique of Vallancey's project,[34] but Jones's letter was quoted in Dublin as evidence of the great orientalist's support for Vallancey's work.[35] Jones gave his honest estimation to a more intimate correspondent:

> Have you met with a book lately published with the title of a *Vindication of the ancient history of Ireland*? It was written by a friend of mine, Colonel Vallancey; but a word in your ear — it is very stupid .... Do you wish to laugh? Skim the book over. Do you wish to sleep? Read it regularly.[36]

However, a number of other orientalists, many of them employed by the East India Company, offered Vallancey definite encouragement to proceed in this direction. For example, Thomas Maurice adopted, albeit hesitantly, Vallancey's thesis about an Indo-Scythic migration to Ireland.[37] As Schwab has shown, orientalist scholarship was itself affected by colonial experience and was often conducted along political lines. Thus, Maurice was motivated by a fear of the seductiveness of Hindu religion as an alternative, and possibly older, system of belief to Christianity, and he enlisted Vallancey in his campaign to prove that

---

32. Vallancey, *Vindication*, 365.

33. Jones to Joseph Cooper Walker, 11 Sept. 1787, in *The Letters of Sir William Jones*, ed. G. Cannon, 2 vols, Oxford, 1970, II, 770-71.

34. *Ibid.*, 771n.

35. Joseph Cooper Walker to Lord Charlemont, 5 May 1788, R.I.A., ms. 12/R/15.

36. Jones to the second Earl Spencer, 10 Sept. 1787, in *Letters of Sir William Jones*, ed. Cannon, II, 768-69.

37. Thomas Maurice, *Sanscreet Fragments: Or Interesting Extracts from the Sacred Books of the Brahmins, on Subjects Important to the British Isles*, London, 1798, 8-9.

Hinduism was derived from biblical theology.[38] Frances Wilford also used information supplied by Vallancey, in an effort to show that "the white islands" of Hindu mythology were the British Isles, thus projecting the beginnings of Indo–British contact back into the remote past.[39] It seems appropriate that such questionable, and ultimately colonial, ideas about Indian civilization, which had echoes of English views of the Gaelic world in the sixteenth century, depended to some extent on the support of the dubious scholarship of an English army officer serving in Ireland.[40]

Thus, Vallancey constantly extended the Irish past *geographically* as far away from Ireland as possible, and tried to incorporate his work into the colonialist scholarship of the East India Company. Nevertheless, he continued to insist that his work was based on Gaelic manuscript sources and that he was a defender of Irish tradition, publishing *A Vindication of the Ancient History of Ireland* in 1786, and *A Further Vindication* in 1804. However, the tradition he defended was largely of his own creation. In 1784 he wrote to the English antiquary, Thomas Burgess, explaining that his conviction of the "perfect correspondence of the Irish with the Oriental tongues" had led him to defend the "ancient Irish History" and to produce "a new System of the History of the continent and of the Britannic Isles".[41] His phrase, "a new System", echoed the title of Jacob Bryant's monumental analysis of Greek mythology, *A New System: Or, An Analysis of Ancient Mythology*, which appeared between 1774 and 1776. Bryant's influence can first be seen in the second edition of Vallancey's *Grammar of the Iberno–Celtic*, published in 1781, which included an additional essay "shewing the importance of the Iberno–Celtic or Irish dialect, to students in history, antiquity, and the Greek and Roman classics". The dedication, which in the first edition had been to Sir Lucius O'Brien (at that time president of the Select Committee on Antiquities of the Dublin Society), was changed to "To Jacob Bryant, Esq.; author of an Analysis of Ancient Mythology and

---

38. Schwab, *Oriental Renaissance*, 339. Maurice, *A Dissertation on the Oriental Trinities*, London, 1801, 21–22, 287–91; Maurice included a piece by Vallancey, which alleged that the god Krishna was worshipped in early Ireland, in *Sanscreet Fragments*, 53–62.

39. Frances Wilford, "An Essay on the Sacred Isles in the West", *Asiatick Researches*, XI (1810), 132, 140.

40. Nicholas Canny, "The Ideology of English Colonisation: From Ireland to America", *William and Mary Quarterly*, XXX (1973), 575–98.

41. Vallancey to Thomas Burgess, 2 Jan. 1784, NLI, ms. 3,899.

several other learned works", a public indication of the trajectory of Vallancey's interest.[42]

In his *Analysis*, Bryant compared biblical history with certain Greek classical histories, in order to prove that the former was "most assuredly true" in every particular. Though wrong in much of the substance of his thesis, Bryant had a sophisticated view of mythology, which did not assess it wholly on the basis of either truth or fable, but saw it as growing organically from tribal memory. He set out

> to divest mythology of every foreign and unmeaning ornament; and to display the truth in its native simplicity: to shew, that all the rites and mysteries of the Gentiles were only so many memorials of their principal ancestors; and of the great occurrences, to which they had been witnesses.

This approach, reflected also in the phrase "It is to be observed, that when colonies make anywhere a settlement, they ingrafted their antecedent history upon the subsequent events of the place",[43] was adopted wholeheartedly by Vallancey in *A Vindication of the History of Ireland* (1786).

Without stating so directly, this *Vindication* was predicated on Geoffrey Keating's *Foras Feasa ar Éirinn* — the most influential seventeenth-century history of the pre-colonial period — underlining how this work, in its English translation, stood for the whole corpus of Irish medieval historiography, rather than being regarded as a relatively recent narrative account based on it.[44] However, Vallancey's defence of Keating's work was not founded on the argument that it was an accurate record of the remote Irish past, but rather the opposite: that its particulars related to the wanderings of the early tribes of Asia and the Middle East, who were the ancestors of the "ancient Irish".[45] Vallancey

---

42. Vallancey, *A Grammar of the Iberno–Celtic, or Irish Language: The Second Edition with Many Additions*, Dublin, 1781, dedication.

43. Jacob Bryant, *A New System, or, An Analysis of Ancient Mythology*, 3 vols, London, 1774–76, I, xii–xiii. On Bryant see Frank E. Manuel, *The Eighteenth Century Confronts the Gods*, Cambridge: Mass., 1959, 274–75.

44. Vallancey, *Vindication*, 23. The first English translation of Keating's work appeared in 1723: *The General History of Ireland, Translated by Dermod O'Connor*, London, 1723. For a scholarly translation see Geoffrey Keating, *Foras Feasa ar Éirinn: The History of Ireland*, eds and trs David Comyn and P.S. Dineen, 4 vols, Dublin, 1902–14.

45. Vallancey, *Vindication*, xlvi.

ascribed previous misguided attempts to historicize purely mythic elements, which had led to a "general disgust" with traditional accounts, to "the ignorance of the Translators, who, zealous for the antiquity of their Country, did not, or would not see, that the early periods of this History, related not to Ireland, but to those parts of Asia their Ancestors came from". These translators had misunderstood the term "Eirin", taking it to mean Ireland, when it really referred to Iran or Persia.[46] Thus, what was "improperly called the ancient history of Ireland" was in fact a compendium of the "fabulous history", or myths, of the "ancient Persians", narrating "a chain of historical events, (whether real or fabulous, I do not pretend to determine) which illustrate the early part of Persian history, and prove that both the Persian and the Irish ... anecdotes, must have been handed to us by one and the same people".[47] Though wrong in all respects, Vallancey's radical re-reading of Keating nevertheless introduced a new and major concept into Irish historical discourse which had hitherto revolved around the oppositional ideas of truth and fable, the twin poles of European rationalist thinking in this field.[48] In advocating the appreciation of myth as an important field of study, Vallancey was in the vanguard in Ireland of reaction against Enlightenment thinking in this area. Since the scientific revolution of the seventeenth century, myths had been categorized among the "prejudices" that had to be swept away in order to make room for the methodological development and application of scientific knowledge.[49] Romanticism, particularly in Germany, reacted against this jettisoning of tradition, and against the unsatisfying incompleteness and tentativeness of science, and often called for "a new mythology" or a return to old myths.[50] Later Celtic scholars of some repute, such as H. d'Arbois de Jubainville in the late nineteenth century, and T.F. O'Rahilly in the 1940s, were to argue that the Irish origin legends contained in texts like the *Leabhar Gabhála*, a twelfth century compilation of earlier sources, were just such a repository of Indo-European mythology or of memories of the Celtic

---

46. *Ibid.*, 50, 170–71.

47. *Ibid.*, xlvi.

48. Burton Feldman and Robert D. Richardson, *The Rise of Modern Mythology, 1680–1860*, Bloomington: Indiana and London, 1972, 3–5.

49. Manuel, *The Eighteenth Century Confronts the Gods*, 147–48.

50. *Ibid.*, 283–87, 306–9; see also A. Leslie Willson, *A Mythical Image: The Ideal of India in German Romanticism*, Durham: NC, 1964.

migrations, although they would hardly have accepted Vallancey as a pioneering forebear in this respect.[51]

Thus, no matter how wrong-headed and fanciful Vallancey's work, it is no longer possible to depict him as simply eccentric or naive. While it has been established that his theories on the links between Irish and Carthaginian are part of contemporary linguistic speculation, he was also open to scholarly influences in Indic studies and mythology. Seen in these contexts, Vallancey emerges as no less colourful but perhaps more interesting a figure than before. This may not be enough to change the dominant view of Vallancey as a writer who, in the words of Seamus Deane, purveyed "absurd historical fictions with a serious purpose",[52] but it demonstrates that his motives and contexts were more complex than hitherto recognized. Vallancey's response to the Irish past was shaped primarily by his position as a British army officer charged with devising and implementing imperial defence policy in Ireland. While he may well have supported the "Patriot" position of Henry Grattan in regard to parliamentary independence, he was not an upholder of Catholic rights in any real sense, despite his friendship with Catholic antiquaries such as O'Conor and O'Halloran. In the heated political atmosphere of the 1780s and 1790s he deliberately detached himself from Irish antiquarianism as traditionally conceived. The trajectory of his writing mirrored his political journey, away from Ireland and into the ambit of British scholars in the East India Company, where he hoped to find kindred spirits.[53]

51. H. d'Arbois de Jubainville, *The Irish Mythological Cycle and Celtic Mythology*, Dublin, 1903; T.F. O'Rahilly, *Early Irish History and Mythology*, Dublin, 1946. For a recent interpretation of the *Leabhar Gabhála*, see R.M. Scowcroft, "'Leabhar Gabhála', part 1: The Growth of the Text; part 2: The Growth of the Tradition", *Eriu*, XXXVIII-XXXIX (1987-88), 81-140, 1-66.

52. Seamus Deane, "Irish National Character, 1790-1900", in *The Writer as Witness*, ed. T. Dunne, Cork, 1987, 94.

53. I am grateful to Tom Dunne, Máire Herbert, Joep Leerssen and Norman Vance for help and encouragement, and to the Fellows of Clare Hall, Cambridge for funding to attend the Leiden conference at which this paper was originally delivered.

ARCHAEOLOGY AND THE IDEOLOGY OF COLONY AND NATION: THE CASE OF NEW GRANGE

NORMAN VANCE

In the Boyne valley not far from Drogheda in Co. Meath, at a place now called New Grange, there is a great burial mound containing a decorated megalithic passage-grave. Similar mounds have been found close by, at Knowth and Dowth. These have been seen as a puzzle or a potent mystery since early Celtic times. Antiquarian discussion of them, and literary allusion to them, provide a unique opportunity to inspect the evolution of contending attitudes towards the Irish past and Irish identity as colony and nation.

The story starts with the tales of the so-called Irish Mythological Cycle, which seem to have acquired their present form in the eighth century. Echu Ollathir, otherwise known as the Dagdae, the Good God, was chief of the pagan gods, a famous king of the Tuatha De Danaan who performed miracles and saw to the weather and the harvest. In the narrative of "The Wooing of Étain" we learn that the Dagdae seduced Boann, wife of Elcmar of Bruig na Bóinne.

Bruig na Bóinne, the dwelling on the Boyne, is now generally identified as the mound of New Grange (thanks to William Wilde, Oscar's father).[1] The union of the Dagdae and Boann produced the great Angus Mac Oc, well-skilled in magic arts, who by a very Irish combination of calculated violence and legal chicanery took over Bruig na Bóinne for a day and a night and then claimed successfully that this meant for all time, since day and night make up all time.[2] Douglas Hyde, writing in 1899, records that "down to the present century" Angus

---

1. William Wilde, *The Beauties of the Boyne*, Dublin, 1849, 188.

2. For a recent translation of "The Wooing of Etain" (*Tochmarc Etaine*) see *Early Irish Myths and Sagas*, tr. Jeffrey Gantz, Penguin, 1981, 39-59.

of the Boyne was "reverenced as the presiding genius of the spot".[3]
Bruig na Bóinne was renowned as a fairy palace of fabled hospitality
which could not be burned by fire or drowned by water or spoiled by
robbers.[4] Some legends suggest that the Dagdae and other kings of the
Tuatha De Danaan lie buried there and that the Boyne burial-mounds are
the fairy-mounds of the Sidhe, the location of the Celtic otherworld.[5]
The stories are persistent and very old, but the place is older still, and
its strange numinous potency is reflected in the magic with which Celtic
legend invests it.

For centuries the mystery and magic were undisturbed. The first
known archaeological investigation was undertaken by the Welsh Oxford-
based Celtic scholar and naturalist Edward Lhuyd in 1699–1700 in the
course of an extended tour of Scotland and Ireland. It seems likely that
Lhuyd intended to follow in the tradition of the Elizabethan topographer
William Camden: he had already revised the Welsh portion of Camden's
Britannia for the new 1695 edition and he planned a massive work on
early Celtic Britain to be called *Archaeologica Britannica*. Despite the
endeavours of the Tudor chroniclers and antiquarians and of Camden
himself there was still plenty of political as well as scholarly mileage in
developing and reinforcing the notion of an Irish, Scottish and Welsh as
well as English Britain. Resistance to William III in Ireland and Scotland
was after all a very recent memory. But only Lhuyd's first volume, a
comparative etymology of the Celtic languages, had been published
before his death in 1709. Fortunately the material on New Grange which
he collected for this work has survived.[6] In two published
communications and two unpublished letters Lhuyd speculated on the
significance of "the Mount of New Grange", tentatively concluding that

---

3. Douglas Hyde, *A Literary History of Ireland* [1899], London, 1967, 48. The
version retold by Lady Gregory suggests that Angus took Bruig na Bóinne from his
father the Dagda: see *Gods and Fighting Men*, London, 1904, 79.

4. These details come from the later romance "The Fairy Palace of the Quicken
Trees" (*Bruighean Caerthainn*) translated by P.W. Joyce in *Old Celtic Romances*,
3rd edn, London, 1914, 186 ff.

5. Bruig na Bóinne is described in the *Senchas na Relec* ("History of
Cemeteries") in a twelfth-century manuscript and in the *Dinnseanchas*
("Topography"), a later work, according to William Wilde, *The Beauties of the
Boyne*, 184.

6. There is an early transcript of Lhuyd's notes and drawings in British Library
Stowe MS 1024; for the New Grange drawings, see ff. 126–29.

"it was some Place of Sacrifice or Burial of the Ancient *Irish*".[7] Grasping at straws, because it was not quite like anything he had ever seen before and he may not have wanted to suggest Ireland had anything fundamentally different from the rest of Europe, he wrote to his friend Thomas Molyneux (a founder-member of the Dublin Philosophical Society and brother of the Irish constitutional theorist William Molyneux) that it was "not unlike the ruined monuments in Wormius' *Monumenta Danica*".[8]

This pioneering work, compiled by the polymath Danish professor of medicine Olaus Wormius in six books in 1643, was a much-misused resource for bemused antiquarians of the period.[9] Molyneux, himself a doctor who had studied at Leiden, was glad to take Lhuyd's hint. He prepared a *Discourse concerning the Danish Mounts, Forts, and Towers in Ireland* (Dublin, 1725), subsequently incorporated in his revised and expanded edition of Gerard Boate's *Natural History of Ireland*. Molyneux's essay leans heavily on Olaus Wormius and steals his best quotations. New Grange is used to develop an antiquarian onslaught on the "meere Irish" and their obviously ill-founded claim to ancient civility. Molyneux prefaces a detailed description of New Grange as a Danish sepulchre with the observation that if the ancient Irish really had been "that polite and well-govern'd nation their histories wou'd make us believe they were" there would be some lasting monuments to show for it. But "the oldest monuments of human industry" are the work of foreign invaders, the Danes or Vikings who arrived in the eighth or ninth century. Three mysterious basons in alcoves of the burial-chamber at New Grange are confidently described as shrines for Thor, Odin and Freya.[10] In an age innocent of chronology Molyneux can disregard the

---

7. Letter to Dr Tancred Robinson, 15th December 1699, published in *Transactions of the Royal Society*, XXVII (1712), 505. Lhuyd's other published account was a letter of March 1700 to Rev. Henry Rowlands of Anglesey published in Rowlands's *Mona Antiqua Restaurata*, Dublin, 1723.

8. Lhuyd to Molyneux, 1700, T.C.D. MS quoted in Michael Herity, "From Lhuyd to Coffey: New Information from Unpublished Descriptions of the Boyne Valley Tombs", *Studia Hibernica*, VII (1967), 127–45, esp. 129. I am much indebted to this article.

9. See Stewart Piggott, *Ancient Britons and the Antiquarian Imagination*, London, 1988, 97 ff., 104.

10. Thomas Molyneux, *A Discourse concerning the Danish Mounts, Forts, and Towers in Ireland*, Dublin, 1725, 190, 202; see Olaus Wormius, *Danicorum Monumentorum Libri Sex*, Copenhagen, 1643, Book I, Ch. 6 "De Sepulturis Veterum", 30–40, from which most of Molyneux's allusions come.

centuries, if not millennia, separating Olaus Wormius's Scandinavian burial mounds from the Vikings' arrival in Ireland.

It is tempting to think that this historically dubious attack on the ancient Irish is all that one could expect of the great-grandson of Queen Elizabeth's Chancellor of the Exchequer for Ireland. It participates in a colonial discourse which can be traced back to Tudor polemic and was renewed in 1685 when the Englishman Edward Stillingfleet, later Bishop of Worcester, had provocatively set the agenda for the next century for patriotic Irish antiquarians by denying there was any Irish literature before St Patrick.[11]

But colonialist arrogance and the quest for truth are not necessarily incompatible. As a doctor and key-member of the Dublin Philosophical Society Molyneux had some claims to be a man of science. Molyneux had in his sights the extravagantly self-aggrandizing Irish traditions represented by the *Lebor Gabála* or *Book of Invasions*, the substance of which had been incorporated into the early part of Geoffrey Keating's popular *Forais Feasa ar Éireann* or *Origins of Irish History* half a century before. Molyneux ridiculed the derivation of the Irish from Magog son of Japhet son of Noah, and the "fable of a niece of Noah himself landing in this island", which probably alludes to Edmund Campion's slightly inaccurate account (1571) of the legend of the antediluvian Irish expedition of Noah's grand-daughter Cesara or Cesair with three men and fifty maidens.[12] Such traditions might seem soft targets, but they were still being retailed half a century later.[13]

Half a century later in the history of New Grange, in 1770, the site was visited by Thomas Pownall, sometime Governor of Massachusetts, a friend of Benjamin Franklin's and like Franklin a man with vigorous views about everything. He wrote extensively about economics, colonial administration and antiquities, the common factor being a concern with the spread and development of civil government. He had had first-hand experience of native Americans, if not the native Irish, and was to report

---

11. Edward Stillingfleet, *Origines Britannicae: Or, The Antiquities of the British Churches* (1685), discussed by Norman Vance in *Irish Literature: A Social History*, Oxford, 1990, 68.

12. The ultimate source for Cesair is the *Leabhar Gabhala: The Book of Conquests of Ireland*, trans. R.A. Stewart Macalister and John MacNeill, Dublin, 1916, 9; Molyneux probably encountered her as Cesara in Campion's *Historie of Ireland* (1571) which is incorporated in Holinshed's *Chronicles* (1577) and Sir James Ware's much-consulted *Historie of Ireland* (1633): see D.C. Allen, *The Legend of Noah* [1949], Urbana: Ill., 1963, 118.

13. See, for example, James Parsons, *Remains of Japhet* (1767), x, xiv, 265 ff.

in 1778 that "The mutual feelings of humanity, which have set bounds
to ravage, desolation, and bloodshed among civilized peoples, are totally
absorbed by an unrestrained effusion of the passions of revenge,
bloodthirstyness, and carnage, even to extermination among the
American savages".[14] This linkage of humanity, civilization and colonial
enterprise, and its correlative that lack of colonial development entails
inhumanity and barbarism, made Pownall naturally doubtful about the
native Irish and sympathetic to Molyneux's Danish hypothesis about New
Grange. But he introduced a bizarre refinement by noticing that the
structure incorporated a large, flat, incised stone the markings on which
were neither Irish nor Runic nor Saxon. He concluded that they must be
Phoenician and that the stone was a unique Phoenician coastal memorial
which the Danes had dragged up-river and pressed into service. An
appendix considered the technical problem of transporting megaliths in
some detail.[15]

Phoenician fantasies, common elsewhere at this time and subsequently
because there were no written records to disprove (or prove) anything,
could either be used to vindicate the ancient dignity of the Irish or
adapted into a more refined version of the colonialist dogma that anything
good in the colony must have come from outside. Pownall chooses the
latter course and audaciously suggests that the Phoenician enterprise was
like that of the British East India company and included an element of
cultural and religious outreach comparable, for instance, to the Jesuit
endeavours in Paraguay, so that their enduring legacy to Ireland was the
pagan religious system associated with the Tuatha De Danaan and the
druids.[16] Not surprisingly Pownall's Phoenician-hunting friend Charles
Vallancey turned this to good account and argued on dubious philological
grounds that New Grange meant the cave or den of *Grian*, that is

---

14. *Gentleman's Magazine*, XLVIII (1778), 611, quoted in P.J. Marshall and
Glyndwr Williams, *The Great Map of Mankind*, London, 1982, 218. See also G.H.
Guttridge, "Thomas Pownall's *The Administration of the Colonies*: The Six
Editions", *William and Mary Quarterly*, 3rd series, XXVI (Jan. 1969), 31–46 and
John A. Schutz, *Thomas Pownall: British Defender of American Liberty*, Glendale:
Calif., 1951.

15. Thomas Pownall, "A Description of the Sepulchral Monument at New
Grange", *Archaeologia*, II (1773), 236–75.

16. Pownall, "Description", 243.

Mithras or the Sun.[17] He may have been partly right for the wrong reasons, as we shall see.

It is interesting to compare this with some of the nineteenth-century accounts of the ruins of Great Zimbabwe in what used to be called Mashonaland or Rhodesia. These great stone buildings implied a settled and technically accomplished civilization which was not obviously continuous with the mode of life of the surrounding indigenous population. It seemed to satisfy common sense as well as colonial ideology to attribute such building to an earlier, prehistoric race of colonists.[18] But who? The Phoenicians, inevitably, were candidates. Perhaps Mashonaland had been part of some ancient Semitic empire? Just as Molyneux and Pownall had grasped at Wormius's Danish straws so nineteenth-century archaeologists grasped at unscientific sixteenth-century Portuguese speculation. The Portuguese had found ancient mine-workings as well as impressive ruins: perhaps this was the biblical land of Ophir from which gold and precious stones were taken by Hiram King of Tyre and the Queen of Sheba (Ethiopia)?[19] Investigators of Great Zimbabwe were particularly impressed by the sophistication of an astronomically oriented temple apparently used for worshipping the sun.[20]

This strangely recalls Vallancey's zany imputation of Mithraic sun-worship at New Grange. The nineteenth-century surveyors of Great Zimbabwe were technically as well as intellectually closer to the modern archaeology which has been applied to New Grange than to eighteenth-century antiquarianism. Brendan Purcell for one, building on the discoveries of M.V. O'Kelly in 1969, has reported recently on the intricate solar alignments of the Boyne valley burial mounds, including New Grange, which suggest that sun-worship, or at least ritual

17. Charles Vallancey, *A Vindication of the Ancient History of Ireland*, Dublin, 1786, 211.

18. One of the most influential accounts was J.T. Bent, *The Ruined Cities of Mashonaland, Being a Record of Excavation and Exploration in 1891* (1892), 3rd edn, London, 1895.

19. See David Chanaiwa, *The Zimbabwe Controversy: A Case of Colonial Historiography*, Eastern African Studies VIII, Syracuse: NY, 1973, 66–71.

20. See R.W.M. Swan, "On the Orientation and Measurements of Zimbabwe Ruins", in J.T. Bent's *Ruined Cities*, 141–78.

acknowledgement of the winter solstice, was indeed part of the mystery of the place, though not in the Mithraic form posited by Vallancey.[21]

The eighteenth-century antiquarians, like the nineteenth-century archaeologists in southern Africa, are now remembered only for being wrong,[22] though such wrong ideas represent significant episodes in cultural history. It is now an article of faith in Zimbabwe that the great ruins from which the post-colonial state has taken its name are of indigenous and comparatively recent origin, a faith all the easier to hold because it was officially frowned on by Iain Smith's government.

But the situation is less straightforward in Ireland where it has come to be recognized that the colonial paradigm is of limited value in understanding an intricately pluralist cultural history. Archaeology in nineteenth-century Ireland, unlike Mashonaland, combined and fused into a national discourse colonialist and nativist, British and Irish elements, a fusion signalled in the English-descended William Wilde's dedication of *The Beauties of the Boyne* to his fellow-antiquarians the Irish-descended John O'Donovan and the Scots-descended George Petrie. Investigations by both Petrie and O'Donovan had been incorporated into Wilde's account of New Grange, from which modern investigations have proceeded. The aggressively colonialist archaeology of New Grange was discredited by Wilde and his successors but there was no neat post-colonialist myth to replace it. It is now accepted that New Grange is very much older than the Vikings and indeed the Phoenicians. But it has not been unequivocally restored to pre-colonial Celtic Ireland: it is agreed that it is the work of a pre-Celtic people settled in the area some time in the third millennium BC. Celtic tradition annexed but did not inaugurate the mystery and majesty of New Grange. The annexation in a sense continues. Some modern art historians see in the spiral motifs decorating the stones of New Grange an early influence upon Celtic art.[23] Máirtín Ó Cadhain, a distinguished twentieth-century novelist and short-story writer in the Irish language, has reflected that "In dealing with Irish I feel I am as old as New Grange, the old hag of Beare, the great Elk".[24]

21. Brendan Purcell, "In Search of Newgrange: Long Night's Journey into Day", in *The Irish Mind: Exploring Intellectual Traditions*, ed. Richard Kearney, Dublin, 1985, 39–55.

22. See the highly polemical post-colonial accounts by David Chanaiwa, cited above, and Peter Garlake, *Great Zimbabwe Described and Explained*, Harare, 1985.

23. See Bruce Arnold, *A Concise History of Irish Art*, London, 1977, 10.

24. Quoted in Proinsias MacCana, *Literature in Irish*, Dublin, Department of Foreign Affairs, 1980, 61.

He speaks of two thousand years of Irish tradition, but New Grange is at least twice as old as that.

In the poem "Funeral Rites" (in *North*) the more generous contemporary imagination of Seamus Heaney has annexed the numinous mystery of New Grange, "the great chambers of Boyne", as a locus of communal mourning for endemic violence, a place where bitterness and murder might be transformed into beauty and peace.[25] The Boyne valley contains both the burial-place of the Dagdae and the holy place of Irish protestantism, the site of the Williamite victory of 1690 where Governor Pownall had paid his respects in 1770. It was also the home of the soldier-poet Francis Ledwidge, killed in 1917 in the First World War, often regarded in Ireland as England's war. Heaney imagines the shade of Ledwidge accompanied by "silence cored from a Boyne passage-grave". The scourge of division and slaughter in Ireland reaches back through Orangemen and Vikings and Celts, "Though all of you consort now underground".[26] New Grange is older than anything in Ireland's harsh recorded history, and so can stand perhaps as a token of Ireland's better future.

---

25. Seamus Heaney, *North*, London, 1975, 16.

26. Seamus Heaney, "In Memoriam Francis Ledwidge", in *Field Work*, London, 1979, 60.

THE POLITICS AND POETICS OF NATIONALIST HISTORIOGRAPHY: MATHEW CAREY AND THE *VINDICIAE HIBERNICAE*

MARTIN J. BURKE

This essay is part of a larger, ongoing project on the writing of Irish history in America; and the work that is its topic, the *Vindiciae Hibernicae: Or, Ireland Vindicated* of Mathew Carey, is one in which a number of the themes of this conference intersect.[1] Carey's was a pervasive presence in the politics of American literature and the literature of American politics during the late eighteenth and early nineteenth centuries. He was a major force in the development of a self-consciously republican literary culture; and he was an important participant in debates on public policy and political economy.[2] With the publication of the *Vindiciae Hibernicae* in 1819, Carey joined once more in the attempt to

---

1. Mathew Carey, *Vindiciae Hibernicae: Or, Ireland Vindicated*, Philadelphia, 1819. Carey subsequently issued two revised and "improved" editions of the text, in 1826 and 1837.

2. Recent scholarship on Carey and his career includes Alan Axelrod, "Mathew Carey", in *American Writers of the Early Republic*, ed. E. Elliott, Detroit, 1985, 89–95; James Green, "Mathew Carey", in *American Magazine Journalists, 1741–1850*, ed. S.G. Riley, Detroit, 1988, 50–66; James Green, *Mathew Carey: Publisher and Patriot*, Philadelphia, 1985; William Clarkin, *Mathew Carey: A Bibliography of his Publications, 1785–1824*, New York, 1984; Edward C. Carter, "The Political Activities of Mathew Carey, Nationalist, 1780–1814", Ph.D. diss., Bryn Mawr, 1962; Edward C. Carter, "The Birth of a Political Economist: Mathew Carey and the Recharter Fight of 1810–1811", *Pennsylvania History*, XXXIII (1966), 274–88; Edward C. Carter, "Mathew Carey and The Olive Branch, 1814–1818", *Pennsylvania Magazine of History and Biography*, LXXXIX (1965), 399–415; Cathy N. Davidson, "Ideology and Genre: the Rise of the Novel in America", *Proceedings of the American Antiquarian Society*, LXXXXVI (1986), 295–321; Martin J. Burke, *The Conundrum of Class: Public Discourse on the Social Order in America* (forthcoming). See also Earl Bradsher, *Mathew Carey: Editor, Author, and Publisher*, New York, 1912; and Kenneth W. Rowe, *Mathew Carey: A Study in American Economic Development*, Baltimore, 1933.

articulate a Catholic and nationalist interpretation of Ireland's past, and
in so doing he raised serious questions about the poetics and the politics
of Irish historiography. It is for these reasons that I would like to turn to
Carey and his text.[3]

Carey was born in Dublin in 1760, and though he spent the better part
of his life in the United States, he always identified himself as an
Irishman. He was one of the five sons of Christopher and Mary Sheridan
Carey, a Catholic family of the middling sort that had grown prosperous
by provisioning the Royal Navy. Among his brothers were John, a
classical scholar and editor of Dryden's Virgil; William Paulet, a painter
and noted art historian; and James, a political pamphleteer and journalist.
The Careys' careers on both sides of the Atlantic are suggestive of the
degree of social mobility enjoyed by educated Irish Catholics during the
late eighteenth and early nineteenth centuries. Mathew was schooled by
the Jesuits, and was apprenticed in 1775 to Thomas McDonnell, a Dublin
printer and bookseller, and the publisher of *The Hibernian Journal*.
McDonnell was a strong supporter of the rights of the colonists in
America and the Catholics at home, and it was during this apprenticeship
with him that Carey made his initial contribution to the discourse of Irish
politics.[4]

In the autumn of 1779 Carey authored a pamphlet on *The Urgent
Necessity of an Immediate Repeal of the Whole Penal Code Against the
Roman Catholics*, and along with it a short *Appeal to the Roman
Catholics of Ireland*.[5] These pieces were critical of the discrimination
enforced by the state and of the conservatism of the Catholic Committee
in challenging it. Although published anonymously, these works troubled

---

3. The often contentious terms and contradictory assumptions of Irish
historiography are discussed by Jacqueline R. Hill, "Popery and Protestantism, Civil
and Religious Liberty: The Disputed Lessons of Irish History, 1690–1812", *Past and
Present*, CXVIII (1988), 96–129; Donal MacCartney, "The Writing of History in
Ireland, 1800–1830", *Irish Historical Studies*, X (1957), 347–62. See, in addition,
David Hayton, "Anglo-Irish Attitudes: Changing Perceptions of National Identity
among the Protestant Ascendancy in Ireland, circa 1690–1750", *Studies in
Eighteenth Century Culture*, XVII (1987), 145–58.

4. In his *Autobiography*, Brooklyn, 1942, 1–3, Carey emphasizes the modest
surroundings and simple education of his youth. A less self-effacing and more
thorough evaluation of Carey and his family in these years can be found in Carter,
"Political Activities", 2–10.

5. Mathew Carey, *The Urgent Necessity of the Immediate Repeal of the Whole
Penal Code Against the Roman Catholics*, Dublin, 1779; *An Appeal to the Roman
Catholics of Ireland*, Dublin, 1779.

the authorities sufficiently that Carey fled to France. There he found employment at the press of Benjamin Franklin at Passy; and there he became acquainted with the Marquis de Lafayette. Carey returned to Ireland in 1780, where he worked on the *Freeman's Journal*, and wrote on behalf of Catholic emancipation, parliamentary reform, and the American rebellion.[6]

In Dublin Carey associated with many members of the more radical wing of the Volunteers, and it was in support of this movement that he began the *Volunteer's Journal: Or Irish Herald* in 1783. His continuous assaults on the Castle and the Parliament led to his prosecution by both of these bodies in the following year. Faced once more with fines and imprisonment, Carey again went into exile, taking passage to Philadelphia and to permanent residence there in late 1784.[7]

The story of Carey's gradual rise to prominence in American letters and public affairs parallels that of his patron Benjamin Franklin, and its details are concerned chiefly with issues in the cultural history of the early republic.[8] He edited the first nationally circulated periodicals, *The Columbian Magazine* and the *American Museum*, the latter of which had a considerable number of subscribers in Ireland. He published the work of such early American novelists as Charles Brockden Brown and Susannah Rowson. And he managed what by the second decade of the nineteenth century was the largest publishing house in North America, one that would export the works of such writers as James Fenimore Cooper and Washington Irving to the European market. In the arena of politics Carey was an assiduous pamphleteer, producing dozens of tracts on such matters as banking, trade, and international affairs.[9]

His significance in the narrative of the Irish in America is predicated upon this influence — he was the most prominent and most respected

---

6. Carey, *Autobiography*, 4–6; Carter, "Political Activities", 10–14.

7. Carey, *Autobiography*, 7–9; Carter, "Political Activities", 17–30. The subjects of Irish politics and Dublin radicalism in these years are discussed in detail in R.B. McDowell, *Ireland in the Age of Imperialism and Revolution, 1760–1801*, Oxford, 1979.

8. Although published in serial form in *The New England Magazine* in 1833 and 1834 rather than in one volume, Carey's *Autobiography* is clearly indebted to that master-text of American autobiography, Benjamin Franklin's.

9. On Carey's career in publishing see Green, "Mathew Carey"; Clarkin, *Mathew Carey: A Bibliography*; Davidson, "Ideology and Genre"; and Bradsher, *Mathew Carey: Editor, Author, and Publisher*, 1–78. Carey's American political writings are best analysed in Carter, "Political Activities".

Irishman in the first half of the nineteenth century — and upon his charitable and political activities on behalf of that community at large.[10] Carey helped to establish the Hibernian Society for the relief of Irish emigrants, and to promote the activities of the United Irishmen, many of whom were colleagues from his Volunteer days, and many of whom sought refuge in Philadelphia in the wake of the Rising of 1798. These connections with the United Irishmen, and by extension with their French sponsors, led Carey into a series of skirmishes with opponents of these revolutionary causes, among whom was the celebrated William Cobbett. Carey emerged as the victor in this war of words with Cobbett and company, and throughout his career he continued in the role of literary champion of the Irish, both at home and abroad.

The most extensive and the most interesting of his defenses was the *Vindiciae Hibernicae*. The title of the text is a play on James Mackintosh's *Vindiciae Gallicae* of 1791, one of the better known of the tracts written in response to Edmund Burke's *Reflections on the Revolution in France*. But where Mackintosh's was a philosophic justification of Jacobinism, Carey's was an historical argument for Irish nationalism, at least in its Volunteer and United Irish incarnations. It was in addition a defense of the character of the Catholic Irish against the charges of conspiracy and savagery levelled against them by generations of Protestant polemicists and historians.[11]

Carey, in his *Autobiography*, explains that his initial inspiration for writing the *Vindiciae* was the popularity, especially in the United States, of William Godwin's *Mandeville: A Tale of the Seventeenth Century in England*, published in 1817.[12] The first part of that novel is set in

---

10. On the Irish in America in the late eighteenth and early nineteenth centuries see David N. Doyle, *Ireland, Irishmen, and Revolutionary America*, Dublin, 1981; and Maurice J. Bric, "Ireland, Irishmen, and the Broadening of the Late Eighteenth Century Philadelphia Polity", Ph.D. diss., Johns Hopkins University, 1991. Carey's work for and among the Irish is discussed in Carter, "Political Activities", 63–69, 189–95, 214–18. See also Carter, "'A Wild Irishman under Every Federalist Bed': Nativism in Philadelphia, 1789–1806", *Pennsylvania Magazine of History and Biography*, LXXXXIV (1970), 331–41; Carter, "Wild Irishman Revisited", *Proceedings of the American Philosophical Society*, CXXXIII (1989), 175–89; Rex Syndergaard, "Wild Irishmen and the Alien and Sedition Act", *Eire-Ireland*, IX (1974), 14–24.

11. Carey, *Autobiography*, 58–59, 71–75.

12. Carey, *Autobiography*, 58–81; William Godwin, *Mandeville: A Tale of the Seventeenth Century in England*, Edinburgh, 1817. The scholarship on Godwin includes: Don Locke, *A Fantasy of Reason: The Life and Thought of William*

Ireland in 1641, and presents a fictionalized rendition of the rebellion of Sir Phelim O'Neill and his confederates. Its protagonist, Charles Mandeville, is witness at the age of three to the slaughter of his parents and the English garrison at Charlemont, and to the ensuing horrors of civil war. Even though he escapes from Ireland, he cannot escape from sectarian bigotry and the memories of an innocence destroyed. For Godwin, the trauma that is Mandeville's particular history is representative of the "tumultuous and tragic" past that has been Ireland's.[13]

As critical as he was of the "savageness" of the "monster" O'Neill and the Catholic "barbarians" in 1641, Godwin was far from an apologist for English colonization or a romanticizer of the Protestant ascendancy. The thoroughgoing radicalism that he had first introduced in the *Enquiry Concerning Political Justice*, and which he continued to develop in such novels as *Caleb Williams* and *St. Leon*, made Godwin an opponent of "things as they are". And among those things were the manifestly unjust conditions in Ireland; indeed *Mandeville* is dedicated to the memory of his close friend, the Irish reformer John Philpot Curran, with whom Godwin had toured Ireland. Godwin had supported the cause of reform in Ireland since the 1780s, and corresponded with Henry Grattan. He had more recently discussed these issues with his son-in-law Shelley, in the course of the latter's composition of "An Address to the Irish People".[14]

Rather than being hostile, Godwin was sympathetic to the plight of a people oppressed by bad government, and in thrall to traditions of superstition and ignorance. The claims made by the Irish for their rights, no matter how perverted by priestcraft, were just. His antipathy was directed not toward the plain people of Ireland, native or newcomer, but

---

Godwin, London, 1980; Peter Marshall, *William Godwin*, Yale University Press, 1984; B. J. Tysdahl, *William Godwin as Novelist*, London, 1981; Joann P. Cobb, "Godwin's Novels and *Political Justice*", *Enlightenment Essays*, IV (1973), 15–28; Mona Scheuermann, "The Study of Mind: The Later Novels of William Godwin", *Forum for Modern Language Studies*, XIX (1983), 16–30; George Woodcock, "Things as They Might Be; Things as They Are: Notes on the Novels of William Godwin", *Dalhousie Review*, LIV (1974–75), 685–97. On *Mandeville* in particular, see Marion Omar Farouk, "*Mandeville: A Tale of the Seventeenth Century* — Historical Novel or Psychological Study?" in *Essays in Honour of William Gallacher*, Humboldt Universität Berlin, 1966, 111–17.

13. *Mandeville*, 3, 23–32, 36–44, 113–14, 121.

14. On Godwin and Irish affairs, see Marshall, *William Godwin*, 68, 172, 236–37, 296–97.

toward the nobilities and the clergies who had been the beneficiaries of centuries of organized oppression. The Irish wars resulted from a combination of the aristocratic ambition and religious intolerance of the Catholic and Protestant elites.[15]

To Godwin, the most effective means of replacing these malevolent institutions was not through violence, but through an appeal to the reason of the community at large, an appeal best made through literature. He assumed that people, once aware of the distorting power of greed and fanaticism, would take the steps necessary to establish equitable social and political systems.[16] How cognizant Carey was of Godwin's overall project for this admixture of political philosophy and fiction in the cause of reform is unclear. He had admired Godwin's earlier works, but took strong exception to the "perversion of history" that was presented in *Mandeville*. Carey was concerned that this reiteration of the Rebellion of 1641 would evoke not a reasonable discourse about the conditions of the people of Ireland, but would provoke those "unfounded prejudices" about Roman Catholics still ingrained in the Anglo-American world. Where the philosopher was confident of the ameliorative power of his historical fictions, the publisher was wary of the novel's appeal to the passions.[17]

Even though each of these men of letters was "republican" in his political principles, the English radical's republicanism was one predicated on a suspicion of, and a hostility toward, all organized religion. In Godwin's analysis, political justice in Ireland could not be realized until both Catholicism and militant Protestantism were overcome; anti-popery was as distorting a social and political force as was slavish papistry.[18] To the American emigrant, however, the toleration, not the elimination, of existing religious diversity was vital to a republic. While Carey agreed with the charges against colonialism, he

---

15. *Mandeville*, 131–33, 143, 148–51.

16. Godwin's preference for the novel as a vehicle for political philosophy is analyzed by David McCracken, "Godwin's Literary Theory: The Alliance between Fiction and Political Philosophy", *Philosophical Quarterly*, XXXXIX (1970), 113–33. See in addition Cobb, "Godwin's Novels and Political Justice"; Woodcock, "Things as They Might Be".

17. Carey, *Autobiography*, 58–60; *Vindiciae Hibernicae*, 18–19.

18. Godwin, *Mandeville*, 3, 23, 29–32, 39–42, 115, 130–33, 148–49. Godwin's animus against institutionalized bigotry was not limited to the Catholic church. One of the novel's main characters, the Reverend Hilkiah Bradford, is a Presbyterian bigot of the first rank, one who trains the young Mandeville in the traditions of militant anti-Popery. See Cobb, "Godwin's Novels and Political Justice", 23–34; Marshall, *William Godwin*, 23, 337–38.

reversed the terms of Godwin's indictment of Catholicism. For Carey, it was the heritage of English Protestantism that was the source of injustice and intolerance in Ireland.[19]

Significant though the potential appeal of *Mandeville* was for the genesis of the *Vindiciae Hibernicae*, Carey did not compose a five hundred page work solely as a refutation of an imaginative retelling of the tales of 1641. As well as being a piece of literary criticism, the *Vindiciae* is an extended effort in historical criticism of both the sources and the "fraudulent misrepresentations" of the rebellion that *Mandeville* was based upon. In addition to Godwin's work, Carey set out to challenge a tradition of "Anglo-Hibernian" historiography that stretched from the publication of Sir John Temple's *The Irish Rebellion* in 1646, through the Earl of Clarendon's posthumous *History of the Rebellion and Civil Wars of Ireland* in 1719-1720, and to the histories of Ireland by Ferdinando Warner and Thomas Leland, which appeared in 1770 and 1773 respectively.[20] To Carey these historians had replaced the facts of Irish history with fictions in a manner far more thorough and far more malicious than had any novelist.[21]

Though the chronology of the *Vindiciae* moves from the twelfth century to the eighteenth, Carey was particularly concerned with the history of Ireland in the seventeenth century, especially with the "fabulous tale" of murder and rebellion in 1641. A great deal of the volume is devoted to a point-by-point rebuttal of the claims of Temple, Clarendon, *et al.* that the rising in that year was the result of a

---

19. On Carey's political and religious commitments to toleration, see Carter, "Political Activities", 23, 330.

20. Sir John Temple, *The Irish Rebellion: Or, an History of the Beginning and the First Progresse of the General rebellion Raised within the Kingdom of Ireland ...*, London, 1646; Edward Hyde, Earl of Clarendon, *History of the Rebellion and Civil Wars of Ireland*, Dublin, 1719-1720; Ferdinando Warner, *The History of Ireland*, Dublin, 1770; Thomas Leland, *The History of Ireland, from the Invasion of Henry II: With a Preliminary Discourse on the Present State of the Kingdom*, London, 1773. In writing the *Vindiciae* Carey used a 1724 Dublin edition of Temple, and a 1774 Philadelphia edition of Leland. On the historiography of the events of 1641, see Walter D. Love, "Civil War in Ireland: Appearances in Three Centuries of Historical Writing", *Emory University Quarterly*, XXII (1966), 57-72; Joseph Leichty, "Testing the Depths of Catholic/Protestant Conflict: The Case of Thomas Leland's *History of Ireland*, 1773", *Archivium Hibernicum*, XXXXII (1987), 13-28; Anne Wyatt, "Lingard, Lecky, Irish History, and 1641", *Eire-Ireland*, XXIII (1988), 22-34.

21. Carey, *Vindiciae Hibernicae*, 26, 30, 37, 80-81, 85.

conspiracy among the Catholic nobility, and that in the course of the rebellion tens, if not hundreds, of thousands of Protestants were slaughtered in a sectarian frenzy. For Carey neither the evidence relied upon by the established chroniclers — personal papers, state records, and most importantly the volumes of depositions given by survivors of the alleged massacres — nor the principles of common sense supported the "sorry romances" of the Anglo-Hibernian historians.[22]

If the standard authorities were quite wrong in their representations of the "thousand-times-told story of the execrable Irish rebellion", what in fact did transpire? Carey finds little merit in their depiction of Ireland before 1641 as a land of peace, tolerance, and prosperity, except as a rhetorical ploy to emphasize the "barbarous and sanguinary" doings of the Catholics. Carey does not deny that there was a rising by O'Neill and his confederates in that year. Nor does he deny that many innocent lives were lost in the course of the ensuing conflict, although the number of deaths was but a fraction of the figure claimed by Clarendon *et al.* He does deny that there was any "general conspiracy" among the Irish, however, or that the Roman priesthood were the instigators of a pogrom against the Protestants. He makes these arguments through a series of very extensive examinations of the texts — especially Temple's *Irish Rebellion* and the depositions upon which that narrative was constructed — and he is able to point out their inconsistencies, incoherencies, and their "manifest forgeries". The deposition by Robert Maxwell, afterwards bishop of Kilmore, referred to the appearances of ghosts and other suspensions of the laws of nature; while that of Captain Anthony Stratford was little more than a complication of rumour and hearsay. Within the thirty-two bound volumes of expositions Carey finds scant evidence to support the accepted interpretation of the rebellion.[23]

Ready though Carey be to dismiss the charges of a Catholic conspiracy, he is not prepared to reject a conspiratorial interpretation of Anglo-Irish relations. He finds in the periodic discoveries by Dublin Castle of treasonous plots and schemes evidence of a far more

---

22. *Ibid.*, 21, 26–30, 39–63, 85, 105–106, 131–37, 178, 289–305, 313–18; *Autobiography*, 58–81. On the depositions given in the wake of the events of 1641 and their use — or abuse — by historians, see M. Perceval Maxwell, "The Ulster Rising of 1641 and the Depositions", *Irish Historical Studies*, XXI (1978), 144–67.

23. *Ibid.*, 39–63, 105–106, 131–33, 148–52, 283–303, 360–74, 400–403, 408–11, 415–32. Given the lack of statistics, Carey wondered if a reliable reckoning of the number of victims in 1641 could be made. He was certain, however, that the Temple figure of 300,000 was a wild exaggeration. He had more faith in Thomas Carte's estimate of 20,000 deaths.

"bloodthirsty and barbarous project": one intended to dispossess the Irish of their holdings in land, and more often than not of their lives. Carey examines the often thin grounds upon which such charges were made, and demonstrates in the case of 1641 the extent to which justice and reason were perverted in order to declare that the Catholic lords were in rebellion. For Carey, the driving force of Irish history since the Norman invasion was not the vindictiveness of such supposed conspirators as Phelim O'Neill, but the "Machiavellian policy" of the English government. Time after time, he argues, the Irish were "goaded into insurrection"; time after time, Ireland was transformed into a "great human slaughter-house". The dynamic of Irish history was one of provocation answered by legitimate resistance. Instead of the rhetoric of demonization employed by such writers as Clarendon or Temple, Carey seeks to humanize the Irish Catholics, and to universalize their plight. Instead of being the "objects of abhorrence", they have been, and continue to be, the chief victims of "pretended plots", and of the civil strife that inevitably follows.[24]

Carey's criticisms of the "characteristic infidelity" of these writers were both professional and personal. How is Sir John Temple, for example, to be taken seriously when he bases much of his analysis on a combination of obvious untruths and incredible flights of fancy? How much credence, Carey wondered, could be given to accounts of Irish affairs by English writers who had "exhausted the powers of language" in order to transfigure patriots into traitors and rebels? Nor were these texts simply instances of intellectual shortcomings. Carey stresses the interrelationships between these writings and the financial and political interests that they served. Instead of assuming the disinterested stance of scholars dedicated to truth, the "Anglo-Hibernians" had perjured themselves and debased their texts in order to "justify the oppression" of the Catholic landholders and their tenants, oppressions by which they often profited. In addition to the injustices of legislative and legal misrepresentation, the Irish were forced to endure the indignities of a tradition of historical misrepresentation that had begun with the writings of Geraldus Cambrensis, was continued through the texts of Edmund Spenser and William Petty, and still flourished in the works of David Hume and Thomas Leland.[25]

---

24. *Ibid.*, 26–28, 58–66, 77–80, 90–91, 97, 109, 131, 289–305, 313–18.

25. *Ibid.*, 26, 69, 80, 85, 99–100, 106, 131–37, 152, 380–85, 389–91, 424, 432.

In the course of this often impassioned analysis of the "dishonest writers" of Irish history, Carey is especially critical of Hume's *History of England* and its treatment of the events of 1641. Though far less partisan or provocative than the texts of the Anglo-Hibernians, Hume's recapitulation of the rebellion does not stray too far from the traditional interpretation. Nor does Hume demonstrate the "keen penetration" of the philosopher when assessing the documentary sources upon which the narrative is based; rather than exposing the frauds of Temple's Irish Rebellion, Hume employs that "wretched" text as an authority some twenty-seven times. For Carey there is little to indicate that a "powerful mind" was at work in the *History of England*, and much to suggest that Hume was deserving of "unqualified censure".[26]

Thus the *Vindiciae Hibernicae* is both a history and a commentary on the writing of history for partisan purposes. Carey acknowledges that the work is, in many places, a continuation of the eighteenth-century Irish debate between such figures as the Roman Catholic John Curry and the Protestant Walter Harris over the events of 1641.[27] To avoid the parochial dimensions of that argument, however, and to deflect charges of "partiality", Carey relies almost solely on sources and authorities favourable to the Protestant ascendancy for his evidence. By drawing heavily from state papers, parliamentary proceedings, and other public records to refute Harris and his fellow writers, Carey turns the terms of official discourse against the falsehoods propagated by the Anglo-Hibernians.

Sceptical though he was about that tradition of historiography, Carey did not presume that all historical writings were necessarily political or polemical "hotch potch". He had confidence enough in the Enlightenment

---

26. *Ibid.*, 395-97. In the course of his critique of Hume's *History of England*, Carey notes the exchanges between Hume and the Roman Catholic historians John Curry and Charles O'Conor. The latter two had attempted to convince Hume of the errors and exaggerations in the Protestant literature on 1641, and were somewhat successful in their efforts. The 1770 edition of the *History* is less indebted to Temple *et al.* than previous editions. Carey, however, appears not to have noted the changes. See David Berman, "David Hume on the 1641 Rebellion in Ireland", *Studies*, LXV (1976), 101-112; Robert E. Ward, "A Letter from Ireland: A Little-Known Attack on David Hume's *A History of England*", *Eighteenth Century Ireland*, II (1987), 196-97.

27. John Curry, *Historical Memories of the Irish Rebellion of the Year 1641*, Dublin, 1758; Walter Harris, *Fiction Unmasked*, Dublin, 1752. On this debate see Love, "Civil War in Ireland", 57-58, 70-72; Berman, "David Hume on the 1641 Rebellion in Ireland", 101-106.

sciences of man to believe in the possibility and the desirability of a non-partisan, objective representation of the past; there were standards of coherence and truth against which to test historians' narratives. The "chicane" that was Irish historiography, however, had been "an exception to all the general rules on the subject of history". Carey assumed that there was a true rendition of Ireland's past that could be reconstructed from the sources, and that such an effort would produce findings "diametrically opposed" to the "opinions" many of his readers had "entertained from youth". Those yet-to-be-composed narratives would be favourable to political liberty and religious equality for both the Irish Catholic majority and the Protestant minority. Such histories need not be written by Catholics, or by Irishmen, but they must be written by those who subscribed to the universal principles of justice and freedom.[28]

In his *Autobiography* Carey suggested that the publication of the *Vindiciae Hibernicae* was one of the "most important operations" of his life.[29] Many of Carey's contemporaries, Yankee and Irish, considered it to be so, although convincing an early nineteenth-century American readership of the oppressive nature of English colonial rule or of the "self-evident" truths of liberal political analysis was not too difficult a task. Convincing them of the trustworthiness of Irish Catholics and their cause, however, was not as easy. Much of the sympathy expressed for Ireland by American republicans was similar to that of William Godwin's: it was couched in the abstract, and often coincided with a strong distaste for Catholicism.[30]

What the significance of this text is to a late twentieth-century audience is, of course, a matter of perspective. For students of American culture, the *Vindiciae* is yet another item from the prodigious output on politics and economics that was Carey's. For scholars in Irish studies, Carey's is among the most thoroughly researched and most strongly argued of nationalist histories written in the early decades of the nineteenth century. It was a far more successful work than were the historical pieces written by such fellow political exiles as Thomas Addis Emmet, William James MacNeven, William Sampson, and John Daly Burk in the wake of the rebellion of 1798. Through its close analysis of

---

28. Carey, *Autobiography*, 85, 98, 131, 133.

29. *Ibid.*, 75.

30. The most thorough study of American attitudes toward the Irish in this period is by Owen Dudley Edwards, "The American Image of Ireland: A Study of Its Early Phases", *Perspectives in American History*, IV (1970), 199–282.

the continuity of certain arguments and conventions, Carey's is a very effective critical reading of Irish history; and with its emphasis on the durability of such "fictions" as the 1641 massacre, it is suggestive of the political utility of historians' practices and historical memories in both early modern and modern Ireland.[31]

In the *Vindiciae* Carey attempted to develop a counter-interpretation of Irish history that based its arguments on, and made its appeal to, presumedly universal values, not to parochial concerns. This was a history written for trans-Atlantic purposes, with trans-Atlantic audiences in mind. With the *Vindiciae* he hoped to counter the rise of anti-Irish, anti-papal sentiment in the United States, and to contradict a culturally and politically salient Loyalist analysis of history in the United Kingdom that had for too long "defamed" the character and the civic virtue of the Roman Catholics. He wished to vindicate that community from the charges of barbarity and from the burden of Anglo-Hibernian historiography. For Carey, Irish history had often been a "narrow ground" of political and cultural contestation, one in which a battle of the books had more than bibliographic implications. The resurgence of the Irish nation, then, required the reinterpretation of that nation's past.

After almost one hundred seventy years the terms and assumptions of the nationalist emplotment of Ireland's history may appear to be self-evident, save to those few unionists who still subscribe to a narrative closer to Temple's or Clarendon's. Yet in 1819 Carey's attempt at displacing the historical discourse of colonialism was a rather ambitious undertaking. Carey and his successors in the writing of nationalist histories during the nineteenth and into the twentieth centuries were consistent and were generally successful in their identification of the cause of the Irish Catholics with the cause of freedom everywhere. But to the extent that such texts dismissed or glossed over the historical memories of the Protestant minority — be those memories fictional or factual — they may have been as self-serving, or as self-deluding, as the "Anglo-Hibernian" narratives they sought to replace.

---

31. Carey, *Vindiciae Hibernicae*, 137, 458–69.

THE POLITICS OF HISTORIOGRAPHY:
OR, NOVELS WITH FOOTNOTES

JANE STEVENSON

This essay had its origin when it suddenly occurred to me to notice that the early nineteenth-century Anglo-Irish novelists Maria Edgeworth and Sydney Owenson (Lady Morgan) tended to encumber their pages with footnotes, and to ask myself why this should be so. A footnote is intended to refer the reader to supporting fact. What, then, might be its purpose in a work of fiction? The answer seemed to be that Anglo-Irish writers perceived their fiction to have a historiographical function; it was explanatory and didactic rather than simply entertaining. Thus, this paper considers the Anglo-Irish understanding of the Irish past and the work of its historians, in order to context the writing of the novelists themselves.

There are two contrasting types of novelistic footnote. The first is exemplified by Maria Edgeworth, who was prone to footnotes which say simply, FACT. Such footnotes are appended to passages of text which represent the diction and view-point of Irish people. Maria Edgeworth and other members of her family were in the habit of jotting down striking or amusing passages of overheard conversation: where such a note appears in a novel, its purpose is to signal that the passage is more or less verbatim reporting from an actual conversation, and therefore that she is providing a fair and realistic picture of what life in Ireland is "really like". They are a testimony to her need to convince. She presents many of her characters as types: such contrasting characters as King Corny and Ulick O'Shane in *Ormond* are quirky and individual, but the broad tendencies of her writing require that they also be seen to represent something about Ireland and the Irish which is both true and significant. What she seems to have been attempting is essentially alien to twentieth-century theories of the novel, but related to the concept of *verisimilitudo* as it appears in Quintilian and other theoreticians of classical rhetoric: a verbal representation which can be generally agreed to be both emotionally affecting and "like life". The classical theorists were well aware that life itself is often not "lifelike", as the catchphrase "truth is stranger than fiction" admits. Maria Edgeworth's notes which say "fact" do not merely state that on some occasion, an Edgeworth overheard an Irish person utter the words in question. They also imply that the utterance is typical, and therefore significant.

The other style of Anglo-Irish footnote may be represented by this note in Lady Morgan's *The Wild Irish Girl* (1806). It is attached to an ineffable passage in chapter ten, in which the Irish heroine lectures the English hero on Irish dye-plants, showing herself to be a young lady whose education has been both extensive and polite. This is the text:

> "See", she added, springing lightly forward, and culling a plant which grew from the mountain's side—"see this little blossom, which they call here 'yellow lady's bedstraw', which you, as a botanist, will soon recognise; it communicates a beautiful yellow; as does the *Lichen juniperus*, or 'cypress moss', which you brought me yesterday; and I think the *resida Luteola*, or 'yellow weed' surpasses them all."

Lady Morgan then adds a footnote:

> Purple, blue, and green dyes, were introduced by *Tighwmas* the Great, in the year of the world 2815. The Irish also possessed the art of dyeing a fine scarlet, so early as the days of St Bennia, a disciple of St Patrick; scarlet cloths and robes highly embroidered are mentioned in the book of *Glandelogh*.

This is a characteristically heady and intricate blend of the historical and the fantastic, marking Lady Morgan as a not ignoble descendant in spirit of the more creative Irish annalists: the preoccupation with the circumstances of the introduction of anything into Ireland was recognized, and indeed satirized, as early as the ninth century: a Carolingian poem by Bishop Theodulf of Orleans, written to an Irishman called Cadac, poses the impertinent question, "tell me, who was the first Irishman to paint his face?"[1] Lady Morgan guards herself against the charge of complete fantasy in her highly romantic narrative by quoting authorities, ancient and modern, all over the place: *Walker's Essay on Ancient Irish Dress*, *Historical Memoirs of the Irish Bards*, *Smith's History of Kerry*, and even *The Palace of Honour* by Gawain Douglas,

---

1. Bernhard Bischoff, "Theodulf und der Ire Cadac-Andreas", *Mittelalterliche Studien* II, Stuttgart, 1967, 22. One of many genuine examples of this trope of native Irish scholarship is in the eighth-century *Martyrology of Oengus*, which attributes the introduction of bees into Ireland to a saint called Dommoc.

a sixteenth-century Scot. By authenticating the details, she hopes to authenticate the narrative.

What is the background to this kind of fiction which claims the privileges of fact? These pretensions to accuracy and informativeness obviously place the writers in the tradition of the didactic novel. But to write in this way, one has to have some basis for the claim to know. What I will now turn to, therefore, is the tradition of historical writing accessible to the Anglo-Irish writers who did so much to inform the outer world's view of what Ireland was. What Maria Edgeworth and Lady Morgan knew about the history of Ireland is not a trivial matter. Both were infinitely more widely read outside Ireland than any work of Irish history whatsoever, and not merely in the British Isles. Their Irish novels were translated into French and German within a few years of their first appearance.[2]

Irish history of course begins with the history of Ireland written by and for the Irish themselves. Historiography has manifestly been an interest of the Irish people since the beginnings of literacy in Ireland. Vernacular Irish historical writing was a byproduct of the enormous social importance of genealogy, and the evidencing of such matters as claims to the ownership of land or the title of king by means of circumstantial narratives (seanchas). The faking-up of Irish history for propagandistic purposes is visibly in process as early as the seventh century, when the Uí Néill kings emerge into historical visibility "like a school of cuttlefish, in a cloud of ink of their own manufacture".[3]

Foreign invaders, in this as in other respects, showed themselves *ipsi hiberniores Hiberniis*. Gerald of Wales, whose family led the Norman conquest of Ireland, devoted relatively little of his *Topographia Hiberniae* to Irish history and culture, but what there was, was there to prove a point. The disgusting inauguration ritual of the O'Neill of Donegal, greatly though it has excited students of comparative Indo-European folkways with its hint of unspeakable archaism and parallelism with ancient Hindu rites, would have had a different effect on a Norman audience. A ruler who had been publicly seen sitting in a cauldron full of soup made from the flesh of a white mare with which he had previously had sexual intercourse could barely claim to be treated as

---

2. For example, *Glorwina, das wilde Mädchen in Irrland*, Leipzig, 1809–10, *Glorvina, ou la jeune Irlandaise*, Paris, 1813, *Ormond, Roman*, Paris, 1817.

3. J.V. Kelleher, "Early Irish History and Pseudo-history", *Studia Historica*, III (1963), 113–27.

human, let alone civilized.[4]   More generally, Gerald persistently describes the Irish as lazy, irreligious, barbarian, and fundamentally alien in their habits of body and mind. When he comments, "their natural qualities are excellent, but almost all their acquired habits are deplorable",[5] it could almost be Maria Edgeworth speaking. Gerald's work very interestingly offers a sort of preview of the Ascendancy culture of five or six centuries later: ironically, most of his descendants had by then joined the ranks of the despised.

Gerald of Wales was a powerful shaper of the Anglo-Irish historiographic tradition. His work was treated as authoritative by such diverse figures as Edmund Spenser, Edmund Campion, William Camden, Sir John Davies, and even the Old English palesman, Richard Stanihurst. Thus, Gerald set the tone and standard in some important ways for sixteenth and seventeenth-century English and Anglo-Irish historiography of Ireland. The authority of his work was attacked only by some of his descendants, Old English (i.e., Hiberno-Norman and Catholic) writers, such as Stephen White, who published an *Apologia pro Hibernia adversus Cambri calumnias* (*Apology for Ireland, against Welsh slanders*).

The reasons why Gerald became so powerful an influence seem to be twofold. First, he wrote in Latin, and his work was therefore accessible. Second, he was not Irish, which may rather paradoxically be seen as a qualification. His outsider's approach to Ireland as a resident alien, and probably also his sophisticated, punning, highly ornamented style as a Latin prose writer, gave him a claim to disinterested authoritativeness — an example, perhaps, of the successful use of rhetorical skill for dubious ends which Edmund Spenser deplored in the Irish bards.

Richard Stanihurst is the most important of the historians of Ireland after the Elizabethan conquest. He was Catholic, "Old English", of Norman descent, and resident in Dublin. We can see in Stanihurst — and even to some extent in Gerald himself — the beginnings of what was to become a familiar pattern: writer poised uneasily between the two cultures of England and Ireland, and concerned to explain at least the Irish ruling class point of view to the English.

Stanihurst's position also made him a conduit of information: another theme which will arise again and again in the rest of this paper. Vernacular Irish history began, perhaps, with annals kept at Iona in the sixth century, and developed within the Irish-speaking world. Anglo-Irish

---

4. *Topographia Hibernica*, § 102.

5. *Ibid.*, § 94.

history, which began, in a sense, with Bede's *Ecclesiastical History of the English Nation*, completed in 731, but more obviously with Gerald of Wales, is a largely independent, parallel construct. The history of Ireland as written by people who do not speak Irish develops in a trajectory of its own, with only occasional and sporadic input from vernacular Irish history, through the medium of an individual who contrives to bridge the linguistic and cultural gap.

The way in which Anglo-Irish writers used the work of their predecessors is demonstrated by Edmund Campion's *History of Ireland*, which is greatly indebted to both Gerald and Stanihurst, as his first paragraph shows: his first book "includeth the first part of Cambrensis ... which was delivered me, by [James] Stanihurst". The seventeenth-century Irish writer Geoffrey Keating, who will be discussed a little later, was inclined to be dismissive about Stanihurst's knowledge of "real" Irish history, but there is no denying he had some: sufficient, at all events, to draw the contempt of Edmund Spenser, whose work was indebted both to Stanihurst and Campion:[6]

> M. Stanihurst who though he be the same countryman borne, ... yet hath strayed from the truth ... for he thereupon groundeth a very grosse imagination, that the Irish should Descend from the Egyptians which came into that Island first under the leading of one Scota the daughter of Pharaoh .... I would first know of him what ancient grounds of authority he hath for such a senseless fable, and if he have any of the rude Irish books, as it may be he hath, yet, (me seemes) that a man of his learning should not so lightly have bin carried away with old wives tales.[7]

Not only is Stanihurst's use of Irish materials criticized, the authority of the native Irish historical tradition is itself rejected. His source here, directly or indirectly, is the *Leabhar Gabhála*, or *Book of Invasions*, a collection of material some of which goes back to the time of Brian Boru's strife against the Vikings.[8] The origin-legend to which Spenser

---

6. Geoffrey Keating, *Foras Feasa ar Éirinn*, ed. and tr. David Comyn and P.S. Dinneen, 4 vols, London 1902-14, Introduction, § 5, i, 31-43. Stanihurst's knowledge of Irish history is defended by Colm Lennon, *Richard Stanihurst, the Dubliner, 1548-1618*, Dublin, 1981, 120-23.

7. Edmund Spenser, *A View of the State of Ireland*, in *Two Histories of Ireland*, ed. James Ware, Dublin, 1633, repr. Amsterdam, 1971, 39.

8. *Lebor Gabála Érenn*, ed. and tr. R.A.S. Macalister, 5 vols, Dublin, 1938-56, II, 129 and II, 153-54, in vol. II, 41 and 69. See also A.G. van Hamel, "An Lebur

scornfully refers can easily be paralleled by similar stories which
Elizabethan English writers continued to hold dear, and to regard as to
some extent explanatory of important facts about the English, such as the
founding of Britain by Locrine son of Brutus, and the descent of the
English from the Trojans. There is a certain irony in the author of *The
Faerie Queene* being quite so dismissive of the origin legends of others.
The *Leabhar Gabhála* continued to be considered relevant to the Irish
themselves long after Spenser was writing. Fr. Michael O'Clery of the
Four Masters collected and re-edited it in the seventeenth century: despite
the obviously fantastic nature of some of its contents, it was perceived as
a relevant narrative forming an historiographic context which the Irish
could use to understand their subjection to the English.[9] Spenser's
attitude, in which Gerald is an authority, and the *Leabhar Gabhála* an
"old wife's tale", is a testimony to the separation of the two traditions.

One of the fascinating aspects of sixteenth-century Anglo-Irish history
is that, apparently unwittingly, its writers start becoming infected by an
Irish outlook: characteristically Irish historical methodology begins to
creep in. The infection, if we may so call it, presumably spreads out
from the Old English, some of whom read and spoke Irish, and the
adoption of the literary tropes of the "meere Irish" was unconscious. For
example, the English Catholic Edmund Campion lists "severall claimes
to the Land of Ireland".[10]

1. The Irish when in Spain (an origin-legend about Míl and his
sons, deriving from the *Leabhar Gabhála* via Stanihurst) were in
obedience to Gurguntius ("from this coast and citty, now part of
Gascoigne, came the fleete of those Iberians, who in 60 ships met
Gurguntius on the sea, returning from the conquest of Denmarke,
to whom they yeelded oath and service, sued for dwelling, were
by him conducted and planted in Ireland, and became his leige
people"). This was in 376 BC.

2. Mac Gil-Murrow king of Ireland did homage to Arthur at
Caerleon in 519 AD. (this is indebted to another creative Cambro-
Norman, Geoffrey of Monmouth, and his fictional *History of the
Kings of Britain*).

Gabála", *Zeitschrift für Celtische Philologie*, 10 (1915), 97–197.

9. Bernadette Cunningham, "Seventeenth-Century Interpretations of the Past:
The Case of Geoffrey Keating", *Irish Historical Studies*, XXV (1986–87), 122.

10. *History*, in *Two Histories of Ireland*, ed. J. Ware, 71.

3. The conquest of Henry II in AD 1172.

The assumption of the continued relevance to the sixteenth-century political situation of events allegedly occurring in the fourth century BC and the sixth century AD — in both cases, wholly and entirely fictional — is very much in keeping with the native Irish treatment of their own historical and pseudo-historical literature.[11]

A temporary channel of communication between the two historiographic traditions of Ireland was opened up in the seventeenth century by James Ussher and his younger colleague, Sir James Ware. Ussher was the Protestant Archbishop of Armagh, but also a nephew to Richard Stanihurst, a Catholic (his mother was also a Catholic). This perhaps contributed to the unusual enlargement of his sympathies. He devoted considerable (and outstandingly successful) efforts to collecting and preserving Irish manuscripts, both vernacular and Latin, and maintained friendly correspondence with exiled Irish Catholic scholars such as Stephen White and Luke Wadding. He was generous in giving such acquaintances — legally proscribed, as Roman Catholic priests, from being in Ireland at all, and whom he should officially have handed over to the authorities — the use of his library, a genuine and disinterested kindness which says much for him. Stephen White, a distinguished Jesuit, wrote to John Colgan (the Franciscan collector and editor of Irish saints' lives) at Louvain,

> [Ussher] received me with the greatest affability and treated me with candour and unaffectedness ... he often invited me to his house, not only to dine (which I modestly declined) but ... even to his most choice library.[12]

In unexpected and welcome contrast to the ferocious and gloomy bigotry of the mid-seventeenth century, Ussher and his Franciscan and Jesuit colleagues in the field of Irish history passed books, transcripts and information back and forth between Armagh, Louvain and Salamanca. Ussher's work on the early history of the Irish church was thus based on

---

11. Another mild irony of Campion's account is the implication which he chooses to draw from his second "claime": since Arthur also exacted submission from the Anglo-Saxons, logically both the Irish and the English should accept their political subordination to whatever descendant of Owen Glendower remained in the Principality.

12. Richard Sharpe, *Medieval Irish Saints' Lives*, Oxford, 1991, 59. The original language of this letter is Latin.

a knowledge of all the sources available at that time, both Latin and Irish, and though inevitably his introductions insisted that early Irish Christianity resembled seventeenth-century Protestantism more closely than it resembled seventeenth-century Catholicism, his meticulous presentation of evidence made his work very widely acceptable. For instance, we find the last great Gaelic historian, the Roman Catholic priest Geoffrey Keating (Seathrún Céitinn), quoting Ussher as *the* authority on Irish church history,[13] and Fr. John Colgan himself took his information on the seventh-century biographers of St Patrick from Ussher's *Britannicarum Ecclesiarum Antiquitates* of 1639.[14] A principal result of the labours of Ussher and his colleagues, Catholic and Protestant, is that the one aspect of Ireland's past glories which was very widely accepted, and indeed still is, is the proud title of "the island of saints and scholars", a designation which Gerald of Wales would neither have understood nor accepted. The title was known and used in Insular circles in the eleventh, twelfth and thirteenth centuries, but taken up and promulgated by the Irish scholars of the seventeenth century and thence, via the work of Ussher, it came to be an accepted fact among the scholars of England and the Continent that Ireland, though economically backward and politically primitive, had made a massive contribution to the spiritual and intellectual history of Europe.[15]

In ninth-century England, King Alfred of Wessex organized the rescue of English learning and culture which had become moribund in the face of invasion, political disaster and national demoralization: not the least of his title to be called "the Great". There was a similar, equally timely, movement in Ireland in the sixteenth and seventeenth centuries. The collapse of English culture had been merely a byproduct of the Scandinavian invasion; by contrast, the extirpation of Irish culture after the Elizabethan conquest was a matter of deliberate policy. By the seventeenth century, Ussher and his Franciscan friends were like men throwing valuables out of the windows of a burning building, deeply conscious that the documents for early Irish history had to be saved before they vanished completely.

At the same time, the last survivors of the brehon schools were preserving and transcribing manuscripts of vernacular Irish law. Irish

---

13. Céitinn, *Foras Feasa*, book II, § 28, eds Comyn and Dineen, III, 301.

14. Sharpe, *Saints' Lives*, 12. Ussher's account was based on the dossier of documents about St Patrick in the ninth-century Book of Armagh, which was of course in his own library.

15. *Ibid.*, 3-5.

poetry was similarly gathered and copied by men who thought of themselves as possibly the last surviving representatives of its traditional guardians. Many poets, scholars and men of learning were hanged or otherwise murdered in the sixteenth century.[16] The land assigned for their support was confiscated, and earnest attempts were made to suppress the activities of "carroughes, bards, rhymers and common idle men and women".[17] The last great monuments of Irish history were the *Foras Feasa ar Eirinn* (*Elements of the History of Ireland*), which went down to the coming of Henry II, written in 1633 by Geoffrey Keating (Seathrún Céitinn), a continental-trained Roman Catholic priest, the offspring of an entirely Gaelicized Hiberno-Norman family, and the *Annals of the Four Masters*, written in Louvain by Fr. Michael O'Clery and his colleagues, which was completed in 1636. The importance of these two works for Gaelic Ireland was of course enormous, but its impact on the Anglo-Irish sense of Irish history was extremely limited, for reasons both linguistic and cultural. The gap between the two historiographic traditions at this point may be expressed by these parallel quotations, from Geoffrey Keating and Edmund Campion:

> Here is a vindication or defensive introduction to the groundwork of knowledge on Ireland ... which has been gathered and collected from the chief books of the history of Ireland, and from a good many trustworthy foreign authors.[18]

> Concerning the state of that wild people, especially before the conquest, I am persuaded I might have sucked thence [Irish annals and histories] some better store of matter, and gladly would have sought them had I found an interpreter, or understood their tongue.[19]

---

16. J.F. Kenney, *The Sources for the Early History of Ireland I: Ecclesiastical*, New York, 1929, 31–32. See also T.F. O'Rahilly, "Irish poets, historians and judges in English documents", *Proceedings of the Royal Irish Academy*, 36 C (1922), 86–120.

17. Kenney, *Sources*, 31, quoting John Perrot, Lord President of Munster, in 1571 (*The Calendar of the Carew Manuscripts I*, 1867, 410).

18. Céitinn, *Foras Feasa*, Introduction, § 9, eds Comyn and Dineen, I, 95 (see further Introduction, *passim*).

19. From "To the Reader", § 16, prefaced to Campion's *History*, in *Two Histories of Ireland*, ed. James Ware (no page number).

Ussher, as we have seen, bridged it to a great extent in the specialized but highly important field of ecclesiastical history. His younger colleague and associate, the English antiquarian Sir James Ware, extended this work into political and social history. One of the last and greatest representatives of the native learned tradition, An Dubhaltach Mac Firbisigh (Duald Mac Firbis), a man whose knowledge of Gaelic culture was encyclopaedic, went to work for James Ware, who knew no Irish. Thus, Mac Firbisigh, must effectively have done most of Ware's research for him from 1655 until Ware's death in 1666, transcribing and translating documents, and directing his attention to what was important. This, like Ussher's friendly intercourse with Irish clerics in the previous generation, is a rare exception to the general cultural apartheid of the period.

Ussher was the most significant Anglo-Irish historian of the Age of the Saints, and his work has its importance to the assessment of the ultimate value of Ireland by outsiders, but he was not of great relevance to the understanding of secular Irish history. The Elizabethan historians following in the footsteps of Gerald continued to hold their value in this field. James Ware reprinted the Elizabethan Irish histories of Edmund Campion, Edmund Spenser and others, together with a large quantity of unusually well-balanced and learned work of his own, which, as we have seen, owed a great deal to the profound Gaelic scholarship of Dubhaltach Mac Firbisigh. Ware, like Ussher, wrote in Latin. What brings his work directly into the context of the Anglo-Irish novel is that his *oeuvre* was translated into English by his grand-daughter's husband, Walter Harris, as *The Whole Works of Sir James Ware Concerning Ireland*, published in Dublin between 1739 and 1764, which made this outstandingly scholarly and unbiased work easily available to eighteenth-century readers. Ware's work is probably the single most significant link between Irish and Anglo-Irish knowledge of Ireland's history in the seventeenth and eighteenth centuries.

Thus we return, at last, to Maria Edgeworth, Lady Morgan, and their footnotes. Maria Edgeworth was not an enthusiast for Irish history. An intensely practical-minded woman, she lived in the present and looked, with qualified optimism, to the future. The *Essay on Irish Bulls* which she co-wrote with her father is a typical piece of Edgeworthiana in that it stresses the similarities rather than the differences between the Irish and other Europeans. The thesis of this work is that the rhetorical tropes known in her own time as "Irish bulls" can be found throughout English and French literature, and result from an inattentive use of metaphor. The nature of the vernacular Irish rhetorical tradition makes the "bull" commoner among Irish speakers than others, but not peculiar to them.

This facetiously written but seriously intended essay concludes by denying the relevance of the legendary past:

> We are more interested in the present race of its inhabitants than in the historian of St Patrick, St Facharis, St Cormuc; the renowned Brien Boru ... or even the great William of Ogham;[20] and by this declaration we have no fear of giving offence to any but rusty antiquaries.

The strength of the Edgeworths' faith in education rather than heredity carries with it the corollary that an individual, or even a whole culture, can and probably should transcend the past in order to join the mainstream of European culture. There was a natural precedent for this view, the great days of the Roman Empire, which had allowed completely open access to people of the most diverse ethnic and cultural background, provided that they were prepared to abandon their native traditions completely and transform themselves into Romans. Maria Edgeworth used her knowledge of the Irish past to inform and explain the present, but kept the workings very much out of sight. The Irish past was important, in that it explained the character of the Irish people. The peasantry were not degraded because they were Irish, but because they were uneducated. She suggests in *Ormond* that if the English could bring themselves to educate the Irish peasantry without insulting their religion, they were just as capable as anyone else of acquiring competitive, entrepreneurial and bourgeois virtues.[21]

The freight of footnotes under which Lady Morgan's Irish novels labour serve a rather different purpose. What she offered polite English society in a highly popularized and sugared form was the thesis that native Irish civilization was in itself just as good a basis from which to become modern Europeans as English culture had been. Native Irish culture had been honourable, knightly and romantic,[22] and its principal representative in the novel, Glorvina, proves its worth by being

---

20. A pun: intentional or otherwise? The Englishman William of *Occam* (d. c. 1349) was known for the reductiveness of his philosophic approach (Occam's razor), the antithesis of the redundancy of the Celtic rhetorical tradition symbolized by the god *Ogma*, credited with the invention of the Ogham alphabet. It is unwise to underestimate the Edgeworths.

21. *Ormond* (1817), chs 23 and 24.

22. She owes this thesis to Sylvester O'Halloran's *History*, Dublin, 1772. See Clare O'Halloran, "Irish re-creation of the Gaelic past: The challenge of McPherson's Ossian", *Past and Present*, CXXIV (1990), 69–95.

simultaneously a daughter of Irish culture, and a refined and polished specimen of the cultivated young lady. Lady Morgan was of course in many ways a very bad and silly writer, but this was no trivial message to be giving the English in the early nineteenth century.

She also had an implicit point to make about the basis of Anglo-Irish life in Ireland. *The Wild Irish Girl* (1806) remembers in its text (chapter 4) an earlier Prince of Inismore who was deprived of his ancestral lands and his life in the time of Cromwell. The hero, Horatio, is made conscious that he and his family have directly superseded the current Prince and his daughter: he sees the Prince as "a man, who shelters his aged head beneath the ruins of those walls where his ancestors bled under the uplifted sword of mine!". Later, he accidentally introduces himself into the Prince's family on the anniversary of this murder, and in his tour of the Prince's collection of antiquities, is shown the helmet and coat of mail in which this ancestor died. In this way, the position of the Ascendancy hero as the descendant and legatee of violent and unjust conquest is kept continually alive as an issue in the novel. This is not a trivial message, and perhaps only so ingenuous and romantic a writer could have made it palatable to an English and Continental reading public.

The writers of novels with footnotes may have made a genuine contribution to English understanding of Ireland. I think we must at least give them credit for their good intentions, in the light of the highly partial view of Irish and Anglo-Irish history which was available to them.

THE RHETORIC OF RIGHT IN MITCHEL'S *JAIL JOURNAL*

CHRISTOPHER MORASH

Clearing a discursive space

"England has been left in possession not only of the soil of Ireland with all that grows and lives thereon, to her own use", writes John Mitchel in his *Jail Journal*, "but in possession of the world's ear also. She may pour into it what tale she will: and all mankind will believe her."[1] In these opening words, Mitchel, the Irish nationalist leader of the 1840s most strongly committed to military struggle for the "soil of Ireland", acknowledges that an equally important battlefield exists elsewhere, in the symbolic arena of discourse and representation. Indeed, written on prison ships, in detention centres, and finally in the penal colony of Van Diemen's Land, the *Jail Journal* could hardly claim otherwise. From the moment of his arrest at four o'clock on the afternoon of 21 May 1848, Mitchel was effectively precluded from engaging in any form of struggle other than a symbolic struggle against the discourses of imperialism. With the curtailment of any possibility that his texts might act transitively in the political sphere by issuing direct calls for revolution, Mitchel's writing moves into an exploration of the relationship between knowledge and power in the intransitive text. Indeed, in the early pages of his "Introductory Narrative" Mitchel describes this relationship in brutally clear terms:

> Success confers every right in this Enlightened Age; wherein, for the first time, it has come to be admitted and proclaimed in set

---

1. John Mitchel, *Jail Journal, Commenced on Board the "Shearwater" Steamer, Dublin Bay, Continued at Spike Island — On Board the "Scourge" War Steamer — On Board the "Dromedary" Hulk, Bermuda — On Board the "Neptune" Convict Ship — At Pernambuco — At the Cape of Good Hope (During the Anti-convict Rebellion) — At Van Dieman's Land — At Sydney — At Tahiti — At San Francisco — At Greytown — And Concluding at No. 3 Pier, North River, New York: With an Introductory Narrative of Transactions in Ireland*, [1854], Dublin, 1913; rpt Shannon, 1982, xxxvii.

terms, that Success is Right and Defeat is Wrong. If I profess myself a disbeliever in that gospel, the Enlightened Age will only smile, and say, "The defeated always are." Britain being in possession of the floor, any hostile comment upon her way of telling our story is an unmannerly interruption; nay, is nothing short of an *Irish howl* (*Jail Journal*, xxxvii).

An "unmannerly Irish howl" aptly describes the deconstructive readings to which the *Jail Journal* submits the literature of Empire in a symbolic attempt to take "possession of the floor". For example, when, during his captivity, Mitchel finds in his limited library a copy of Lieutenant Alexander Burnes's *Travels into Bokhara*,[2] Mitchel produces a reading which radically subverts the "common sense" assumptions which would form the horizon of expectation for most readers. "In his capacity of a geographical traveller", Mitchel writes of Burnes, "he took notes of the amount of plunder to be got, marked the exact spots where every good booty was to be found, and estimated the strength of the walls, bolts, and bars, with a view to future British burglarious operations" (*Jail Journal*, 105-106). In a textual strategy not without its parallels in contemporary critical practice, Mitchel displaces the imperialist author as the source of a text's authority by branding him as a burglar or spy. Whereas a reader functioning within a rational, liberal humanist concept of knowledge would consider disinterested knowledge of India as an end in itself, Mitchel — acutely aware that knowledge is rarely, if ever, disinterested — recognizes that acquisition of knowledge of a subject can easily form the prelude to material acquisition.

Mitchel's apprehension of the dialectic of power and knowledge does not, however, lead him to seek the elimination of imperial forms of textuality; indeed, as he later indicates, such forms of writing constitute the necessary (but necessarily rejected) foundation for a strategy of textual differentiation. Once a text like *Travels into Bokhara* has been subjected to a deconstructive reading, it becomes a palimpsest upon which Mitchel can inscribe his own textual identity:

It is apparent that the value of any book is not in the mere thoughts it presents to you, expressed in black-on-white, but rather in those it suggests, occasions, begets in you, far outside the intentions and conceptions of the writer, and even outside the subject of his writing. If some dull rogue writes you an essay, on what he does not understand, you are not bound to follow his

---

2. Alexander Burnes, *Travels into Bokhara: Being the Account of a Journey from India to Cabool, Tartary, from the Sea to Lahore in 1831–3*, 3 vols, London, 1834.

chain of reasoning (as perhaps he calls it) — the first link of his chain may fit itself to other links of your own forging, and so you may have whole trains, whole worlds of thought, which need not run upon the dull rogue's line, nor stop at his terminus (*Jail Journal*, 120).

Authenticity, presence and style

Again and again throughout the *Jail Journal*, Mitchel identifies the discourse of imperialism — whether it take the form of a book, a newspaper report, a phrase, or even a metaphor — as a form of writing against which he must define himself. However, as the prolonged intertextual engagement with texts such as *Travels into Bokhara* makes clear, his struggle for textual autonomy requires this imperial discourse, so that it might be parodied and rejected in the quest for an elusive authenticity. Consider, for example, the struggle to achieve an authentic, autonomous literary style in the following passage:

> Some nations that do now bestride the narrow world will learn lessons of true philosophy, but not new philosophy, in sackcloth and ashes. And other nations, low enough in the dust now, will arise from their sackcloth and begin a new national life — to repeat, it may be, the same crimes and suffer the same penalties. For the progress of the species is circular; or possibly in trochoidal curves, with some sort of cycloid for deferent; or more properly it oscillates, describing an arc of a circle, pendulum-wise; and even measures time (by æons) in that manner; or let us say, in one word, the world wags.
>   Another crimson evening is upon us. The sun, in a conflagration of clouds, flames on the very rim of Ocean (*Jail Journal*, 29).

The passage begins with what appears to be an earnest contribution to the discourse of national destiny. However, by developing to the point of absurdity the geometrical metaphor of "circular progress", and making history move in accordance with its tropic logic, following "trochoidal curves", "oscillating", and looping into an arc "with some sort of cycloid for a deferent", the text makes the reader aware of a disjunction between reality and textuality by opening a vista of pure textual play. This parody of the pseudo-scientific imperialist discourse of "the progress of history" is then foreclosed and deflated with the bathetic epigram: "the world wags".

Having dismissed an inauthentic form of writing, the page is now clear for Mitchel himself to make an appearance as an authentic authorial presence in the text. This he does by moving from the abstract language of mathematics to the precise particularity of a sunset over the ocean:

> Another crimson evening is upon us. The sun, in a conflagration of clouds, flames on the very rim of Ocean. He, too, the unwearied Sun, is chasing his own shadow round and round the world. "The Sun also ariseth, and the sun goeth down, and hasteth to his place whence he rose. All the rivers run into the sea, yet the sea is not full; unto the place from whence the rivers came, thither they return again. The waters wear the stones: Thou washest away the things which grow out of the dust of the earth; and thou destroyest the hope of man. Thou prevailest for ever against him, and he passeth". Good night (*Jail Journal*, 29).

By merging the details of his particular situation — watching the sun set from his cabin window — with this passage from Ecclesiastes, Mitchel establishes a contrast between two forms of textuality. The first form of writing — imperialist, scientific, inductive — is signalled as inauthentic by being subjected to parody; that is to say, it exists in a state of disjunction with the world outside of the text. The second form of writing, both poetic and religious, is presented as authentic; indeed, in the latter case, the text is as authentic as the "wonderful and terrible God" (*Jail Journal*, 135) whom Mitchel invokes when he is least concerned with the opacity of language. Moreover, the final conversational "Good night" identifies the personal authorial presence with the Biblical text in an act of reciprocal authorization. Yet, in both the parodied passage and the authenticated passage, Mitchel says more or less the same thing: that history is not linear, but follows a series of rises and falls. What differs radically between the two is the style of writing. It is thus in Mitchel's prose style that we can locate his attempt to create an authorial voice which has not been saturated by the pervasive discourse of empire.

Thomas Carlyle and the discourse of authenticity

While Mitchel's strategic alternation of parodic subversion and self-authentication functions successfully throughout much of his writing, in subscribing to the very idea of authenticity Mitchel compromises his own radical project. This becomes apparent when we begin to examine the intertextual referents and material contexts of the prose style which Mitchel's texts mark out as authentic. In 1847, for instance, when Mitchel was editor of the *Nation*, he began an editorial entitled "Ireland Not the Bravest" with a long quotation from Thomas Carlyle's 1843 *Past and Present*:

In all battles, if you await the issue, each fighter has prospered according to his right. His right and his might, at the close of the account, were one and the same .... A heroic WALLACE, quartered on the scaffold, cannot hinder that his Scotland become one day a part of England; but he does hinder that it become, on tyrannous and unfair terms, a part of it .... Scotland is not Ireland — no, because brave men rose there and said "Behold, ye must not tread us down like slaves, and ye shall not, and cannot". Fight on, thou brave true heart, and falter not, through dark fortune and through bright. The cause thou fightest for, so far as it is true, no farther, yet precisely so far, is very sure of victory.[3]

"It were worth centuries of 'agitation'", comments Mitchel, "could but that text of the Scottish Carlyle, written there above, get recognized ... by one generation of us" — thereby signalling that the text by Carlyle is an authentic form of writing. In so doing, Mitchel is making an intertextual reference which is by no means idiosyncratic for an Irish nationalist of the 1840s, for there are numerous, equally laudatory references to Carlyle by other writers in the nationalist press of the period. One finds, for instance, two poems with the title "Past and Present", one by Michael Tormey in the *Nation*,[4] another by Martin MacDermott in the *Irish Felon*;[5] we also find Lady Wilde's exhortations to the youth of Ireland, "Signs of the Times"[6] (taking its title from Carlyle's 1829 essay of the same name), and "Work While It Is Called Day",[7] a line from John 9:4 which Carlyle's *Sartor Resartus* had transformed into a catchphrase. The *Irishman*, Joseph Brennan's newspaper which took over from Mitchel's *United Irishman* after Mitchel's arrest in 1848, was particularly forthright in its praise of Carlyle, publishing several laudatory surveys of his career ("Literary Gossip";[8] "Thomas Carlyle").[9] In one such essay, the anonymous

---

3. *Past and Present*, X/12; as quoted in "Ireland Not the Bravest", the *Nation*, V, 242 (29 May 1847), 537. For the Carlyle text, see *The Works of Thomas Carlyle*, Centenary edn, 30 vols, London, 1896–1899.

4. The *Nation*, IV/207 (26 September 1846), 792.

5. The *Irish Felon*, I/2 (1 July 1848), 27.

6. The *Nation*, V/234 (3 April 1847), 410–11.

7. *Poems by Speranza*, 2nd edn, Glasgow, n.d., 47–48.

8. "Literary Gossip — Second Sitting: Thomas Carlyle", *Irishman*, I/36 (8 September 1849), 567.

reviewer declared that he was not influenced by any one of Carlyle's works, but by all; moreover, the reviewer claimed to have read all of Carlyle's works when they first appeared, and all remained fixed in his memory ("Literary Gossip", 567).

Indeed, in 1845 a deputation of Young Irelanders, including Mitchel's close friend and fellow solicitor, John O'Hagan, visited Carlyle in London in an attempt to enlist his help in the Irish repeal movement. The timing of the visit coincided with Carlyle's public defence of the exiled Italian nationalist, Guiseppe Mazzini, whose mail had been opened on the orders of Sir James Graham, with whom Mitchel and his colleagues were locked in a conflict concerning the Colleges Bill of 1845. "Mazzini is a man of rank, genius, and knowledge", declared the *Nation*. "He is a man of such character that THOMAS CARLYLE thought fit to write a letter to *The Times*, saying that he had known MAZZINI".[10] "The people are great disciples of mine", Carlyle wrote of the Young Irelanders in an 1847 letter to his brother Alexander. "But I think I have very little credit of them: in fact, they seem not unlikely to get themselves shot, or hanged for treason, by and by!".[11]

In spite of misgivings about his Irish disciples, Carlyle was to meet Mitchel during his first visit to Ireland in 1846, and in a letter written to Charles Gavan Duffy in October, 1848, Carlyle mentions leaving Mitchel "that autumn evening on the pier at Kingstown".[12] In another letter, dated March 1, 1847, Carlyle tells Duffy that he believes Mitchel to be "a noble, chivalrous fellow, full of talent and manful temper of every kind" (*Conversations*, 27). Later, in his *Jail Journal*, Mitchel returns the compliment, making several reverential mentions of "*noster* Thomas" (*Jail Journal*, 86, 116), noting that "Thomas Carlyle is the only man in these latter days who produces what can properly be termed books" (*Jail Journal*, 204).

The testimony of the journalist in the *Irishman* who claimed a comprehensive knowledge of Carlyle notwithstanding, Irish nationalist admiration for Thomas Carlyle in the 1840s was as selective as it was widespread. Diplomatically avoiding or excusing Carlyle's hagiographic study of the *bête noire* of Irish history, Oliver Cromwell, references to

---

9. "Thomas Carlyle; by R.D., Trinity College", *Irishman*, II/11 (16 March 1850), 171.

10. "Sir James Graham", the *Nation*, III/136 (17 May 1845), 505.

11. *The Letters of Thomas Carlyle to His Brother Alexander*, Cambridge: Mass., 1968, 648,

12. Charles Gavan Duffy, *Conversations with Carlyle*, London, 1892, 33.

Carlyle tended to focus on two texts: *Past and Present* (1843) and *Chartism* (1839). In particular, nationalists such as Mitchel turned to passages in Carlyle's texts emphasizing the conclusion towards which his works of the 1830s and 1840s inexorably move: "Might and Right do differ frightfully from hour to hour; but give them centuries to try it in, they are found to be identical" (*Chartism*, xxix, 173-74). Culminating in the apocalyptic power worship of his *Latter Day Pamphlets* (1851), Carlyle asserted his belief in this teleological justification of force with increasing vehemence throughout the 1840s, drawing the events of past ages and his own into orbit around a principle that he saw as an "everlasting polar star in the black tempestuous vortices of this world's history" (*Chartism*, xxix, 147). Moreover, as Carlyle's formulation of his philosophy of "might and right" became increasingly apocalyptic during the period of the ascendancy of the Young Ireland movement in Irish nationalist circles, it became increasingly attractive to the movement's militant wing. Recalling the 1845 meeting of the Young Ireland deputation with Carlyle in London, Duffy wrote:

> The Young Irishmen were greatly impressed by the philosopher and his wife. They did not accept his specific opinions on almost any question, but his constant advocacy of veracity, integrity, and valour touched the most generous of their sympathies, and his theory that under the divine government of the world right and might are identical, as right infallibly became might in the end, was very welcome teaching to men struggling against enormous odds for what they believed to be intrinsic justice (*Conversations*, 4).

Words with power
There is a deep irony in Carlyle's sponsorship by Mitchel, Duffy and their colleagues, for Carlyle's philosophy of "might and right" provided Victorian apologists of British imperialism with a moral justification for economic and military expansionism. For instance, James Anthony Froude, another of Carlyle's disciples and his future biographer, was to use the doctrine as the basis of a defence of British imperial rule in Ireland. Froude's *The English in Ireland in the Eighteenth Century*[13] was written to justify the use of force in the maintenance of the British presence in Ireland at a time when Gladstone's ameliorative gestures were being read by some as a tacit admission of the failure of British

---

13. James Anthony Froude, *The English in Ireland in the Eighteenth Century* (1872-74), rev. edn, 3 vols, London, 1881.

colonial government. In what amounts to a thesis statement at the beginning of the opening volume, Froude declares:

> Among reasonable beings right is for ever tending to create might .... There is no disputing against strength, nor happily is there need to dispute, for the strength which gives a right to freedom, implies the presence of those qualities which ensure that it will be rightly used (*Ireland*, I, 2, 12).

"If we examine", writes Carlyle in *Chartism*, "we shall find that, in this world, no conquest could ever become permanent, which did not withal show itself beneficial to the conquered as well as to the conquerors" (Carlyle, *Chartism*, xxix, 146–47). Indeed, Carlyle had an almost mystical vision of the British Empire as an entity capable of using "might" as a means of spreading righteousness throughout the world. "The stern Destinies have laid upon England a terrible job of labour in these centuries", he wrote in 1848; "governing, regulating, which in these days will mean conquering dragons and world-wide Chimeras, and climbing as high as the zenith to snatch fire from the gods, and diving deep as the nadir to fling devils in chains!"[14]

We know that Mitchel had no illusions about Carlyle's attitudes towards Irish nationalism, for in his *Jail Journal* he notes: "Carlyle cannot write rationally about Ireland; and he believes that Carthage [England] has a mission to conquer the world" (*Jail Journal*, 204). And yet, in spite of his recognition that Carlyle is one of the most eloquent defenders of the Empire to which he is so adamantly opposed, Mitchel's texts share his fellow nationalists' debt to Carlylean discourses. For instance, writing in his *Jail Journal*, Mitchel declares his understanding of the role of the nation in Carlylean terms:

> Neither for man nor nation is happiness the end of living — least of all for those who utter new truths and lead in new paths. Let a nation act with all the energy of its national life — do with its might what its hand findeth to do — the truth it has got to speak in thunder. Therein let it find its "happiness", or nowhere. (81)

The comparison with Carlyle in this passage goes beyond a mere similarity in the belief in a national destiny (which, after all, was common throughout the century, and can be traced back at least as far as Herder's *Reflections on the Philosophy of History* of 1784-91). The

---

14. *Rescued Essays of Thomas Carlyle*, ed. Percy Newberry, London, 1892, 34.

similarity here extends to a rhetorical style which determines the epistemological status of belief. In fact, it could be said that Mitchel is writing in "Carlylese". In both writers, we find a distinctive use of Biblical archaisms ("hither", "therein", "findeth") and vocabulary consciously echoing that of the King James Bible — words like "utter", "speak in thunder" and "sackcloth". By blurring the distinction between their own texts and the Biblical passages which pepper their writings, both Carlyle and Mitchel indicate that forms of writing authenticated by such Biblical references are not open to question. Indeed, at one point in his *Jail Journal* Mitchel declares in unambiguous terms that the establishment of rhetorical might lies at the basis of his textual practice: "It is all assertion. I declaim vehemently; I dogmatise vigorously, but argue never. You have my thought. I don't want you to agree with me; you can take it or leave it" (*Jail Journal*, 88).

Lessons of empire

In exercising this neo-Biblical rhetorical force, claiming for their texts the status of revelation, both Mitchel and Carlyle are making the stylistic assertion of a textual "might" which is self-justifying. If a point can be carried through rhetoric, their texts indicate, it must be valid. Hence, at the level of style, their texts reaffirm the claim that "right equals might", accepting the sheer world-creating force of language and rejecting both inductive reasoning and what they refer to as "metaphysics".

In the case of the latter, there is a particularly interesting connection between Mitchel and Carlyle. For Carlyle, any attempt to move beyond a limited conception of "right" was to encourage the cancerous growth of "the disease of metaphysics" ("Characteristics", xxviii, 25). Throughout the entire body of his work, Carlyle never lapses in his praise for the man who eschews speculative thought. Speculation, Carlyle writes, leads to doubt. Action, on the other hand, or work, demands a conviction which must ultimately be based upon righteousness. "The mere existence and necessity of a Philosophy is an evil", writes Carlyle in "Characteristics":

> Man is sent hither not to question, but to work .... For truly, if we look into it, there is not a more fruitless endeavour than this same, which the Metaphysician proper toils in: to educe Conviction out of Negation .... The Irish Saint swam the Channel, "carrying his head in his teeth"; but the feat has never been imitated ("Characteristics", xxviii, 27).

Eighteen years after Carlyle wrote this passage, Mitchel found himself in a prison hulk moored off the coast of Bermuda, in a position of almost perfect impotence, able neither to act, nor to inspire action. Indeed, while his fellow convicts worked breaking stones, Mitchel was not even allowed this activity, for the prison authorities considered him to be a "gentleman". Thus, precluded from work and action, Mitchel finds himself pondering an abstract question at great length, at which point he interrupts his text:

> But what is this? Is it the abyss of metaphysics I see yawning before me? Assuredly, I will not plunge into that bottomless pit again, after having drawn myself out of it, with pain and labour, full fifteen years ago — just so long is it since I endeavoured to walk with my own head in my teeth, like the decapitated Christian martyr celebrated by Mr. Gibbon — to rival that "Irish Saint", known to Thomas Carlyle, who swam across the Channel with *his* head so secured — "a miracle", saith Carlyle, "which has never been repeated" (*Jail Journal*, 121-22).

Not only does this journal entry show Mitchel to have had a deep enough knowledge of Carlyle to have been able to cite "Characteristics" from memory (Mitchel does not mention having the essay amongst the volumes in his prison library); it also tells us that shortly after the essay was published in 1831 ("full fifteen years ago" — Mitchel was writing in January of 1849), Mitchel made a conscious choice to give up speculation for direct action.

The kinship between the ideological positions of Carlyle, the British imperialist, and Mitchel, the Irish nationalist, becomes more readily apparent once they entered into a discursive arena removed from the Irish nationalist–British imperialist opposition. Both Mitchel and Carlyle were staunch supporters of slavery, and during the American Civil War both supported the Confederate side from a strong commitment to the idea of racial hierarchy. Duffy claims that Carlyle "taught Mitchel to oppose the liberation of negroes and the emancipation of Jews" (*Conversations*, 117), and there is good reason to believe him. In his notorious "Occasional Discourse on the Nigger Question" (1849), Carlyle bitterly describes "beautiful Blacks sitting there [the West Indies] up to the ears in pumpkins, and doleful Whites sitting here without potatoes to eat" ("Nigger Question", xxix, 351). Mitchel echoes this sentence twelve years later in his *Last Conquest of Ireland (Perhaps)*,[15] when he rails

---

15. *The Last Conquest of Ireland (Perhaps)* (1861), rpt London, n.d.

against the British government granting compensation to slave owners for "turning negroes wild (setting them 'free' as it was called)" (94), and then refusing to grant adequate relief money to the Irish during the Famine.

The ironies and contradictions of the convergence of Mitchel and Carlyle are compounded, moreover, by the circumstances surrounding the writing of Carlyle's "Occasional Discourse". Written in 1849, the same year in which Carlyle made a tour of Ireland and wrote a number of essays on Irish subjects, it is as much about the "Irish Question" as the "Nigger Question"; indeed, he saw little difference between the two. Similarly, Froude, in his companion volume to *The English in Ireland*, *The English in the West Indies*,[16] makes frequent mention of Ireland, warning that to have abolished slavery "is to have created in the Antilles and Jamaica so many fresh Irelands" (*West Indies*, 372). Indeed, he defines the imperial imperative in terms which make it clear that he wants the racial justification of empire to apply equally to Ireland and the West Indies:

> If you choose to take a race like the Irish or like the negroes ... who are not strong enough or brave enough to defend their own independence, and whom our own safety cannot allow to fall under any other power, our right and our duty is to govern such races and to govern them well, or they will have a right in turn to cut our throats. This is our mission (*West Indies*, 208).

Mitchel learned the lessons of imperialism well. In accepting Carlyle's doctrine that basic human rights and freedoms are not intrinsic but earned through force — "right equals might" — he was accepting the terms (but not the conclusions) of the argument behind the moral justification for colonialism. Froude would use the Carlylean philosophy of self-justifying power retrospectively to justify the imperial *status quo*; Mitchel used it to argue for a revolution more violent than the oppression by which it was occasioned. Both polemics proceed from the principle that a colonized people had the right to "cut the throats" of inept colonizers. "I prescribe copious bloodletting", writes Mitchel in his *Jail Journal*, "upon strictly therapeutical principles" (92). The difference between the two positions arises from differing interpretations of historical and political discourses. By taking possession of "the world's ear", and deconstructing British interpretations of Irish history, Mitchel clears a space both for his

---

16. James Anthony Froude, *The English in the West Indies: Or, The Bow of Ulysses*, London, 1888.

own writing, and for political action. Hence, whereas Carlyle, and later Froude, would warn that *unless* the colonial powers gave up conciliatory policies and reasserted their superior strength they would lose their right to govern, Mitchel interpreted conciliation and negotiation as abnegation of that right. Indeed, in Mitchel's attacks on British rule in Ireland, particularly in his vilification of what he calls "ameliorations",[17] there is a note of contempt, as if he despised the British more for their weakness than for their harshness. However, while Mitchel's texts ostensibly set out to deconstruct and supplant the literature of empire, his intertextual engagement with Thomas Carlyle, and his acceptance of the terms of the Carlylean analysis of power and righteousness, leads him into an area of contradiction, as he celebrates at the level of syntax and vocabulary that which he castigates. In asserting at a stylistic level that rhetorical "might equals right", Mitchel's radical nationalism is itself subverted, becoming a mirror image of the imperialism it seeks to overthrow.

---

17. For example, Mitchel refers to the Colleges Bill as one of "the Premier's ameliorations" in *The History of Ireland from the Treaty of Limerick to the Present Time*, 2 vols, 3rd edn (1868); Dublin, n.d., II, 382.

ROSA MULHOLLAND, W.P. RYAN AND IRISH CATHOLIC FICTION AT THE TIME OF THE ANGLO-IRISH REVIVAL

JAMES H. MURPHY

The canon of literature is at best a regrettable necessity. For it to retain any credibility the assumptions which govern the canonization of authors and texts at a particular time must be reviewed periodically. Over the years we have tended to present late nineteenth and early twentieth century Ireland as being the era of a literary revival, led by Anglo-Irish Protestants, who wrote poems and plays. Of course, Joyce, the ex-Catholic novelist, does not fit into this pattern. Literary historians have tended to shrug off this embarrassment by placing him in a category of his own. He is to be seen as *sui generis*.

This version of the era we are considering elides much of what was actually going on. In his catalogue of Irish novels, *Ireland in Fiction*, first published in 1916 and revised in 1919, Stephen Brown records many hundreds of novels written in the late nineteenth and early twentieth centuries in Ireland. A substantial proportion of them were written by Catholics and it is certain that there were many other novels written by Catholics which did not find their way into Brown's book.

Most of these works have never received any critical attention. What follows, however, is an attempt to offer a model for understanding this vast body of fiction which relates it to the mentality and concerns of the various social classes from which its authors sprang. It will not be claimed that what is found in fiction can be used as evidence for what was happening in real life. However, it will be argued that such fiction can be seen to reflect the values and mentality of the social groups to which its authors belonged. Much of the material is not of any great literary worth. It is, nonetheless, as significant as the Anglo-Irish literary revival for what it reveals about the development of Irish culture.

In reading Irish Catholic fiction, during this period, one is struck by a change which overtakes it in the 1890s. This change reflects an alteration in Irish society which Emmet Larkin has persuasively described as the coming to power of a new lower middle class Catholic establishment. This substantial group in Irish society, made up of farmers and shopkeepers, was the one which was to dominate life in the Irish Free State after the granting of independence to southern Ireland in 1922. By 1890, though, it had already secured its position as what Larkin calls "the nation-forming class".[1]

The decade of the 1890s then marks a watershed in Irish society. It also marks a watershed in fiction written by Catholics in Ireland. Before the 1890s Irish Catholic fiction reflected the distinctive outlook of the Catholic upper middle class. After the 1890s it reflected the concerns of an emerging Catholic intelligentsia, opposed to the values of the new establishment. Rosa Mulholland's *Marcella Grace*, published in 1886, and W.P. Ryan's *The Plough and the Cross*, published in 1910, will serve as good illustrations of these trends.[2]

Rosa Mulholland was the daughter of a doctor and the wife of an historian, Sir John Gilbert. Her sister married the lawyer Sir Charles Russell, later to be Lord Chief Justice of England. His brother was Father Matthew Russell, editor of *The Irish Monthly*, the journal which was to publish the early work of Oscar Wilde and W.B. Yeats. Rosa Mulholland belonged firmly to the Catholic upper middle class. It is a group which has received little scholarly attention. Its own distinctive ethos and aspirations to take a leading part in Irish society have been lost to sight. The rise of the new lower middle class establishment put pay to the aspirations of the upper middle class to become Ireland's nation-forming class. Indeed, so pervasive did the culture of lower middle class Catholic Ireland become that the culture of the upper middle class became assimilated to it. That which was distinctive about upper middle class culture and aspirations was forgotten. Yet we can still catch a glimpse of it in Rosa Mulholland's novels, particularly in her seminal work, *Marcella Grace*.

Above all things, the Irish Catholic upper middle class feared provincialism and aspired to a certain cosmopolitanism.[3] The problem

1. Emmet Larkin, "Church, State and Nation in Modern Ireland", *The American Historical Review*, LXXX (1975), 1244–76.

2. For a fuller exploration of issues which it is only possible to outline in a short article see James H. Murphy, "Catholic Fiction and Social Reality in Ireland, 1870–1922", PhD dissertation, University College Dublin [N.U.I.], 1991. This work is the first to offer a social model for Catholic fiction during the period.

3. Rosa Mulholland's *The Wild Birds of Killeevy* (1883) and J.H. McCarthy's historical novels *The Illustrious O'Hagan* (1906) and *The King over the Water*

was that Ireland was involved in a fraught political and cultural relationship with Britain, centre of that cosmopolitan culture of which the Catholic upper middle class aspired to partake. Victorian society saw Ireland as a whole and saw it in a very negative light, influenced by stereotypes of Irish national character and by the adverse publicity which Irish agrarian and revolutionary agitation generated.[4]

The Catholic upper middle class knew that the only way by which its own position might be normalized within Victorian society was if some resolution could be found to the difficulties between Ireland and Britain, particularly to the land question. Between 1880 and 1882, during the first phase of the land war, over 10,000 agrarian outrages took place in Ireland, constituting more than half of all reported crime.[5] The Catholic upper middle class placed its hopes for peace, not in tenant ownership, but in the replacement of a Protestant with a Catholic gentry, dedicated to the fair treatment of the tenantry. A rural Ireland ruled by a Catholic gentry would be a country ruled by a class of an identical outlook to that of the urban Catholic upper middle class.[6]

Marcella Grace is the most significant example of a novel which makes a bold attempt to tackle the complexities of the land question and to make out a case for a Catholic gentry solution. It charts the experiences of a young Catholic girl, born into poverty in Dublin, who inherits an estate in the west of Ireland. It is precisely Marcella's background, enabling her to understand the experiences of ordinary

---

(1911), among others, can be seen as attempting to soothe the fear of provincialism by presenting Irish characters as being involved in cosmopolitan adventure.

4. Irish people were seen as either the simian monsters of *Punch*, or as the hapless idiots which upper middle class Catholics so despised in the novels of Lover and Lever and in *The Real Charlotte* (1894) by Somerville and Ross. The upper middle class project was to convince the English that "we are very like other people only nicer", to use an oft repeated phrase of *The Irish Monthly* (XVIII [1890], 614, and XIX [1891], 379). Novels by Catholics such as Justin McCarthy's *A Fair Saxon* (1873) and James Murphy's *Convict No. 25* (1883) try to modify English perceptions about Irish violence and wrongdoing.

5. T.W. Moody, *Davitt and Irish Revolution 1846–82*, Oxford, 1982, Appendix E1, 565.

6. Apart from Rosa Mulholland's *Marcella Grace* (1886), other novels which advocate a Catholic gentry solution include Dillon O'Brien's *The Dalys of Dalystown* (1866), in which Henry Daly envisages "a tenantry whose interests and mine shall be one" (518), and R.B. O'Brien's *D'Altons of Crag* (1882) whose landlord–hero values the "affection and devotedness" of his tenants above "miserable gains" (Preface).

people, which is adduced as the reason for her suitability to be a benign landlord.

She finds herself surrounded by a variety of other responses to the situation. Firstly, there is the absentee response which had been the one reluctantly adopted by her predecessor, Mrs O'Kelly, a Catholic unionist, who had lived in Dublin for fear of attack from the "Fenians", here used in a generic sense as a label for those involved in agrarian violence. Secondly, there is the confrontational response of the rack-renting O'Flahertys, cousins of Mrs O'Kelly. Thirdly, there is the egalitarian response of the Kilmartins, who had given their lands away to their tenants, as a point of principle. Finally, there is the violent response of the "Fenians" themselves, which is seen as sinister and counterproductive.

Though the response of the Kilmartins is seen as having something to commend it, Marcella decides to adopt the response which the parish priest, Fr Daly, urges on her. His vision of her is of a benign landlord looking after her tenants and thus giving no excuse for the development of agrarian violence. Marcella determines to be a good landlord and not to follow the example of the O'Flahertys. With the help of Fr Daly, whose protégée she becomes, Marcella improves conditions on her estate and wins over the tenants, though she has to face an assassination attempt *en route*.

Rosa Mulholland was not an advocate of the Catholic gentry solution to Ireland's land question, without qualifications. After all, she depicts Mrs O'Kelly and the O'Flahertys as both Catholics and bad landlords. Though Catholicism itself was an advantage, it would have to be matched by the development of a prudent and productive relationship between landlord and tenant, if peace was to ensue. Thus Marcella is seen to steer a successful and moderate course between the extreme solutions of the O'Flahertys and the Fenians. Mulholland's solution to Ireland's problem is embodied in a heroine who turns out to be the benign ruler of a grateful and dutiful people:

> Were not these poor overjoyed creatures her actual children? Had they not been given bodily into her charge? Had not providence ordained that enough sustenance should be derived from the land for her and for them?[7]

If *Marcella Grace* illustrates the distinctiveness of the aspirations of the Catholic uper middle class it also reflects its principal flaw, a capacity

---

7. Rosa Mulholland, *Marcella Grace* [1886]; New York, 1891, 149.

for delusion about its own role in a future Ireland. Even as *Marcella Grace* was being written, tenant ownership and the new Catholic *petit bourgeois* establishment were becoming realities. By the turn of the century not even the Catholic upper middle class could delude itself into imagining that it would ever be in the driving seat of the nation. Its ethos began to adjust to that of the new establishment. It became more vigorously nationalistic and Catholic in tone. Even Rosa Mulholland herself adjusted to the new situation, an adjustment which is reflected in some of her later novels.[8]

The assimilation of the ethos of the Catholic upper middle class to that of the dominant lower middle class in the early twentieth century resulted in cultural historians losing sight of the fact that it had ever had an independent existence.[9] However, recovering a sense of that distinctive ethos is important for the social history of nineteenth-century Ireland. It is also important for understanding much of the literature produced by the Irish Catholic community during the period.

Marcella Grace itself was a widely read and very influential novel in its day.[10] Yet it is now largely forgotten in spite of its author being anthologized by Yeats, in *Representative Irish Tales* (1891); in spite of Mrs Humphrey Ward using the name Marcella for the heroine of a series of her novels; and in spite of the fact that *Marcella Grace* provoked a still unidentified author to attack all that it stood for in a novelistic riposte, *Priests and People: A No-Rent Romance* (1891).[11] This latter work was reissued in 1979 in New York as part of the Garland series,

---

8. *The Return of Mary O'Morrough* (1908), in particular, reflects both a new note of nationalism and a lingering regret over the failure of conciliation between Irish and English culture.

9. Katharine Tynan's *The Way of a Maid* (1895), M.E. Francis's *Miss Erin* (1898), Justin McCarthy's *Mononia* (1901) and J.H. McCarthy's *The Fair Irish Maid* (1911) are all novels in which writers who had worked within the conventions of upper middle class Catholic fiction can be seen to adjust, with varying degrees of alacrity, to the more Catholic, nationalist outlook of the newly dominant lower middle class.

10. Originally serialized in *The Irish Monthly*, XIII (1885), *Marcella Grace* went through several editions in Britain and the United States. In "What Our Country Folk Read", *The New Ireland Review*, I (March–August 1894), 65–67, Rosa Mulholland's novels are said to have been more popular than those of Gerald Griffin, the Banims and William Carleton, and only surpassed by C.J. Kickham's *Knocknagow* (1873).

11. The assertion that it was a riposte to *Marcella Grace* is made on the basis of convincing internal evidence.

though without any reference to *Marcella Grace* which it had set out to attack.

The waning of the upper middle class and the rise of an intelligentsia class opposed to Ireland's new *petit bourgeois* establishment are the key contexts for understanding Irish Catholic fiction in the late nineteenth and early twentieth centuries. Before going on to describe the features of fiction produced by intelligentsia writers, with special reference to W.P. Ryan's *The Plough and the Cross*, it is worth noting how the settings of the Irish fiction of George Moore reflect the changes in Irish Catholic society and fiction which we have described. *A Drama in Muslin*, published in 1886, is set in the world of the Catholic gentry. It thus comes from the context of Catholic upper middle class fiction, even though its realism is far from the sentimentality of the romantic comedies which Catholic upper middle class writers produced. Indeed, Moore obviously intended his realism to act as a rebuke to their *insouciance*.

When George Moore returned to fiction set in Ireland nearly two decades later, his work is best understood within the context of Catholic intelligentsia fiction. *The Untilled Field* (1903) and *The Lake* (1905) enact the intelligentsia struggle against Catholic Ireland. Both works focus on the struggle of individuals for self-realization within an anti-modern society in which such self-realization is denied. The short stories of *The Untilled Field* constitute a cumulative case for an alliance of the intelligentsia and peasantry against Catholic Ireland. *The Lake* adduces the case of a priest as a significant example of the triumph of modern values over those of Catholic Ireland.

The issues of modernization and self-realization were at the heart of the Catholic intelligentsia struggle against *petit bourgeois* Catholic Ireland. Whether they were journalists, teachers, writers, priests or members of other professions, the members of the Irish Catholic intelligentsia were all convinced of the need for modernization, education, individual freedom, a liberal spirit in society and a critical stance with respect to current Irish realities.[12] The Catholic intelligentsia

---

12. See Tom Garvin, *Nationalist Revolutionaries in Ireland, 1858–1928*, Oxford, 1987. This work argues that these new Catholic intellectuals themselves came from a lower middle class background and were helped by the 1878 education act; the number of Catholics in second-level education nearly tripled between 1861 and 1911. The number of Catholics receiving secondary education as a percentage of the total number receiving such education rose from 51.1% to 73.6% over this period (45). Part of the thesis of this work is that resentment at being excluded from the social and career elites of society was among the factors which led a proportion of new Catholic intellectuals to involvement with revolutionary movements in the first two

was a growing force in two senses. The number of those who might be classed as intellectuals was on the increase and they felt that the tide of history was moving in their direction.

The first two decades of the twentieth century were a period of intellectual ferment in Ireland. In spite of the strength of the new establishment, members of the Catholic intelligentsia felt that the country was on the verge of change and that a new Ireland was about to be brought to birth. Indeed, the sub-title of Ryan's novel, *The Plough and the Cross*, is *A Story of New Ireland*.

Members of the intelligentsia looked to a variety of contemporary movements to act as sources of renewal which would replace Catholic Ireland with a new Ireland. Radical nationalism, the Gaelic League, the Cooperative Movement and the literary revival were all seen as repositories of the values of true Ireland. From these sources of true Ireland a new Ireland could be created. This new Ireland would foster a modernity which valued the rights of the individual over those of society.

In Ireland novels have always been read not only as works of fiction but as works making statements about Irish life. This tendency was especially pronounced during the first two decades of the twentieth century. At this period the novel was perceived to be an only semi-fictional *locus* both for autobiographies of the struggle with Catholic Ireland and also for testing whether various new Irelands could be brought to birth out of the expected decay of *petit bourgeois* society. Of course, in many of the most powerful of these novels, the vision of a new Ireland is so personal as to be inseparable from the autobiography. Nonetheless, it is important to underline the fact that these novels have a double focus and are concerned both with modernization in society and with self-realization.[13]

Whereas Catholic upper middle class writers almost unconsciously reflected the economic and social concerns of their class, Catholic intelligentsia writers were self-consciously individual. The upper middle class had a common vision of its true Ireland. On the other hand, each intelligentsia writer's quarrel with the establishment consensus was different. And, though there were always points of similarity between

---

decades of the twentieth century.

13. A list of such novels for the period under consideration would include not only Moore and Ryan's novels but also James Joyce's *A Portrait of the Artist as a Young Man* (1916) and novels by Gerald O'Donovan, particularly *Father Ralph* (1913), Patrick MacGill, Brinsley MacNamara, Seumas O'Kelly, Aodh De Blacam, Edward MacLysaght and Eimar O'Duffy.

them, intelligentsia writers, prizing individualism as they did, tended to arrive at different solutions to what they saw as Ireland's problems.

Therefore, each author exhibits a different balance between the political and the personal, the communal and the individual. For all Stephen's talk of forging "in the smithy of my soul the uncreated conscience of my race",[14] Joyce's concerns tilt in favour of the individual. George Moore's priorities are political in the general sense that his writing champions his own version of true modern Ireland. The concerns of W.P. Ryan, who was a politically committed journalist, are more formally political while, for all his concern with changing society, Gerald O'Donovan's primary focus is on the personal.

What was central to W.P. Ryan's vision was his belief that Catholicism could be reformed. Liberalism and socialism were his chosen instruments for that reform. *The Plough and the Cross*, which was published in 1910, presents the reader with an Ireland in which such a reform is attempted.

The hero of the novel, Fergus O'Hagan, is the editor of a radical paper. He is a campaigner for the nationalist and Gaelic causes and for the cause of modernizing Catholicism in conjunction with some liberal priests. The narrative recalls what one of them had written to Fergus:

> The great modern task of freeing Catholicism in Ireland from formalism and literalism, on the one hand, and of patronage or forgetfulness of the poor rather than love of them, on the other, and making it a profoundly moving and enlightening spiritual and social force again demanded the most subtle delicacy as well as courage.[15]

This is a position echoed by O'Hagan himself during a confrontation with a bishop who has joined in the general denunciation of O'Hagan's paper as un-Irish because of its questioning of clerical power in Ireland:

> Is there any reason why we should not have broad minded, democratic and intellectual churchmen in Ireland — men who would show that the Church so far from being afraid of science, culture, democracy and progress, appreciates them and encourages

---

14. James Joyce, *A Portrait of the Artist as a Young Man* (1916), St Alban's, 1977, 228.

15. W.P. Ryan, *The Plough and the Cross: A Story of New Ireland*, Dublin, 1910, 3.

them and has a mission and a spirit immeasurably greater than them all?[16]

As with so many Catholic intelligentsia novels, *The Plough and the Cross* ends with the defeat of the movement to bring about a new Ireland. O'Hagan's paper collapses and, like the heroes of other such novels, he is left struggling to create a space for his own survival as an individual with integrity. He is buoyed up by his insistence that his own values are still representative of true Ireland:

> When you come to think of it ... the great Ireland is in ourselves, and it is full of beauty, divine activity and boundless hope. The outer Ireland, agitated or stagnant, is something incidental to keep our souls in training.[17]

The novel ends with O'Hagan looking forward optimistically to the day, perhaps ten years ahead, when progressive ideas would at last triumph. In the real world, Catholic intelligentsia hopes for a new Ireland were to be decisively dashed by the consolidation of the new *petit bourgeois* establishment, with the founding of the Irish Free State. The sense of expectation about change which had so charged the intelligentsia with enthusiasm was to dissipate.

If the Catholic intelligentsia had a flaw it was that the weakness of its position in society left it prone to a certain paranoia, though this is not over-pronounced in Ryan's novel. In general, though, the intelligentsia case against Catholic Ireland was diminished by the severity of its anger and by its general inability to imagine how anyone could embrace the values of Catholic Ireland with integrity. It lacked the confidence and perspective to be able to distinguish between an oppression which is the result of a minority feeling that society has allowed no room for its particular values and an oppression which is the result of a malicious and villainous plot.

This article has attempted to draw attention to the vast body of fiction which was produced by the Catholic community in Ireland in the late nineteenth and early twentieth centuries. Though the work of Joyce and several others has been the subject of much critical interest, the attention it has received has often not properly situated it within the context of the fiction of the Catholic community.

---

16. *Ibid.*, 306.

17. *Ibid.*, 373.

Elaine Showalter has noted that canon-formation "is now understood as an historically grounded process, rather than an assertion of aesthetic value".[18] The canonization of the writers of the Anglo-Irish literary revival and the scholarly oblivion which has overtaken all but a few of the Catholic novelists of the time is remarkable.[19] A study of the processes by which this came about would be instructive. One suspects that the general anti-intellectual haze which hovered over Catholic Ireland and the fact that many of the most distinguished scholars of Irish writing in English were from an Anglo-Irish background may have had something to do with it. Certainly the time is now ripe for a renewed interest in these writers and their social background, if only because their novels provide a rich source for a deeper understanding of Irish society at a crucial period.

18. Elaine Showalter, "Feminism and Literature", in *Literary Theory Today* (1990), eds Peter Collier and Helga Geyer-Ryan, Cambridge, 1992, 193.

19. For instance, no upper-middle-class Catholic novelist appears in *The Field Day Anthology* (Derry, 1991). On the other hand, John Wilson Foster, *Fictions of the Irish Literary Revival: A Changeling Art* (Dublin, 1987, xii–xiv) draws attention to the large numbers of novels written by both Catholics and Protestants at the time which did not form a part of the literary revival. Adverting to the dearth of scholarly work on such novels Foster rightly comments that "This popular fiction would make a fascinating study in its own right".

LITERATURE REWRITES HISTORY:
JAMES CONNOLLY AND JAMES LARKIN
LARGER THAN LIFE

BARBARA FREITAG

The historical background

Until the appearance of Connolly and Larkin on the Irish scene, the plight of Irish labourers was desperate indeed, and particularly so in Dublin where unskilled workers lived in appalling conditions, often described as the worst in Europe. Most of the trade unions in Ireland were branches of British unions. When the Irish Trade Union Congress was formed, this was initiated by men who were nearly all members of British unions, and who were not prompted by any spirit of Irish nationalism. The Irish congress was not intended to supersede the British TUC, the reasons for its formation being of a practical not ideological nature. Most Irish trade unions simply could not afford the expense of sending delegates to Britain, and furthermore those who did go found the British congress offered very little by way of benefit because the British delegates tended not to deal with Irish problems. "The only real interest that the British TUC had in anything Irish was to make sure that Irish workers in Britain were organised into trade unions so that they would not undercut the wages of British workers."[1]

For years the Irish TUC adopted a policy of carefully avoiding treading on anybody's toes by eliminating all controversial political questions from their agenda and dealing with routine matters only. In this way, they had managed to maintain a good relationship with all political parties. Now, however, with the appearance of the two socialists from Great Britain on the trade union scene, the whole political direction was to change dramatically.

Larkin was sent to Belfast in 1907 as organizer for the National Union of Dock Labourers, with the mission to create a trade union for the dock-labourers of the city. Within only a few weeks he was making such

---

1. Andrew Boyd, *The Rise of the Irish Trade Unions*, Dublin, 1976, 69.

unexpected progress that he alarmed the Unionist newspapers. They denounced him as "a socialist and a Catholic" warning the Protestant labour force to stay away from him. But the working people of Belfast who for generations had been ambushing, maiming and murdering one another in the name of religion, stood by Larkin, and all factions marched together taking part in non-sectarian Labour demonstrations. Larkin had fired their imagination.

When the Belfast dock-labourers protested against having to work alongside non-union labour they found themselves locked out, and their jobs taken by strike-breakers who were imported overnight from Liverpool. Other sections of the labour force promptly struck in sympathy, bringing the docks to a virtual standstill. The subsequent drafting in of thousands of extra policemen and soldiers for the protection of the strike-breakers sparked off a crisis whose suddenness, bitterness and explosive nature struck fear into the hearts of employers and politicians alike. After weeks of demonstrations, then rioting, and eventually bloodshed and death, the use of overwhelming military force brought the bitter conflict to an end. Demoralized and dejected, the workers returned to work, being forced to sign a document which said that "no person representing any union would be recognized by employers".

In the bitterness of the aftermath, old sectarian fears were rearoused which destroyed all feelings of loyalty to their union. But instead of addressing these issues or restructuring the sadly diminished organization, Larkin soon departed from Belfast, leaving behind him neither funds, nor able organizers nor even a coherent political programme for the union. He spent the following years shuttling back and forth between Liverpool, London and Dublin founding new union branches, agitating for wage increases and organizing strikes.

However, his militant activities were not only met by the combined opposition of the employers, the police and the clergy, but also with antagonism from his union headquarters in England.

Dismissed at the end of 1908, Larkin immediately founded his own Irish Transport and General Workers' Union (ITGWU) in Dublin. His magnetic personality and gifts of oratory soon had thousands of workers enrolled. Most importantly, however, James Connolly joined the ITGWU, and was appointed organizer of that union. Under the combined talented leadership of these two men, the labour movement went from strength to strength. During the next few years membership of the ITGWU rose from 4,000 to 14,000. Despite occasionally disastrous results, each strike enhanced the ITGWU's standing, because this union was beginning to give "the most downtrodden of the workers a sense of identity and of self-respect".[2]

But then the employers reacted in the same manner as they had in Belfast. In August 1913, the Employers' Federation decided to break Larkin's union by locking out all those employees who belonged to it. Other employers' associations speedily followed suit. Within a couple of weeks, about 100,000 were thrown out of employment. Despite being reduced to starvation, they kept up the struggle for eight months, in an atmosphere of increasing bitterness and violence, savage baton charges and mob rioting. At the end of it all, after dozens of people had been arrested and imprisoned (Connolly and Larkin among them), three people killed and many hundreds wounded, the workers gradually drifted back to work. Many of them were not reemployed, and most of those who got their jobs back were forced to sign a document disowning the ITGWU. Union militants were victimized and in many cases wage cuts were imposed. Larkin publicly admitted, "We are beaten, we will make no bones about it", and Connolly wrote with bitterness, "We Irish workers must again go down into Hell, bow our back to the lash of the slave driver ... and eat the dust of defeat and betrayal".[3]

Six months later, Larkin went to the United States on a fund-raising tour. He did not return to Ireland until nine years later. After first getting involved in a campaign against the 1914-18 war, he started to promote socialism and support for the Soviet Union. For these activities he was tried and found guilty of criminal anarchy in 1920, and served three years of a ten year sentence in Sing Sing prison. Upon his return to Ireland he was given a rapturous welcome, but he soon discovered that he could not take up where he had left off in 1914. There were ugly rows with the committee of his union which refused to reinstate him in the position of general secretary. The dispute ended in his expulsion. Larkin founded a new organization, the Workers Union of Ireland, but he never again reached the same degree of public influence. For the rest of his life he remained dissatisfied with his country, and when he died in 1947, leaving only £4.50 and a few personal belongings, he died a disappointed man.[4]

Connolly, who had taken charge of what was left of the ITGWU after Larkin's departure to America, was faced with a situation not unlike that

---

2. F.S.L. Lyons, *Ireland since the Famine*, London, 1978, 279.

3. Curriculum Development Unit, *Dublin, Divided City: Portrait of Dublin 1913*, Dublin, 1978, 102.

4. *Ibid.*, 109.

of Belfast in 1907. "The Union was completely bankrupt of funds, very heavily in debt and reduced to a very few members."[5] Beside his attempts to keep the Union alive, Connolly devoted most of his time to perfecting the organization of the Irish Citizen Army, founded for the protection of the locked-out workers in the heat of the 1913 struggle. He took part in the secret preparations for the Easter Rising, and was appointed military commander of the Republican forces in Dublin, including his own Citizen Army. He was in command of the GPO during Easter Week, badly wounded, and executed in 1916.

The two big labour struggles in Belfast and Dublin both failed to achieve their immediate objectives, and the hopes of the labour leaders who had had wider aspirations were dashed. Not only was Larkinism successfully repelled, but subsequently organized labour as a whole suffered a setback, particularly so in Belfast where it was subjected to successive catastrophic defeats.[6] Despite this, however, a heroic and revolutionary mythology, revolving around Larkin and Connolly, is associated with the events. The two men inspired poets, writers and dramatists to sing their praises.

Biographical determinants

In his work on revolutionary heroism, the sociologist M. Naumann[7] maintains that it is not so much the successful outcome of a revolutionary struggle which determines who is to become a hero and who is not, but rather the self-perception of the individual who has heroic aspirations. If we apply this to Larkin and Connolly, then it may be seen that the hero-worship of the two labour leaders was actually deliberately orchestrated by the two men themselves.

Rather than discussing the validity of Naumann's contentions, I will simply confine myself to applying some of his findings to our two labour heroes. One of his arguments is that, generally speaking, revolutionary personalities tend to have lost their parents in childhood and come from broken homes. As they find the memory of these early experiences painful, they seek to eradicate it from their minds.

5. Frank Robbins, *Under the Starry Plough: Recollections of the Irish Citizen Army*, Dublin, 1977, 27.

6. John Gray, *City in Revolt: James Larkin and the Belfast Dock Strike of 1907*, Belfast, 1985, x.

7. Michael Naumann, *Strukturwandel des Heroismus: Vom sakralen zum revolutionären Heldentum*, Frankfurt, 1984.

Without wishing to over-emphasize this point, I find it intriguing that both labour leaders made a mystery of their childhood, which is why there are conflicting accounts of their early life. Most of Larkin's biographers contend that he was born in Liverpool, England, in 1876 while he himself swore in Court that he was born in Newry, Northern Ireland, that year. W.P. Ryan, writing about Larkin's childhood, also claims Newry to be his birthplace while the editor of the booklet, in a footnote, changes this to Liverpool.[8] Indeed in the 1920s, anti-Larkin pamphlets were published, intended to expose him as a liar, which showed a copy of his birth certificate. According to their version, he was born in Liverpool, though not in 1876, but in 1879.[9]

There are the same uncertainties with regard to Connolly. Some biographers state that he was born in Edinburgh, while others say he was born in Ireland. 1866, 1868, 1869 and 1870 are the different dates of birth given, and various small villages in County Monaghan are claimed to be his place of birth. Connolly never wrote anything about his childhood, and it struck his friends that "Nobody will ever know anything about Connolly. He will never tell anything about himself."[10]

In this connection it is interesting to note that Connolly wrote a play, called *Under Which Flag*, which saw its first performance in March 1916 (*ibid.*). Although it is an anti-recruitment play set in Ireland in 1867, it reads like a thinly disguised anamnesis of Connolly's early experience. The main character is 18-year-old Mary O'Neill, the orphaned child of a neighbour who lives with the farmer Pat O'Donnell and his wife Ellen, whom she calls Uncle and Aunt. However, halfway through the play she twice refers to "Uncle" as her father. At one stage she suddenly says to her aunt: "Did you not take me in ... when my poor mother died and I had no one left me in the whole wide world. And my poor father, God be good to him, that I never saw". This passage, as indeed the idea of her being adopted, is totally irrelevant with regard to the play as a whole.

Mary's foster parents have two sons, John and Frank, one of whom is about to emigrate to America and the other is about to enlist for service in the British Army. The only other character in the play, Dan Mahon, is one of the old guard of the Fenian movement. He teaches Mary a patriotic lesson that makes her change her outlook completely; she now urges Frank to join the Fenians and fight for Ireland.

---

8. W.P Ryan, *Jim Larkin: Irish Labour Leader*, Cork, n.d., 11.

9. National Library Dublin: LO, 113 (item 79).

10. National Library Dublin: W. O'Brien's Papers, Pos 6993.

The Connollys indeed also had two sons, John and Thomas, one of whom emigrated while the other entered the British Army. Furthermore it is widely known that Connolly was taught Irish nationalism by an old Fenian veteran whom he called Uncle McBride. Given these startling parallels between the O'Donnells and the Connollys, it seems a fair assumption that James Connolly was in fact writing about himself when he created "Mary". This would suggest that he was adopted as a child, either because he was orphaned or illegitimate, but in any case he considered his background to be problematic.[11]

Let me return to Naumann's study. In blotting out the undesirable past, he claims, the revolutionary personality is seeking for a new identity in the future. Not only does he wish to destroy the existing society and replace it with a fundamentally different social system, but he wants his name to be associated with the forcible action that brought about the change. In other words, he wants to go down in history as a revolutionary hero.

Although they held different ideas with regard to methods and timing, Larkin's and Connolly's ultimate aim was to change Irish society from capitalism to socialism. To achieve this goal, they advocated direct action by the working class. "Add to this the concept of one Big Union embracing all, and you have ... the most effective ... combination for industrial warfare", Connolly taught. "Political power", he maintained, "must come straight out of the Industrial battlefield".[12]

Doubtless both men genuinely believed in Socialism which they almost compulsively fought for all their lives, but at the same time it is also quite obvious that they wanted to become the heroes of the masses and be remembered for their deeds.

In his play *Under which Flag?* Connolly has Mary express the desire to become "the most talked of girl in Ireland" with "all the people, high and low running to see [her]". Being but a girl, however, seriously limits her scope of activities, "Wish I was a man", she sighs, "so that I could do something to make a stir in the world".

In order to become the "most talked of" man in Ireland, both men went forth with extraordinary single-mindedness, engaging in breathtaking and attention-seeking activity. Larkin, blending and borrowing what suited him best, from Marxism, populist radicalism,

---

11. Naumann comes to the same conclusion; however, there are a few errors in his analysis of the play (particularly with regard to the setting).

12. James Connolly, *The Re-Conquest of Ireland*, [1915], Dublin and Belfast, 1972, 62.

Christian socialism, syndicalism, Bolshevism and Catholic nationalism, seems to have been driven more by revolutionary instinct and perpetual restless movement, rather than by any theoretical certainty about the future. Connolly, on the other hand, displaying equal zeal and stamina, was following more sharply articulated ideas and goals.

Neither of them drank, nor did they have any diversions beyond studying and writing. About Larkin, we are told, that "even when [he] amused himself, it was within serious context".[13] They both lived in dire poverty all their lives. They subjected their wives and young families (Connolly had five children, Larkin had three) to constant moves, not only between three different countries, but from one slum tenement to another. Connolly's biographer tells us how he struggled, slaved, starved and "studied on an empty belly while the problem of keeping his family gnawed at the back of his mind".[14] Larkin mentioned in 1913, "Thirty-six years of hunger and poverty have been my portion".[15]

As far as appearance goes, the two men had nothing in common. Larkin was of great height (being over 6 feet), distinctive in appearance, with a broad forehead, thick dark hair and a vigorous stride. His voice was tremendously powerful, and when he spoke it was, according to O'Casey, "in rugged, passionate, vitalising phrases".[16] Countess Markievicz felt that he was not so much a man, but some great primeval force, from whose power of speech tornadoes and storm-driven waves emanated.[17] Connolly on the other hand was small, squat, looking "more like a quay-side publican than a social revolutionary" according to O'Faolain,[18] and O'Casey, too, portrays Connolly in somewhat unflattering terms as having a sparsely-covered round head, a rather

---

13. Emmet Larkin, *James Larkin, 1876-1947: Irish Labour Leader*, [1965], London, 1977, 9.

14. C. Desmond Greaves, *The Life and Times of James Connolly*, London, 1976, 146.

15. Emmet Larkin, 128.

16. Sean O'Casey, *The Story of the Irish Citizen Army*, [1919], London, 1980, 3.

17. Emmet Larkin, 160.

18. Sean O'Faolain, *Constance Markievicz, or the Average Revolutionary: A Biography*, London, 1934, 186.

common-place face with a thick nose, two short pillar-like legs, slightly bowed, causing him to waddle a little in his walk.[19]

When the two men teamed up in 1910, time was beginning to run out for Connolly. It was his second attempt at a career in Ireland. Originally he had started working for the socialist movement in Scotland, without making any impact in seven years. For a further seven years he tried in vain to propagate his ideas of Socialism among the Irish. His uncompromising leadership of the "Irish Socialist Republican Party" came under severe criticism, forcing Connolly to resign and emigrate to America. Not a single comrade came to bid him farewell. In disgust, Connolly wrote, "I regard Ireland, or at least the Socialist part of Ireland ... as having thrown me out, and I do not wish to return like a dog to his vomit".[20] He then committed himself to the Socialist cause in America, for yet another seven years, but fared no better there. After many rows, he in fact found himself in quite a similar situation as in Ireland: rejected and isolated. "I ... confess that I regard my emigration to America as the great mistake of my life", he admitted.[21]

Larkin, on the other hand, was already a formidable figure in the Labour movement. Not only was he the founder and General Secretary of a powerful union, but his paper *The Irish Worker* was a tremendous success with a circulation figure of something over 20,000 a week.

Understandably enough, Connolly resented Larkin who overshadowed him in every respect. "That man is utterly unreliable — and dangerous because unreliable", Connolly wrote to a friend; and elsewhere: "Larkin seems to think that he can use Socialists as he pleases .... He will never get me to bow to him" (*ibid.*). On an increasing number of occasions Connolly pleaded mysterious "violent headaches" preventing him from taking part in joint rallies with Larkin.[22]

Connolly knew of course, that after 21 years of tireless campaigning for the Socialist cause and nothing to show for it, he would soon have to make or break it. He was not only under pressure from Larkin, but there began to emerge numerous other movements which all looked like potential competitors. Sinn Féin was one of these, with a policy that differed from all other nationalist movements in that it championed

---

19. Sean O'Casey, *Drums under the Windows, Autobiography: Book 3*, London, 1973, 14.

20. Samuel Levenson, *James Connolly: Socialist, Patriot and Martyr*, London, 1977, 109.

21. National Library, Dublin: W.O'Brien's Papers.

22. Naumann, 181.

industrial development as a key issue facing the country. Its call for protection for Irish industry appealed to the urban middle class and the working class alike.

During the six years that were left to him, Connolly recklessly plunged himself into hectic activity. But no matter how hard he tried, he just could not extricate himself from Larkin. The Socialist Party of Ireland which he reorganized and campaigned for, never really took off. The far more promising Labour Party which Connolly had proposed and had been instrumental in founding, was promptly taken over by Larkin, whereupon Connolly resentfully wrote, "He does not seem to want a democratic Labour movement; he seems to want a Larkinite movement only .... He must rule, or will not work, and in the present stage of the Labour movement he has us all at his mercy .... I am sick of all this playing to one man .... In fact ... [I am] sick and sorry I ever returned."[23]

By 1914 both men had fiercely stepped up their agitation, enduring arrests, imprisonment and hunger strike, in a last desperate bid for a place in the pantheon of Irish heroes. Their language, belligerent and full of religious and nationalistic undertones, revealed that they had grown far more violent, had accustomed themselves to the thought of using physical force, and were in fact impatiently looking for an opportunity to die a martyr for the cause.

Larkin had convinced himself that he was the chosen one for the salvation of the working classes. "I care for no man. I have got a divine mission ... to make men and women discontented .... I am out to do it, and no ... creature can stop me carrying out the work I was born for .... I am out for revolution." Getting killed in action did not worry him: "What do I care? They can only kill me, there are thousands more to come after me." In fact sacrificing himself would virtually guarantee him the desired hero-worship. "I promise", he declared, "that living or dead, they will never break me, and dead I will be a greater force against them than alive". There was frequent reference to the immortal soul, and to Jesus Christ in whose name Larkin fought. "We are determined that Christ shall not be crucified in Dublin by these men", he announced, and pointing to the miserable conditions of the working class, he said, "All this is done two thousand years after Christ appeared in Galilee ... these men are making people atheists — they are making them godless. But we are going to stop that."[24]

---

23. Samuel Levenson, 215f.

24. Emmet Larkin, 128, 123, 135.

Larkin had not only convinced himself of his divine mission, but also his followers. When "William Partridge, his most loyal and faithful lieutenant, stated that he believed Jim Larkin was sent by God to save the working classes of Dublin", he only expressed what most Dublin workers felt. But in the gloomy aftermath of the Great Lockout, with all hopes for a glorious victory dashed, Larkin suddenly lost interest in the salvation of the working class. Both Jesus Christ and the Socialist cause were now replaced by Cathleen-Ni-Houlihan. "No longer were the social revolutionaries ... the first off his lips or his pen but rather the heroes of national resistance and insurrection — Wolfe Tone, Emmet, and Dwyer." Ireland had become the new mystical body. A few weeks before he left for America, Larkin called for recruits willing to fight for Erin with the Citizen Army, openly warning, "You may have to seal your faith, love and loyalty for her in your blood".[25]

Connolly also thought that the time had come for "less philosophising and more fighting", and the idea of sacrificing himself to liberate the proletariat was firmly planted in his mind. He stated that to die for the practical brotherhood of the human race, was to die for the holiest of all causes, and like Larkin he believed in the power of the dead martyr. "If you ... kill us, out of our ... graves we will evoke a spirit that will thwart you, and ... raise a force that will destroy you." However, the defeat of Labour in 1913 necessitated a reorientation for him, too, which resulted in Nationalism taking precedence over Socialism. With astonishing frankness, he also called upon those young men, ready to shed their blood, to join the Citizen Army. "We want young men prepared to die for Freedom in Ireland", he wrote in 1914.[26]

Now that Larkin was in America and out of his way at long last, Connolly had to strike soon if ever he wanted to immortalize his name. To embrace the Nationalist cause was the obvious option. But time was of the essence: Larkin might return soon. Or worse still, Padraic Pearse, one of the leading figures within the Irish Volunteers and fanatically intent on bloodshed and self-sacrifice, might claim the martyr's crown.

Connolly, determined not to let this last chance slip by, intensified the drilling and training of the Citizen Army week by week. "We believe in constitutional action in normal times. We believe in revolutionary action in exceptional times. These are exceptional times", he wrote.[27] Though cautioned about such talk and action by the Volunteers, Connolly pressed

25. *Ibid.*, 159, 183, 182.

26. Naumann, 190, 191, 189.

27. Seán Cronin, *Irish Nationalism*, Dublin, 1980, 121.

for an immediate insurrection, "repeating his by now well-worn theme that whether or not the Volunteers came out, the Citizen Army would fight".[28] He knew full well that his 200-odd men would be slaughtered; but that was exactly the point. "Without the slightest trace of irreverence, but in all due humility and awe", he boldly stated, "we recognise that of us, as of mankind before in Calvary, it may truly be said, 'without the shedding of Blood there is no Redemption'."[29]

His own obituary in mind, he wrote, "The best men in Ireland, the only men the Ireland of the future will care to remember, have decided long ago that if they must fight they will fight in Ireland, for Ireland, and under Ireland's flag".[30] And indeed, this is exactly what the heroes of his play *Under Which Flag* do. All the "true sons of Erin" have "gone to fight for Ireland, gone to give their heart's blood ... that poor Mother Erin might be a nation among the nations of the earth". The last words before the final curtain are spoken by Dan, the Old Fenian, who is down on his knees: "God's blessing with ... them, and with the brave girls that sent them out to battle, and God's blessing be with the cause of the land that bore them. Amen."

Larkin, far away in America, was stunned when he heard of the rising. "Though fate denied some of us the hope of striking a blow for human freedom, we live in hopes that we, too, will be given the opportunity", he wrote, acknowledging "that the most glorious thing that has happened ... was the self-sacrifice and devotion of these men to a cause which they believed in".[31] So Connolly had triumphed in the end, and Larkin was not given another opportunity, at least not one quite so dramatic.

Larkin and Connolly: socialist heroes in drama
In socialist drama there is always an implicit or explicit condemnation of the social status quo. Specific social abuses are often focused on as symptomatic of a deeper, more fundamental wrong in the political structure. In revolting against any corrupt or unjust practice, the socialist hero therefore poses a considerable threat to the whole fabric of that society. Plays which identify and highlight social injustice, even communicate its avoidability, are not simply meant to entertain or to add

---

28. Lyons, 346.

29. Naumann, 205.

30. *Ibid.*, 198.

31. Larkin, 213–14.

to the audience's knowledge about human society. The ultimate effect, in John Arden's words, should be "an assistance and inspiration to the activity of Socialists both now and in the future".[32] Thus, while the function of the stage heroes is to serve as a pattern for the audience to imitate, the heroes of reality, as we have seen, hope that their action will be absorbed into literature. There is, in other words, an interchangeability of models from literature and reality.

As a symbolic figure whose importance goes far beyond his individual achievements, the socialist hero always acts in the interest of the common good; never for his personal gain. His qualities are individual, but his actions are collective. The hero in legend and literature differs from other men by his peculiar energy, spontaneity, magnanimity and unbending character, and indeed the socialist hero shares all these qualities with his traditional counterpart. In order to prove his worth, he needs to be confronted with a concrete cause. As already suggested, in his case the evils are largely external, identifiable and remediable; and generally the conflict tends to be a straightforward one: the established power of Church and State against the downtrodden working classes. Willing to undergo hardships in fighting against the social abuses meted out to the masses, the social hero, splendid in his courage and assertive in spirit, sets examples for others to follow. His efforts need not necessarily be crowned by triumphant success, in fact a complete realization of all his goals might undermine the revolutionary spirit in others. It is often pointed out that the most moving revolutionary figures are those who die unfulfilled.

Against this backdrop, how do Connolly and Larkin measure up as heroes? In order to find out I shall analyze the following plays: Sean O'Casey, *The Star Turns Red*; James Plunkett, *Big Jim* and *The Risen People*; Eoghan Harris, *The Ballad of Jim Larkin*; Eugene McCabe, *Pull Down a Horseman*; Margaretta D'Arcy and John Arden, *The Non-Stop Connolly Show*.

Freud held that there is a certain correspondence between the subject matter of a literary work, particularly the hero, and its creator. Subconsciously the writer transfers his own feelings and latent wishes to his protagonist, he claimed. Thus, in disguised form, the hero reflects the writer's day-dreams. This proposition certainly seems to be borne out when we look at the abovementioned playwrights and their choice of hero.

---

32. John Arden, "A Socialist Hero on the Stage", in John Arden, *To Present the Pretence*, London, 1977, 95.

As is well documented, Sean O'Casey had a lifelong admiration for Larkin, upon whom he bestowed the highest possible praise in his *Autobiographies*, in numerous articles, letters and interviews. The two men had a lot in common: humanitarians with a great capacity for charity, laws unto themselves, excitable, given to intemperate verbal attacks which alienated friend and foe alike. Averse to any kind of doctrine, neither of them could ever fully embrace any political ideology. Despite various protestations that they were this, that and the other, both remained eclectics, with an emotional leaning towards Communism. Even in religious matters they thought alike. Though often outspokenly anti-clerical, they were not anti-Catholic. In fact, both seem to have felt a close affinity to Jesus Christ whom they frequently quoted. Larkin when addressing crowds, would draw comparisons between Jesus and himself, and O'Casey would often do the same in letters, saying, "Jesus Christ did it before me, and I occasionally follow in His steps".[33] As far as O'Casey was concerned, there was not much to choose between Larkin and Jesus. Asked why he had lost his faith in the Church, O'Casey replied: "I never lost my faith, I found it. I found it when Jim Larkin came ... and organised unskilled workers .... He was the saviour of Dublin."[34]

For a very brief period Larkin and O'Casey worked together in the Citizen Army, and later, when Larkin was imprisoned in America, O'Casey tirelessly campaigned for his release. They remained in personal contact with each other until Larkin's death.

When O'Casey, referring to Larkin's return to Ireland in 1923, wrote, "Jim's person was so lovable, so persuasive, that I realised I would be in jeopardy if I saw him too often",[35] he was expressing his fear that Larkin might persuade him to actively join the Labour Movement. O'Casey felt, however, that Irish Labour at that time was a spent force, held down by enemies from within the Movement and checked by a Church-backed Home Government. The stranglehold of the Catholic Church irritated him above all else. "I didn't think that the Church would get such a grip on Ireland's throat", he commented. He would be wasting his time acting in support of Larkin's cause. Instead he had begun to see

---

33. *The Letters of Sean O'Casey*, ed. David Krause, London, 1975, I, 602.

34. David Krause, *Sean O'Casey and His World*, London, 1976, 12.

35. Ronald Ayling, "Sean O'Casey and Jim Larkin after 1923", *Sean O'Casey Review*, (Spring 1977), 103.

"that my fight would have to be made with all [these] enemies, and that I'd have to make it almost alone; a big egotistical stand".[36]

In *The Star Turns Red*, O'Casey fights alongside Larkin in spirit; what is more, he makes him victorious. Although the play centres on the 1913 Dublin lockout, and is in fact dedicated to the men and women who fought through it, there are many echoes of other historical events which took place in later years, such as the Russian Revolution, the Nazi take-over in Germany, the Spanish Civil War and the rise of the fascist Blue-Shirts in Ireland. In transferring the Labour struggle to a higher political plane, O'Casey gives it a deeper significance. In fact he creates the opportunity (denied to Larkin in real life) to strike "a blow for human freedom". This is Larkin's Easter Rising, or what would have happened had he, and not Connolly, been in command of the Citizen Army. O'Casey did not like Connolly very much (he even expressly denied him the honour of having fallen the first martyr to Irish Socialism);[37] nor did he like the type of country Ireland had become as a result of the Rising. Hence, the play is written very much with the subsequent political developments in mind. But in typical O'Casey fashion there is no lamentation about these. He simply creates an alternative 1913/1916 in which his own hero triumphs, and there is no mention of Connolly.

O'Casey allows Larkin to beat almost single-handedly all the enemies which he himself set out to fight "almost alone". Basically the fight is between two opposing forces which are both trying to win over the apathetic working class: on the one side, the ruling class, composed of the Church Hierarchy, the Fascists and the Bourgeoisie, protected by the police and the military; on the other side, Jim Larkin and his revolutionary workers. Larkin, portrayed here as the fiery tornado he has so often been called, passionate, careless of his own safety in the face of real danger, strong and brilliant, having to overcome a conspiracy within his own ranks, in the end wins gloriously. Soldiers refuse to fire on the workers and join in the "Internationale". It is Christmas Eve, the silver Star of Bethlehem turns into the red Star of Communism to indicate the nativity of Christ-Jim. Clerical fascism which had put such a terrible stranglehold on Ireland is broken at long last, and the true inheritor of the Christian ideal of peace emerges in the shape of James Larkin.

James Plunkett was also personally acquainted with Larkin. Having joined the Workers' Union as a young man, he was made Branch Secretary at the age of 23, a position he held for four years until Larkin's

---

36. *Ibid.*, 103.

37. O'Casey, 64.

death occurred in 1947. Plunkett made three attempts at coming to terms with his own Larkin experience. The first was *Big Jim*, a play written for radio in 1954, which gives a rather enthusiastic account of the 1913 lockout. This was revised for the stage in 1958 and became *The Risen People*,[38] a much gloomier version of the same event. Out of that grew *Strumpet City* in 1963, the novel which made Plunkett famous, and which expressed, according to himself, what he really wanted to say about the events at the time. The latter was written in response to a request from his publishers, Hutchinson, who were really looking for a book on Connolly, but it turned out to be yet another tribute to Larkin.[39] Connolly plays no role in any of Plunkett's works. Nevertheless, Larkin, the full-blooded centre and soul of his first work, is given less room in the second and simply fades away into the background in his last work.

What kind of hero does Larkin prove to be in Plunkett's plays? Plunkett is no iconoclast. Gentle and kind, subscribing to most values of Irish society, a Catholic with much respect for the Church and a true chronicler of his time, Plunkett presents us with quite a different picture. With *Big Jim* he wanted to give his hero an ovation. The play, full of authentic. excerpts from speeches Larkin delivered in 1913, shows many facets of Larkin's controversial character: impatient, intemperate, yet loving and caring, and with an acute feel for the popular momentum, we see him struggle and fight for the workers. But this is no revolutionary fight, it is a Labour conflict. Decent wages and better working conditions are fought for, and the immediate target are the employers; these work hand-in-glove with the Church representatives who are also criticized for their stance during the lockout. The play ends on a positive note: the workers return to work with a new confidence and feeling of solidarity. Robert Fitzpatrick, the one foreman to go on strike, is the only worker who is not reinstated, but he is given full approval and support by his wife. From the frame narrative of the play we are relieved to learn that he did succeed in the end. He turns up at Larkin's funeral with all the other protagonists. All of them have prospered in the meantime and gratefully acknowledge that this was due to James Larkin.

The Risen People is a less positive account of the same events, presented in a more stylized fashion. Gone are the dramatic confrontations, disputes and emotional scenes. Larkin's prime enemy, the anonymous employers, are no longer overtly supported by the clergy,

38. James Plunkett, *The Risen People*, Dublin, 1978.

39. "Dublin's Advocate: Interview with Eavan Boland", *This Week*, 12 October 1972, 40.

and Robert Fitzpatrick, the model foreman of *Big Jim*, is seen to falter in the end. In the earlier Abbey production of 1958, Fitzpatrick, after having unsuccessfully searched for a job, is left by his disgruntled wife, and is now prepared to sign the form disowning Larkin's union. In the later Project Theatre production, also in the printed version of the play, Fitzpatrick, abandoned by wife and family is about to join the British Army. Both ends are bleak and quite different from the elevated mood of *Big Jim*.

Eoghan Harris, an ex-leading member of the Workers' Party, who is strongly critical of present-day Irish society and seems to have a particular dislike of what he calls the stagnant provincial bourgeois class, wrote his play *The Ballad of Jim Larkin* in 1988. He himself calls it revisionist and anti-Nationalist. Not unlike O'Casey, but strictly from a Labour point of view, Harris regrets the political developments which took place in Ireland in the aftermath of the Easter Rising. He firmly puts the blame for these on Arthur Griffith and Sinn Féin. Instead of British Capitalism, independent Ireland ended up with Irish Capitalism. Larkin, humanitarian, courageous and compassionate, emerges here as a modern Wolfe Tone: capable of uniting North and South. "The capitalists tried to divide us on religious and political grounds, and while we were talking, they robbed both of us", he has Larkin comment after the Belfast strike, referred to as "a heroic effort" in which Catholic and Protestant had stood together. "But the Orange employers and Hibernian bigots had between them choked off the cry of solidarity."

Larkin, hitting Ireland and the Irish employers "like a tornado", breaks up their complacent, comfortable world, "leaving it in smithereens" so that the workers might march in. Thus for the first and only time in the history of their country, the Irish working class are put in a position to take over. The play suggests that if Larkin had succeeded in 1913, there would have been no political division, Labour would be in control, and clerical power would have been curbed.

McCabe and D'Arcy and Arden chose Connolly as their hero. All three of them have responded to crucial historical events in Ireland, and have written plays about these which seek to make apparent the underlying political forces at work. While D'Arcy and Arden are more radical playwrights with a firm political commitment, McCabe is content to offer deeper insights into social issues.

Pull down a Horseman[40] is entirely about the historical meeting between Pearse and Connolly which took place in January 1916, at a

---

40. Eugene McCabe, *Pull Down a Horseman / Gale Day*, Dublin, 1979.

time when Connolly had been propagating the Nationalist cause for over a year and a half, and had (presumably) written his own Nationalistic play. Yet McCabe would have us believe that Connolly still only has one aim in mind: to liberate the working class. He repudiates Pearse's ideas of bloodshed and sacrifice, and says with "passionate contempt": "Patriotism and Blood: Flags and Dreams. We are sick ... of this teaching. The working class is the only foundation on which a free nation can be reared." Surrounded by a hostile chorus of employers and gombeen men, Connolly becomes a hero of almost tragic proportions. Fate has presented him with two options; either he starts a revolution with the Citizen Army (in which case they might get "crushed, shelved and shrugged at"), and he would "die alone, for what [he has] worked and hungered", or he joins forces with the Volunteers (in which case they might end up in "her Majesty's dungeons by Easter"), and he would perish in the patriot trap. Unintimidated by these prospects, Connolly decides in favour of the latter, shouting, "Workers unite, the first round's won, our fight has just begun".

The Non-Stop Connolly Show[41] is a massive drama in six parts which runs for 26 hours. Although the play is an account of Connolly's life, from the cradle to the grave, it focuses on his political life and public activity, rather than on his personal affairs. It was begun in 1969, completed in 1974 and first performed in its entirety at Liberty Hall in Dublin over Easter 1975. The two playwrights had neither planned to write a play of such length, nor indeed to base it solely on Connolly. Originally it had been their intention to compose a series of plays about various revolutionary characters which were to include Jesus Christ, Gandhi, Rosa Luxemburg and many more, but in the end everybody else was dropped from their list of candidates.[42]

The basic conflict of the play is between socialism and capitalism. Connolly's whole life is seen to be devoted to destroying the "Capitalist Monster" which oppresses people everywhere. This internationalist Capitalist, represented by a "demon king" figure, called Grabitall, occasionally becomes specific people, but he wears the same mask throughout; employers, Church representatives and the military are dealt with in same fashion. Though the emblematic figure of Grabitall is the prime enemy, there are others. These are the proponents of reform within the Labour movement. In watering down Revolutionary demands,

41. Margaretta D'Arcy and John Arden, *The Non-Stop Connolly Show*, London, 1977.

42. Arden, 103.

the Labour reformists throughout the play are seen to be playing straight into the hands of the Capitalist Monster. But despite the grinding poverty he and his family are subjected to, Connolly pursues a relentless battle with all the enemies to liberate the oppressed.

As we have seen, Connolly and Larkin may not have been able to achieve their primary political objectives, but they were certainly successful in inviting their own literary canonization. They emerge triumphant in literature, and given the intended effect of the socialist hero on stage, they will no doubt inspire others to follow in their footsteps.

Robert Mahony, Center for Irish Studies at the Catholic University of America, is preparing *Jonathan Swift: The Irish Identity* for Yale University Press. He has published on English and Irish writers of the eighteenth century and, with Betty Rizzo, compiled *Christopher Smart: An Annotated Bibliography, 1741-1983* (1984), and edited *The Annotated Letters of Christopher Smart* (1991).

Susan Fisher Miller wrote a doctoral dissertation on W.B. Yeats and has published on Swift, Yeats, William Trevor and Mennonite church history. In 1994 she published *Culture for Service: A History of Goshen College, 1894-1994*.

Christopher Morash, Department of English, St Patrick's College, Maynooth, is author of *Writing the Irish Famine* (1995); has edited *The Hungry Voice* (1989), a collection of Famine poetry, as well as a collection of essays on the Famine, *"Fearful Realities"* (1995); has edited the keynote addresses of the 1992 IASAIL conference in a volume entitled *Creativity and Its Contexts* (1995); is a contributor to the forthcoming *Oxford Companion to Irish Literature*, *Blackwell's Companion to Irish Culture* and other reference works. He has also published a number of articles on nineteenth-century Irish culture.

James H. Murphy, Department of English and director of post-graduate research, All Hallows College, Dublin, has edited *No Bland Facility* (1991) and *Beginnings in Ministry* (1992). He has written articles on Irish fiction and on cultural and religious issues in nineteenth-century Ireland. He is at present working on a cultural study of Irish education.

Ciaran Murray, Department of English at Chuo University, has written extensively on the Japanese sources of Romanticism. He is currently completing a comprehensive survey of the subject.

Clare O'Halloran, Department of History, University College Cork, published *Partition and the Limits of Irish Nationalism* (1987), and is preparing a study of Irish and Scottish antiquarianism in the eighteenth century based on her doctoral thesis.

Jane Stevenson, Department of History, University of Sheffield, has published articles on Irish Studies, Latin, Literacy and Liturgy. She is the author of *Laterculus Malalianus and the School of Archbishop Theodore*, forthcoming from Cambridge University Press.

Wim Tigges, Department of English, Leiden University, published *An Anatomy of Literary Nonsense* (1988); is preparing (with Peter Liebregts) the Proceedings of the Leiden October Conference on "Beauty and the Beast? Walter Pater, Christina Rosetti, R.L. Stevenson and Their Contemporaries"; has published Dutch translations of works by Malory, Pope, Samuel Johnson and Edward Lear, and articles on various literary topics, including "The Land of Cokaygne", Flann O'Brien and James Joyce.

Norman Vance, School of English and American Studies, University of Sussex, has published *Irish Literature: A Social History* (1990), *The Sinews of the Spirit* (1985), a literary study of Victorian Christian Manliness, and essays on Irish, Victorian, classical and biblical topics. His book *The Victorians and Ancient Rome* is nearing completion and a study of Irish writing since 1800 is now in preparation.

Richard Wall, Department of English, University of Calgary, is the author of *An Anglo-Irish Dialect Glossary for Joyce's Works* (1986), a translation and edition of Brendan Behan's *An Giall* and *The Hostage* (1987), and many articles on Irish literature and language. Among his current projects are *A Dictionary and Glossary for the Irish Literary Revival* (forthcoming) and *A Dictionary and Glossary for Irish Literature*.

Adriaan van der Weel, Department of English, Leiden University, has published extensively on twentieth-century Anglo-Irish writers, especially James Joyce and Samuel Beckett, and translated their work into Dutch.

Bart Westerweel, Department of English, Leiden University, published *Patterns and Patterning: A Study of Four Poems by George Herbert* (1984), edited *Something Understood: Studies in Anglo-Dutch Literary Translation* (1990) and has published articles on Shakespeare, emblem studies, Philip Sidney and George Herbert. A collection of essays on Anglo-Dutch relations in the field of the emblem which he has edited will be published shortly.

NOTES ON CONTRIBUTORS

C.C. Barfoot, English Department, Leiden University, published *The Thread of Connection: Aspects of Fate in the Novels of Jane Austen and Others* (1982); has most recently edited *Shades of Empire in Colonial and Post-Colonial Literatures* (with Theo D'haen, 1993), *In Black and Gold: Contiguous Traditions in Post-War British and Irish Poetry* (1994) and *"Een Beytie Hollansche": James Boswell's Dutch compositions* (with K.J. Bostoen, 1994). Amongst his many publications are articles on Goldsmith and Yeats.

Peter Davidson, Department of Comparative Literature, University of Warwick, is preparing *The Penguin Book of Cavalier Verse* and the Clarendon edition of the poems and translations of Sir Richard Fanshawe; has written articles on Yeats, Scottish literature, Renaissance studies and music history; and has recently published an edition of Sir Walter Scott's *Old Mortality* and an emblem book, *The Eloquence of Shadows* (with the painter Hugh Buchanan). His study of Ezra Pound and the Classics will be appearing soon.

Barbara Freitag, School of Applied Languages, Dublin University, is the author of numerous articles on Anglo-Irish Literature and of *Keltische Identität als Fiktion* (1989).

Arthur Green is a Board Member of the British Council and former Under Secretary, Northern Ireland Civil Service.

Joep Leerssen, Department of European Studies (Modern European Literature), University of Amsterdam, has published widely on the history of ideas and scholarship (e.g., *Komparatistik in Großbritannien, 1800-1950*, 1984), Irish literary and cultural history (e.g., *Mere Irish & Fíor-Ghael*, 1986; *The "Contention of the Bards"*, 1994) and national and cultural difference and stereotype (e.g., as editor of the *Yearbook of European Studies*, since 1988). He is at present working on a book provisionally entitled *Idyll and Ideology*, on aspects of nineteenth-century Irish literature and culture.

www.ingramcontent.com/pod-product-compliance
Lightning Source LLC
Chambersburg PA
CBHW020345270326
41926CB00007B/318